Labor of Fire

In the series *Labor in Crisis*,
edited by Stanley Aronowitz

Labor of Fire

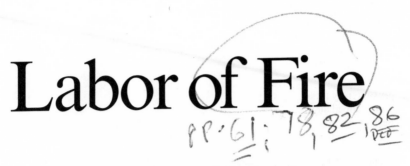

PP·61; 78, 82, 86 DEC

The Ontology of Labor between Economy and Culture

BRUNO GULLÌ

TEMPLE UNIVERSITY PRESS
Philadelphia

Temple University Press
1601 North Broad Street
Philadelphia PA 19122
www.temple.edu/tempress

⊗The paper used in this publication meets the requirements of the American
National Standard for Information Sciences—Permanence of Paper for Printed
Library Materials, ANSI Z39.48-1992

Library of Congress Cataloging-in-Publication Data

Gullì, Bruno, 1959-
Labor of fire : the ontology of labor between economy and culture / Bruno Gullì.
    p. cm. — (Labor in crisis)
Includes bibliographical references and index.
ISBN 1-59213-112-3 (cloth : alk. paper) — ISBN 1-59213-113-1 (pbk. : alk. paper)
1. Labor—Philosophy. 2. Work—Philosophy. 3. Marxian economics. 4. Capitalism.
5. Economics—Philosophy. I. Title: Ontology of labor between economy and
culture. II. Title. III. Series.

HD4904.G82 2005
331'.01—dc22

2005044023

2 4 6 8 9 7 5 3 1

In fertility time grew.
—Pablo Neruda, *Canto General*

Contents

Acknowledgments

THERE ARE MANY PEOPLE who, in many ways, contributed to the making of this book. First and foremost, I have to thank Stanley Aronowitz, in whose 1996 seminar on Marx the first ideas of this study were formulated and who provided the structure and the space for them to be developed and printed. I need to remember the late Robert Dombroski, who constantly encouraged me, and I thank Frank Rosengarten, who carefully read the manuscript as a doctoral dissertation. Michael Hardt read the manuscript for Temple University Press and gave me important structural suggestions, which I almost entirely incorporated into the text. Sandro Mezzadra and Pedro Canò also read the whole manuscript, at different stages of its development, and especially to Sandro I owe thanks for many insightful comments and suggestions. I wish to thank Micah Kleit, of Temple University Press, for his constantly supportive comments. I also want to thank Peter Bratsis and Michael Menser for reading an earlier version of Chapter 2, perhaps the most important chapter in the book, for *Found Object*. Thanks are also due to Michael Menser, to whom I owe my interest in Bookchin. David Siar also read an earlier version of Chapter 2 for *Cultural Logic*. Sandra Luft gave me the opportunity to study Heidegger's critique of Nietzsche when I was a student at San Francisco State University. A special thanks to my twin brother, Nino, who has read virtually everything I wrote; to my sister, Angela, and Nino Quaranta, with whom I experimented, in the summer of 1998 in the Calabrian countryside, the viability of a different economy, geared toward the production of use-values; and to Vera K., who provided an important structure of support and care over the years.

Labor of Fire

Introduction

THE THESIS EXPLORED in this book is that the category of labor as constructed by political economy under the capitalist mode of production does not correspond to what labor is in itself, to its concept. Indeed, it does not correspond to but, rather, betrays, the true potentiality of labor, of the many concrete forms of labor. For political economy and capital, labor is either productive or unproductive, and this means productive or unproductive *for* and *of* capital. However, labor in itself, the concept of labor, is neither one of these categories. I call it *neither-productive-nor-unproductive,* or refer to it as the *neither/nor* of labor, as labor in its neutrality. This neutrality is not something new in philosophy. John Duns Scotus, for instance, builds his metaphysics on the neutrality (or univocity) of the concept of being, that is, on the notion that being, the most common concept, is included in all of its qualified occurrences (such as finite or infinite being), but they are not included in it; so being is different from them, it is neutral with respect to them. I intend to address something similar to Scotus's model when I speak of the neutrality of the concept of labor. In fact, I hold that "labor" is to political and social ontology (or poetic metaphysics) what "being" is to pure ontology (or pure metaphysics).

In the metaphysics of John Duns Scotus, neutral is not being but the concept of being. In fact, "being" can be finite or infinite, created or uncreated, and so on; once it is so qualified (or modified) it no longer is simply "being." But because the human intellect also can conceive the concept of being as such, it means that this latter is different from the other concepts, such as finite being or infinite being. As Étienne Gilson very clearly explains in his great study of Duns Scotus, the concept of being is certainly included in both concepts, that is, for instance, the concepts of finite being and infinite being, but they are not included in it. Thus, properly speaking, it is neither of them; it is *neutral* with respect to them; it is *univocal.*[1] In a footnote, Gilson adds that neutral is the concept, not the really existing being. And he continues, "The common concept of being is formally neutral with respect to the finite and the infinite, but a real being is necessarily either one or the other" (Gilson 1952: 100).[2]

The same holds true with labor. The concept of labor is certainly included in the concepts of both productive and unproductive labor, but they are not included in it. Thus, the concept of labor is neutral with respect to them. Moreover, the concept of labor is included in all the concrete forms of labor, which, although reduced to the categories of productivity and unproductivity under capital, are in reality moments of creative, living labor.

Perhaps here a complication arises because we equate labor with living labor (and throughout the book these expressions will be understood as synonyms). It must then be said immediately that the word "living," which apparently qualifies "labor," is such a qualifier only from a grammatical, not an ontological, point of view. "Living," in the expression "living labor," does not address the "how" or "which" of labor, but it is the most essential constituent of its "what," of its substance. In fact, how could labor be "not living"? The expression "dead labor," by which one denotes capital, does not erase the fact that *life* is the substance of labor, of all labor, and thus that all labor is living labor. We will see this point with more clarity when we deal with the question of machinery, in which this "dead" labor becomes able to act with relative autonomy. What makes it "dead" is the fact that capital, just like a vampire, sucks its substance; for machinery itself, that is, accumulated living labor and social knowledge, would simply give back to social life, in the form of life, what it has received from life itself. Living labor then is the subjective power of labor, whose deadly objectification begins when it is constructed and expended as labor-power. I will discuss this point in Chapter 1.

However, to say that we deal with the *concept* of labor does not imply the notion of a logical abstraction. The concept of labor is *real* labor in the same way in which, in Scotus's metaphysics, the concept of being is real being, and not a logical universal. Thus, we deal with labor neither from the merely abstract point of view of logic nor from the empirical point of view of political economy but, rather, from the point of view of ontology. And, in keeping with Scotus's teaching, we hold that the object of ontology (or metaphysics) is something real. This means that even though we grasp the *concept* of labor, this concept is not an ideal being, but a real being, which is contracted and becomes singular in many individuating and essential differences; certainly not only and not necessarily in the forms predicated and prescribed by the productivist logic of capital. To start from labor in its empirical existence would be to have, by means of intuition alone, what Marx calls a *chaotic conception* (Marx 1973: 100). But the concept one grasps at the level of thought, although in part also abstract, is not *merely* abstract, that is, it is not a simple object of reason, it does not have in abstraction or predication its full and only reality. Rather, it is abstract and yet concrete, for it is a determinate abstraction, which can be grasped as concrete only at the end of a process of analysis and synthesis. In this sense, as Gilson explains with respect to Scotus's metaphysics of being (but the same holds true of labor in the field of political ontology), commonality (i.e., the fact that labor is present in all manifestations of the social) precedes and determines universality. And the universal is actually the singular.

THE "BIRTH" OF LABOR

Labor has always existed. The idea of a beginning, or even more so, the notion of the "invention" of labor, rests on the equivocal way in which the word "labor" is used. If by that word one means wage labor under capitalist conditions of production, or what Karl Polanyi calls the "self-regulating market," then labor has a beginning; hence it also can have an end. But this is not what labor necessarily means. As Polanyi says, "Labor is only another name for a human activity which goes with life itself, which in turn is not produced for sale but for entirely different reasons, nor can that activity be detached from the rest of life, be stored or mobilized" (1944/1957: 72). In other words, for Polanyi, labor is *not* a commodity, or, together with land and money, it is a "fictitious" commodity. This seems to be completely at odds with the Marxian analysis, but in reality it is not. And this not simply because a fictitious commodity is still a commodity. What Polanyi is pointing out is the distinction between labor as an ontological category: "another name for a human activity which goes with life itself" and labor as a solely economic category, which is constructed as a commodity. Polanyi then concludes that in the self-regulating market labor *becomes* a commodity, rather than stay with the initial proposition that it is *not* a commodity; he thus recuperates the correct analysis of the distinction between ontology and political economy, which otherwise is lost. The element of "fiction" remains within his analysis, but it becomes "the organizing principle of society" (p. 75). Polanyi says that a "self-regulating market demands nothing less than the institutional separation of society into an economic and political sphere" (p. 71). It is this institutional separation that we are trying to understand, describe, and challenge: the notion that this separation is irrevocable. Polanyi continues:

> It might be argued that the separateness of the two spheres obtains in every type of society at all times. Such an inference, however, would be based on a fallacy. True, no society can exist without a system of some kind which ensures order in the production and distribution of goods. But that does not imply the existence of separate economic institutions; normally, the economic order is merely a function of the social, in which it is contained. Neither under tribal, nor feudal, nor mercantile conditions was there... a separate economic system in society. Nineteenth century society, in which economic activity was isolated and imputed to a distinctive economic motive, was, indeed, a singular departure. (ibid.)

In other words, not simply capitalism, which also was present in mercantile society, but its institutionalization, or what Marx calls its *specificity*, really gives rise to a separation of the economic sphere and its dominance over society as a whole. Other historical periods did not, of course, lack the economic dimension, but it was integral to the totality of life. A future society, based on the communal mode of production, would not lack it either but, again, it would be part of the totality of life, and not separated from the rest of life expressions. Labor was not absent in past society, and it will not disappear in the future. As "another name for a human activity which goes with life itself," labor would simply lose its commodity character, and be what it most essentially is: the univocal and common concept of the social.[3] Those who predict the end of labor are as mistaken as those who think that labor *as such* emerged at one point in time. The human adventure begins with labor and it will end with labor; this is the meaning of Polanyi's definition—regardless of the

NB

changes that labor undergoes in the course of history. What makes societies different is not whether they have or do not have labor, but whether this labor is geared toward a modality of use, in which the economic and noneconomic motives are in synthetic unity, or toward a modality of possession and money-making. The primacy of the noneconomic in ancient societies, with its three principles of *reciprocity, redistribution,* and *householding,* has the following general characteristics: "[T]he absence of the motive of gain; the absence of the principle of laboring for remuneration; the absence of the principle of the least effort; and, especially, the absence of any separate and distinct institution based on economic motives" (Polanyi 1944: 47). But all these do not entail the absence of labor. In this sense, theorists such as Aronowitz and DiFazio (1994), who are often misunderstood as predicting the end of labor, are correct in distinguishing between labor (work) and "job." Thus, a jobless society is not one in which there will no longer be work to be done but, rather, one in which wage labor, alienated labor, will hopefully disappear, and the work that remains to be done will be done reasonably and communally. To disappear will be *productivity,* which is proper to the concept of wage labor and "job," not labor or production. It is on the question of productivity that any analysis of labor will show where it stands: in the capitalist or in the anticapitalist camp.[4]

THE CENTRALITY OF LABOR IN THE AGE OF GLOBALIZATION

The word "globalization" is highly equivocal, and although much has been, and is being, written on the phenomenon, there is little agreement as to what it really is, whether it is a new phenomenon or not, whether it is "good" or "bad," and for whom it would be good or bad. It is not our intention to give any answers to the questions concerning globalization. Certain it is that the phenomenon appears, as Ronaldo Munck says following Polanyi, as "the great transformation of our time" (Munck 2002: 6). And toward the end of his study, referring to Polanyi again, he says that globalization, "if it is nothing else, is the worldwide application of laissez-faire principles" (p. 175). From our point of view, because we start with Marx, it suffices to say that Marx himself spoke of the essential tendency of capitalist development toward globalization, and that the phenomenon itself can certainly be seen in the mercantile economy of the sixteenth century; that, in other words, the expansion of global trade that changed the world around the year 1500—a movement that had begun even before the so-called Age of Discovery (by land, rather than sea, route)—was a movement of this kind. The fact that the globalization process had been happening even before our contemporary age does not mean that radical changes have not taken place in the latter. At the same time, this does not cancel the possibility that the present-day phenomenon of globalization is the development of the same principle defining capitalist expansion, and not something other than it. To be sure, capitalism itself can only be understood as one of the *essential differences* (Marx's phrase) of historical development.

Indeed, as Manfred Steger points out (Steger 2003), the beginning of the globalizing process can be seen as coeval with the beginning of the human adventure. Thus, even before the invention of agriculture, an early and limited form of globalization can be discerned in the prehistoric migrations of bands of hunters and gatherers throughout the globe (Steger 2003: 20). Certainly, the changes that have occurred since 1970, in both the economic and noneconomic spheres of the world's societies, are of such a magnitude that speaking of a new period is justified. Yet it is necessary to stress that this new period still remains within the "general illumination" (Marx 1973: 107), or the specificity, of the capitalist mode of production. The changes that have taken place within the production process, notably, automation, or in the nature of wage labor, for example, flexibility and informalization,[5] have not altered the essential relation between labor and capital but only brought to completion the process of subsumption of the former by the latter. For instance, the fact that transnational corporations can bypass organized labor on a national level, only displaces the immediate site of the antagonism between capital and labor, but it does not cancel it; in fact, the antagonism is augmented and becomes, indeed, *global*. In this sense, from a pragmatic and political point of view, it is on capitalist globalization that we need to focus, always bearing in mind, of course, the fundamental truth that the history of capitalism is not equal to history as such.

As Marx and Engels say in *The Communist Manifesto,* "The need of a constantly expanding market for its products chases the bourgeoisie over the whole surface of the globe. It must nestle everywhere, settle everywhere, establish connexions everywhere" (Marx 1994: 162). And again: "The bourgeoisie has through its exploitation of the world market given a *cosmopolitan character* to production and consumption in every country... it has drawn from under the feet of industry the national ground on which it stood" (ibid.; emphasis added). In his study on globalization and labor, Ronaldo Munck calls attention to the centrality of labor in the globalized economy, which is usually ignored by both globalists and their opponents. Labor remains central because of the centrality of production but also because, from a subjective viewpoint, it embodies the will or agency for social change. Munck says,

> Today, in the era of globalisation, as much as in Marx's time, production is at the heart of social and economic development. Financial fluidity and e-commerce notwithstanding, down-to-earth people still work. The death of the working class, the end of work, and so on, are slogans that have come and gone. The transformations wrought by globalisation may have reconfigured the world of production but they have not done away with it. So, labour is centre stage in terms of the dynamic of contemporary society, and the labour movement has also gone through a reconfiguration which at least leaves it with the possibility of impacting the future trajectories of globalisation. (2002: 64)

As Munck notes, the problem with most of the literature on globalization is that, whereas capital is seen as the active element behind it, labor is only conceived as a "passive victim" (p. 67), a "static" and "reactive" element (p. 68). In truth, when labor is considered in its ontological sense, as the human activity that goes with life itself, considered in its broadest meaning, and that is, all labor, all *labors,* productive as well as unproductive, material and "immaterial,"[6] intellectual and manual, artistic and affective, and so on, then it can be grasped as the power that moves and shapes the entire spectrum of the social: the form of unrest of social movements and struggles is the unrest of living labor. It is after all true that if all labors united and stopped, following the closing call of *The Communist Manifesto,* the world of capital, thus "globalization" as we know it, would collapse. This is usually deemed an impossible event; yet, the notions of possibility and impossibility should be reconsidered.

Giorgio Agamben, in all of his recent works, calls attention to the dual structure of potentiality and impotentiality (the potentiality not to), constitutive of the very essence of potentiality itself. He does that by going back to Aristotle's distinction between potentiality (*dynamis*) and actuality (*energeia*) and by seeing within potentiality the structure of its suspension. The potentiality not to, the ability to say no, to withdraw, is freedom itself. The inability to make use of one's impotentiality is the clearest demonstration that the freedom we experience today is false, an empty word, a useless concept, which hides the truth of our servitude. If all concrete labors do not spontaneously make use of their ability to not pass into actuality, it remains the task of a radical ontology of labor to show the viability of such an option, at least at the level of theory; and that is, show that other and better worlds are indeed possible once the logic of exploitation is destroyed, as well as show once again that it is on the shoulders of labor that the global machinery of capital rests— shoulders that are stronger than is commonly thought. Given the fact that labor, in its broadest ontological sense, is the motor of social transformation, for there is no social movement today, or in the past, which is not informed and moved by it, it is absolutely demagogical to predict and preach its end, to say, in other words, that nothing has remained but the dead world of capital, whose automatic motions have replaced or will replace the autonomy and power of living labor. I will discuss the question of automation later.

For now, it may be important to mention that automation and globalization, the two main features of present-day capitalism, are themselves the result of the doing of labor—a labor that has been institutionalized in a certain way, yet not of any thing different from it. About these essential moments of capital, one can say what Munck says of globalization alone: that we should not think "as though some blind or mystical force just created globalisation one day—and the whole world becomes its passive victims" (p. 63). The concept of "the world" is here the key concept, for *world* is nothing but the *making* and the *having been made* of labor, and this must be said not simply from a Marxian perspective but also in accordance with the philosophy of Giambattista

Vico. What labor does is constitute a *praxis* that makes the world. The power of praxis, that is, labor, is at one and the same time the power of *poiesis,* of that poetic metaphysics that, for Vico, is responsible for the synthesis of experience, that is, responsible for the equation between *making* and *judging as true.* Judging that *what has been made* is a system that goes under the name of globalization does not cancel the fundamental principle enunciated by Vico, reiterated by Marx, with the qualification, by the latter, that historical circumstances always condition the making itself.

But it is in this making that one finds the active principle, the agent, and the subject: the concrete will, as well as the desire, which alone is able to decide whether to remain or not within the new situation created. It is here that the concepts of potentiality and impotentiality (the potentiality not to)—and that means, the concept of freedom—become important. It is evident that "the world" is not the passive victim of the globalizing process, much less of globalization seen as an event. It is as evident that labor is not a passive and reactive element but, rather, the true force behind all this. What remains to be ascertained is whether there is an outside to subsumption and globalization—but this outside does not have to be spatial in character: it is of an ontological and political outside that we are speaking here. Our answer is positive, for, otherwise, we should accept the idea that the world is a passive victim of a blind force, rather than the conscious construction of labor, regardless of the coercive and oppressive conditions in which labor often finds itself. The question is then whether, besides the narrow equation of potentiality with productivity, the dual structure of true potentiality and the potentiality not to, which in political terms has been theorized and practiced as the *refusal to work* for instance, will be able to give the world a new direction. Again, we say that this is possible. The notion of a global economy in itself is very interesting, for it says that the law (*nomos*) regulating the management of the *oikos* (the habitat, the world) has acquired a global character. Using elements of Agamben's analysis of the law, we can say that this amounts to a deactivation of the law.

As we have seen, the notion of a global economy really means the worldwide application of laissez-faire principles. This in turn means that local economies are overruled, overturned, and neutralized. From the point of view of capital, of capitalist deregulation, and, again, of capital's regulating the suspension of laws and regulations (thus, of new forms of regulation or neo-regulation),[7] the direction is very clear: an infinite expansion of production for its own sake, that is, for the sake of productivity and profit—an infinite expansion of consumption for the same reason. From the point of view of labor, the direction is that of the reduction of its potentiality to productivity alone, rendering useless and void all activity which does not fit that category. By withdrawing and returning to itself, to the neither/nor of its pure potency, labor can bring the capitalist machinery to a halt. Then it will be able to judge in a more adequate manner the world it has made and redirect its effort and power toward the making of a better world.

THE RETURN OF LABOR TO ITSELF

Marx often makes use of the phrase "the return of labor to itself," which is of Hegelian origin. In Hegel, what returns to itself is the Spirit, and it describes the circular movement of the Absolute. The phrase, both in Marx and in Hegel has a precise technical meaning. Giorgio Agamben has written an essay on the question of such a return, focusing on Hegel and Heidegger but drawing conclusions which go beyond both. The article is: "*Se:* Hegel's Absolute and Heidegger's *Ereignis*" (Agamben 1999b: 116–137). He says that in "Indo-European languages, the group of the reflexive *se*... indicates what is proper... and exists autonomously" (p. 116). In English, the reflexive *se* is present in "self." Philosophically, it determines the meaning of the Absolute: "The Latin verb *solvo,* from which the adjective "absolute" is derived, can be analyzed as *se-luo* and indicates the work of loosening, freeing (*luo*) that leads (or leads back) something into its own *se*" (p. 116).

I will not now follow Agamben's interesting analysis of the Absolute in Hegel and of *Ereignis* (enowning, appropriation) in Heidegger. It suffices here to state the basic difference between the two, which is that, whereas the circular movement of the Absolute describes a movement of identity in Hegel—a movement of withdrawal from having found itself in the other, and this is close to Marx's use of it: a withdrawal from the condition of alienation—in Heidegger, the concept of *Ereignis,* which is similar to, but not identical with, Hegel's Absolute, means that "Being itself is experienced as such" (quoted in Agamben 1999b: 128). Thus, whereas for Hegel, according to Heidegger's reading of him, the Absolute's coming-to-itself implies the overcoming [*Aufhebung*] of man's finitude, for it is *in man* that this event takes place, for Heidegger "it is precisely finitude that comes to view—not only man's finitude, but the finitude of *Ereignis* itself" (quoted in Agamben, ibid.). The emphasis on finitude brings us again close to Marx. What is important for us here is Agamben's concluding remark, according to which *se,* "the proper," whose idea is already contained in Heraclitus's concept of *ethos* ("dwelling place, habit"), is "the social praxis itself that, in the end, becomes transparent to itself" (p. 137).

Social praxis is understood as labor. It is labor that returns to itself in the constitution of a new social praxis. Of labor, in its absolute mode and totalizing activity, can be said what Aristotle says of absolute thought: *thought is the thought of thought* (*Metaphysics* 1074 b 35; quoted in Agamben 1999b: 119). Then, *labor is the labor of labor.* To say this means that labor, absolutely speaking, does not belong to capital, but to itself. Not only that, what capital appropriates for itself as fixed capital, which relatively speaking replaces labor in the automation age (see Remark: The Productive Power of Capital), really belongs to labor.

But the phrase also says at least two more things. On the one hand, the essential relation between production and consumption becomes here evident, and the two modalities of productive consumption and consumptive production are brought to bear on the reflexive nature of a labor that is equal to life itself: labor produces labor and is consumed by labor. Yet, on the other hand, the dialectic of production and consumption is not limited to the transformation of the most visible world of matter, which labor necessitates in the creation of value. Rather, as labor enters into the constitution of a social praxis, that is, the work of ideas, the constitution of communities, the structures of governance, the shaping of individuality, and so on, it also *makes* what is properly called *a world,* for the idea of "world" is not contained in the satisfaction of the basic needs of life, and this is already apparent in Aristotle's distinction between *living* and *living well.*[8]

Insofar as the world made by labor is appropriated by what labor is not, the former loses what is proper to it, and it loses its autonomy. The return cannot be a simple holding back from everything it has made, for even that holding back is not actually possible. It is not possible for two different but essentially related reasons. On the one hand, the return is not a departure in the sense of going to *another* place, for the place in which labor finds itself is already *another.* On the other hand, there is really no other place to go: all labor, really all life, being subsumed under capital, there is, as Hardt and Negri say among others, *no outside* (Hardt and Negri 2000). To the first reason we can add that the point is not going somewhere else, for the return implies the destruction of the essence of alienation, which makes *this place,* which is proper to labor, *other;* in substance, it implies the destruction of capital. By leaving "the factory," that is, the whole network of institutions subsuming and directing labor, and returning to itself, labor subtracts from capital the main source of its power and lets it die.

To the second reason we can add that, if it is true that there is no outside in the spatial sense of the word, yet an outside of otherness as alienation, which is the immanence and autonomy of what is proper, can be regained by accomplishing the return. Once this is done, the question of whether there is or there is not an outside—a question that belongs to traditional metaphysics—can be abandoned as useless. The return of labor to itself does not imply the construction of a new world somewhere else, as it would be the case with a thinking that thought in the spirit of the most romantic utopias but, rather, the transformation of *this* world, which is neither inside nor outside, but is, as Nietzsche says, *the only world.*

AS THE UNIVOCAL AND COMMON concept of the social, labor is capable of being included in the synthetic mode of praxis and gives substance to it; otherwise praxis would be a pointless doing and be reduced to mere motion. Substantiated by labor, this praxis, which is already united with poiesis, and that is, with a particular activity of making, defines both the economy and culture, no longer seen as two separate and juxtaposed spheres. In fact, economy and culture (base, or structure, and superstructure, to use Marxian categories), are united in this synthesis and thus constitute a totality, a total social fact.

TOTALITY, ATTACKED BY A CERTAIN modernist, and certainly by the postmodernist, project, is what a radical ontology of labor needs to recuperate, or else be totally annihilated. We have seen how today, under the regime of "globalization," the centrality of labor is diminished in discourse and representation, and that is, diminished by means of a special ideology. Labor is totally subsumed under capital, and the latter constitutes a totality of its own, which is, however, an apparent and disfigured totality, and in fact a mere partiality. The politics of deregulation enhances distribution and consumption for some, but it humiliates and practically weakens the world of labor. Deregulation is a return to the self-regulating market system, of which Polanyi spoke, which gives primacy and autonomy to the economic sphere, which, in other words, detaches the economic from the rest of everyday life, but in so doing, gives it the power of determining all aspects of everyday life.

The same process of deregulation we witness in the economic sphere is also present in the sphere of culture—and this is indeed what goes under the name of postmodernism. There, too, deregulatory practices bring to the fore, as an alternative for some, the logic of *both/and,* that is the idea that choosing is no longer necessary; but they throw the world in a condition of double negation, a *neither/nor,* from which only a truly revolutionary set of practices, able to cover and reshape the totality of everyday life, can save it. However, the point now is not choosing between regulation and deregulation, that is, between two different forms of capital. Deregulation may in fact be the totality of capital moving toward mature globalization, and thus spinning through its typical spiral of madness without the ability to detotalize itself. But totality, as Christian Godin points out with a particular reference to Sartre (Godin 1997), can be seen as a double movement of totalization and detotalization, and in this sense it is a fully positive concept: nothing to do with totalitarianism or any-centric conception of the world. This totalizing/detotalizing movement, which is the same as the movement of the cursed dialectic, remains open, and, within the plane of contingency, which is the true plane of being, it constantly singularizes itself without losing its universal aspiration.

The idea that singularity is opposed to totality must be corrected. The singular is itself a total fact; by converse, a totality is singular. The many aspects constituting the totality of the singular, or the singularity of the total, are merely analytical pointers useful to the examining mind, but they are not such in the synthesis of experience. A fragment does not exist. In the synthetic contraction of *haecceitas,* in its individuating mode, which is the mode of life, a fragment is already a totality.

THE RETURN OF LABOR to itself shows labor's ontological nature in all its clarity. When this happens, labor still shows its presence in production as production (what we shall sometimes refer to as "mere" production), but it also goes beyond it. Indeed, a new understanding of production becomes necessary, one that does not limit production to the sphere of political economy and the market; one that does not, at the same time, distinguish between

NB

economic production and social life, and, in particular, between economic production and artistic production. It is what we attempt to do here, to provide a concept of production based on an adequate understanding of the concept of labor: production without productivism, labor without capital—a production that spans the range of human activity from economy to culture: a poetic praxis, a practical poiesis.

That this is not impossible has been shown, among others, by Karl Polanyi who, on the basis of cultural anthropology and economic history, has argued that, not only capital but also the market has not always existed. Obviously, a return of labor to itself does not imply a recuperation of past historical models, but the study of history certainly shows that what is taken today as an absolute impossibility by the advocates of the autonomy and primacy of the economic sphere, is actually theoretically still possible. And what is possible in theory is also possible in practice, as Aristotle shows.

The present work is a stand against productivity and productivism, as it is against the aesthetic[9] and social idiocy that characterizes our contemporary age. It seeks to be a contribution to the formulation of a concept of praxis, perhaps to the gathering of the elements for a *new science* of praxis, capable of confronting the crisis that at all levels of the social threatens to destroy humanity, annihilate reason, freedom, and hope.

This crisis is mainly brought about by the aberrant way in which we look at production—not as a form of human, sensuous, creative power, not as an activity for the improvement of social welfare and the quality of everyday life, certainly not for the construction of a solid structure for the good life at the global level (where the good life becomes an irreversible totality through the elimination of poverty and the establishment of adequate measures for the equal redistribution of social wealth),[10] but, rather, as a mere means for incrementing profit, with all that this principle entails: cementing the injustices present in the new international division of labor: roughly speaking, the division between a global North and a global South, deepening the system of exploitation and uneven distribution of wealth, increasing the suffering of an ever greater number of people. This happens with the greatest possible indifference toward poverty and toward the often tragic heroism people have to endure for reasons of mere survival—this, in a world which could guarantee a decent life to everybody. Yet, a change will not occur if this indifference (the social idiocy I mentioned earlier) is not destroyed, and that means destroying the culture of productivity and productivism, the firm belief that any change has to pass through the channels of capital in its most mature form, through the channels of a deregulated and self-regulating market. Thus, the widespread notion that productivity growth will ultimately ameliorate the material conditions of life in the world as a whole. Yet, between this indifference and the *essential difference* we are describing there is an absolute contradiction, an irreducible antagonism.

WE LOOK AT LABOR as a neutral concept (*neither-productive-nor-unproductive labor*), which is not a logical abstraction, but an ontological reality. It is *creative labor,* always present within production, regardless of the *mode* of production. However, a mode of production, and that means, a set of institutions and a "general illumination," is capable of reducing this creativity to nothing, as it happens with the capitalist mode. Yet, even when the creativity of labor is reduced to nothing at the institutional and empirical level, it still maintains intact its immense ontological power, its potentiality and the potentiality not to. It is for this reason that capital is not content with using and abusing labor for its own ends, but it also wants the political and social control over it. For, notwithstanding the ideologies saying the opposite, capital is aware of its transitoriness and dependence from labor, whereas the finitude of labor, which is equal to the finitude of history and time, exceeds the "thisness" of any mode, its singularity and specificity; it becomes, rather, the transhistorical ground of history—transhistorical in the sense that, regardless of the institutional form it takes, it is present throughout the various historical stages. In this sense, it is history proper. Thus, following Marx's *critique* of political economy, our task is to stress that capital is a transitory concept and reality but labor is not. Creative labor is then also the free labor (and free time) of the future.

THE UNIVOCAL CONCEPT of being, which constitutes the central moment of Duns Scotus's metaphysics, a pure ontology, becomes living labor in the construction of a radical social ontology. The neutrality and commonality (or diffusion) of being are the neutrality and commonality of labor. Duns Scotus's concept of *thisness* (*haecceitas*) is also used in the present work as the historical contraction of what otherwise remains transhistorical. However, this transhistoricality must be understood not as a realm outside history but, rather, as history itself, as what in history sustains and makes possible the coming to be and passing away of stages, ages, and modes. In its empirical character, history acquires then a contingent dimension. But contingent is also the process of causation of historical facts—a process that, subjectively, requires the intervention of the rational will. Contingency and the rational will open up the sphere of the possible within an otherwise too narrowly defined concept of the real.

There is here a rejection of what-is, of the merely given, not its inclusion in the concept of an alternative. Yet this rejection does not entail the elimination of the concept of empirical reality; it is only its actual and present form that is challenged: *this* what-is, which impedes transformation and change, not the idea that another *this,* inclusive of the potential of labor and, consciously, of possibility in general, another mode of production, inclusive of creativity, must be there. Following the affirmation of the logic of neither/nor, this necessary rejection opens the realm of the *could,* what-could-be, which would otherwise remain closed to both speculation and praxis; in other words, the time when what-is is equal to what-could-be. This modality of the "could," also used to counter the ontotheological "ought," is of course essentially related to both contingency and the rational, or concrete, will. It relates to the concept of contingency insofar as the latter displaces the merely given—a displacement that occurs at the ontological level of its formation.

In this sense, what might otherwise be constructed as a metaphysical category (i.e., necessary, eternal, immutable) is revealed in the light of a contingently caused *this*, caused in the freedom of the *could*. Within this structure of freedom and contingency, which has the configuration of an open disjunction (or... or... or... or....), there remain the ever-germinating seeds of an alternative, of a plurality of alternatives, of radical change, subversion, and actual freedom. Duns Scotus gives a concrete image of this structure—a structure that bridges the gap between the ontological level and the level of concrete, historical occurrences—when, adapting a figure from Avicenna, he says, "... those who deny that some being is contingent should be exposed to torments until they concede that it is possible for them not to be tormented" (Duns Scotus 1987: 9).

IN ADDITION TO THE CONCEPTUAL aid coming from the philosophy of Duns Scotus, a radical ontology of labor also must make use of some of Vico's invaluable concepts and insights. Vico is one of those audacious thinkers who shuns the dull formality of the merely rational (often an unreasonable form of rationality) and, without falling into the irrational, welcomes the work of the imagination and poetic thinking. The result is a form of reason, poetic reason, much more in touch with the exigencies and complexities of the concrete than the prevalent form of reason might be.

Thus, the sense of Vico's poetic metaphysics pervades the whole philosophical framework of the present study, particularly the last chapter on artistic production. With Vico, before Marx, *poiesis* and *praxis* are identified. This means that poetic metaphysics is also practical metaphysics, and this synthetic modality is essentially related to the concepts of doing (praxis) and making (poiesis)—the basis of all social ontology. In fact, Vico's identification of the *verum* with the *factum* is much more than a simple argument against Cartesian epistemology: it is a new ontology of the social being, the making of "this world of nations"—of this world. The concepts of possibility and change are here also present, perhaps often only implied, for the world we make we also can subvert and transform.

IN *THE NEW SCIENCE,* Vico calls his metaphysics a poetic metaphysics. In the conclusion to *On the Most Ancient Wisdom of the Italians Unearthed from the Origins of the Latin Language,* the subtitle of which is *Book of Metaphysics,*[11] and that contains Vico's critique of Descartes as well as his own principles of *verum ipsum factum* and of the limits of human reason, he speaks of a "metaphysics compatible with human frailty," and that is a metaphysics of finitude (Vico 1988: 109). Vico's is not the metaphysics of the certainty of the *cogito* that has God as a guarantor but the metaphysics of the human being as a being in the world with the material and spiritual needs of dwelling in it and making sense of it. His metaphysics is then immediately *practical.* Traditionally, metaphysics is not practice but the principle of practice; it is the principle of all doing (praxis) and of any specific making (poiesis). Yet in Vico the two coincide or at least should not be thought of as separate constitutive moments.[12]

Vico begins the *Book of Metaphysics* with the famous axiom that *verum* (the true) and *factum* (what is made) are the same. This is the "first truth" on which Vico's metaphysics is based. The distance he takes from traditional metaphysics is immediately evident. This first truth means that, in the human world, *being is what is made to be*. The metaphysical, ontological value of this axiom lies in Vico's awareness that "what is done cannot be undone" (p. 107). What is done becomes *fate;* fate, however, does not precede but follows the making. At the beginning, which begins with metaphysics,[13] Vico posits the *factum* and that by which the *factum* is made: making itself, action, doing. However, this making is not thoughtless. Indeed, metaphysics involves and is based on thinking; better, thinking is the essence of metaphysics—a dialectical essence, for metaphysics "seeks its proofs not in the external world but within the modifications of the mind of him who meditates it" (Vico 1968: 374).[14] Thus, in Vico's metaphysics, a metaphysics that is an anthropology and a making of history, thinking is not merely a speculative but also a practical occupation: to think is, Vico explains, to gather or put together things that are separate. It is a synthetic activity.[15] Thinking is a doing in the practical sense that we gather what is already there (namely, what is given and what is made) and that, in so doing, we make something new, a new *factum* and a new *verum*. We make the truth and add to it. Thinking as gathering is, in other words, a human practice that is inseparable from the making of truth.[16]

Vico says, "Just as divine truth is what God sets in order and creates in the act of knowing it, so human truth is what man puts together and makes in the act of knowing it" (p. 46). The difference between divine truth and human truth is very important. From the human standpoint, the former constitutes what is simply *given* (a given that, however, must be interpreted); the latter constitutes what is *made*. Of course, what is given to humans is, for Vico, made by God. A thoroughly secular thought would simply note that not everything is manmade. Certainly, men and women make their world; they—as Marx says after Vico—"make their own history; but they do not make it just as they please; they do not make it under circumstances chosen by themselves, but under circumstances directly encountered, given and transmitted from the past" (Marx 1994: 188). Perhaps less stressed, this truth is also valid for Vico, who begins his metaphysics from a time in which there is supposedly no past, the time of the "first men, stupid, insensate and horrible beasts" (Vico 1968: 374). Although what is given at the beginning is, for Vico, given by God, the fact remains that, fundamentally, "man is neither nothing nor everything" (Vico 1988: 63). The neither/nor modality, which here we encounter again, defines the human condition. It is in this sense that a metaphysics of finitude must be one that is "compatible with human frailty."

Vico's metaphysics moves away from representation and contemplation toward action. But this action is not thoughtless action; it is not "pure." Instead, it is an action that, though it moves from and is grounded in thinking, is immediately practical: a "gathering" ("andar raccogliendo").[17] As he says in the chapter on causes in his *Book of Metaphysics, causa* means *negotium* (activity, absence of rest). In this sense, Vico says, cause and effect are the same. And, he explains, "... if the true is what is made, to prove something from causes is the same as to make it" (p. 64). Making, *poiesis,* is then the ground of Vico's practical metaphysics. This thought is similar to Duns Scotus's notion of contingent causation.

With Vico, the concept of philosophy is the concept of poetry. But the proper material of poetry is the "credible impossibility" (p. 383), which goes beyond the merely given and opens up onto the field of what-could-be. The poets, the interpreters of the gods (381), whom the poets themselves have conceived and created, pass the limit when they believe that the impossible is an integral part of reality as a whole. They cross the metaphorical bridge between what immediately presents itself to their senses (what-is) and the "nothing" that lies beyond (what-could-be). Poetry and thought arise when the world is shaken, when language and reason break down,[18] when human beings need to make sense of things because their usual sense is lost or there has never been one. However, it is precisely this deficiency that turns man into a maker and a creator; thus the axiom "that man in his ignorance makes himself the rule of the universe" (p. 405).

This last statement, from the section on the poetic logic of *The New Science,* is a repetition of what Vico said in *The Book of Metaphysics,* namely, that "man is neither nothing nor everything," and it is also a clear indication of the continuity between these two works. Then, Vico's poetic metaphysics is nothing but a metaphysics "compatible with human frailty," and that means a metaphysics of finitude. What is left outside of this metaphysics is neither reason nor its negation but, for Vico, the infinite and pure intelligence of God. In other words, Vico's system does not lead to irrationalism but to a proper, that is, adequate, use of human reason, its adequate grounding in the power of the imagination. In describing the difference between rational and imaginative (or poetic) metaphysics, Vico says, "... as rational metaphysics teaches that man becomes all things by understanding them (*homo intelligendo fit omnia*), this imaginative metaphysics shows that man becomes all things by *not* understanding them (*homo non intelligendo fit omnia*)." And, in obvious opposition to Descartes' understanding of the relationship between reason and the will,[19] he continues: "[F]or when man understands he extends his mind and takes in the things, but when he does not understand he makes the things out of himself and becomes them by transforming himself into them" (p. 405). This is the transformation of living labor, and it is in this sense that labor, adequately understood, cannot be but *living*—always exceeding the deadly attacks of the subsumption mode.

1   The Ontology of Labor

Problems of the Relationship between Philosophy and Political Economy

> ... something can be changed, for something is possible
> ("possible" being defined as contrary to "necessary")
>
> —John Duns Scotus

POLITICAL ECONOMY OBSCURES the ontological ground of labor and gives the impression of constituting a totality. Yet ontology shakes the ground as well as the edifice of political economy. It then makes sense to begin not with a work of Marx in which the critique of political economy becomes thematic but with one in which the ontological ground of labor is first shown. This will allow us to stress the subjective dimension of the ontological concept of labor and show how this subjectivity, in itself an objective capacity, can unleash that elemental power of subversion whereby the concept subsumed under the categories of political economy and capital goes back to itself, its ground, and its freedom. If this is not done at the outset, that is, if labor does not posit itself in its freedom, one risks remaining prey of the very categories one wished to destroy—destroy in practice as well as in theory. By contrast, when this is done, when labor fully masters its freedom and power, namely, itself as *sensuous human activity* and *practice;*[1] in other words, when it masters its subjectivity, then the subsumptive mode in which it has fallen under capital becomes evidently its antagonistic other, which must be fought in ways similar to those employed against capital—fought not insofar as it is labor but insofar as it is labor subsumed under capital, and then already notlabor, already capital. But this is not the same fight that labor wages against capital proper, a fight to the death; rather, it is a fight that seeks liberation and a return. Or, rather, antagonistic is not the "what" which is subsumed, that is, labor, but rather subsumption proper, the modality of subsumption, the way in which the original "what" is now essentially modified.

It is in Marx's *Economic and Philosophical Manuscripts of 1844* that we find a clear distinction between ontology and political economy. Here, the concept of labor, understood as a category of political economy, undergoes a critique, and this critique is worked out from the point of view of ontology.[2] The ontology of labor recuperates all that political economy neglects: the time that for political economy does not count as labor, that is, as *economic, productive* labor. This is the time of *living labor,* of which productive labor is only an expression—and indeed an aberrant one, for productive labor is the time when living labor enters the process that will transform it into dead labor. But the

Key idea. From this, he moves into the logical analysis of being & not being…

ontology of labor recuperates all social time, for it has to do with all human sensuous activity, all practice, and with subjectivity.

It also has to do, as Marx says, with *the time when the worker is not working.* But this time is not simply "leisure" time as the time during which the worker is physically away from the workplace; rather, it is present even during the labor process, at the point of production, for the attempted reduction of the subjective power of labor (living labor) to labor-power (the commodity form by and through which living labor enters the phase of its consumption and death) can never be thorough and complete. Or, rather, labor-power can never be separated from the living, human being whose capacity it is. Marx defines it as "the aggregate of those mental and physical capabilities existing in the physical form, the living personality, of a human being, capabilities which he sets in motion whenever he produces a use-value of any kind" (1977: 270). Thus, the expenditure of labor-power during the labor process necessitates the actual presence of the worker, but the worker is never completely and only a worker. This means that even when the worker is working, he or she is also *not working,* also *not a worker.* Concretely, during the labor process the worker may choose to spend time daydreaming, organizing the next struggle, implementing an act of sabotage against production itself. But for political economy a human being only has value insofar as he or she can work and work productively, only insofar as he or she can be reduced to the status of a worker. And the essence of the worker lies in his or her labor-power, his or her labor-time; the rest of the time is not of political economy's concern.

Of course, the human being that political economy considers as a possible worker is not any human being, but the proletarian. Political economy defines the *proletarian* as a *worker,* and only looks at him in that respect. Here lies the origin of estrangement and alienation, the proletarian's loss of his humanity. He loses his humanity, not insofar as he is a proletarian, but, rather, insofar as he becomes a worker. He loses his humanity *and* his subjectivity by becoming an element in the objective nexus created by capital, by changing his living labor into a commodity, into labor-power. When the proletarian becomes a worker, then all living labor takes on the form of appearance of productive labor (or its counterpart, unproductive labor.) Then there is apparently no exit, no escape, from the categories with which capital and political economy construct the world. Yet "proletarian" and "worker" are not identical concepts.[3]

THE TIME OF THE PROLETARIAN

Marx says, "It goes without saying that political economy regards the *proletarian,* i.e. he who lives without capital and ground rent from labour alone, and from one-sided labour at that, as nothing more than a *worker.* It can therefore advance the thesis that, like a horse, he must receive enough to enable him to work. *It does not consider him, during the time when he is not working, as a human being.* It leaves this to criminal law, doctors, religion, statistical tables, politics and the beadle" (Marx 1975: 288; last emphasis added). This

time is social *and* institutional time; the time that later became the object of
Foucault's studies on normalization, discipline, and control. In fact, even
though it is of no direct concern for political economy, it is a sort of preparatory time, without which the labor process could not take place or, at least,
be effective.

But what is the proletarian? In the passage by Marx, we find a definition
of the *proletarian as a worker* that defies any productivist logic, and thus any
attempt to reduce Marx's theory of revolution to a past theory able to relate
only to a given phase of the capitalist mode of production, that is, the phase
in which the proletarian can be clearly identified with the factory worker.
Today things stand differently. We hardly speak of "the proletarian," and certainly, particularly with the confusion arising from the concept of "immaterial labor" (when literally understood), the category seems untenable. Marx
defines the proletarian as "he who lives without capital and ground rent from
labour alone." This category is much broader than that of the factory worker.
This labor is, Marx stresses, "one-sided and abstract." Today, the one-sided
and abstract dimension of labor has become even more dominant than in the
mid-nineteenth century, and the proletarian, far from disappearing, shows his
presence everywhere. Political economy's narrow understanding of labor
allows the transformation of whoever has no capital or ground rent into a
worker or a potential worker. This is also the origin of the distinction between
productive and unproductive labor. And, in fact, for political economy,
whether labor is productive or unproductive depends only on the need capital has for it. The only labor that counts is, of course, productive labor. Unproductive labor can also be performed by the proletarian, who would in this case
be an unsuccessful worker, a jobless worker. As Marx says, "In political economy *labour* appears only in the form of *wage-earning activity*" (1975: 289). This
means, in the form of money; but of a specific form of its appearance: money
that is immediately capital. And this again means money as the form of
appearance of exchange value.

The second important moment of this passage has to do with the reproduction of the worker's labor-power: "It [i.e., political economy] can therefore
advance the thesis that, like a horse, he must receive enough to enable him to
work." Thus, as far as capital and its science (political economy) are concerned, the time of the proletarian is only his labor time, that is, the actual
time at the point of production plus the time needed for the reproduction of
his labor-power. The distinction between structure (or base) and superstructure can also be detected here. Labor time is structural time. The time that
remains is superstructural time. This is "the time when [the worker] is not
working."—the time when being is nothing. This time, political economy
leaves to criminal law, doctors, religion, and so on; to the state and the institutions. It is the time in which he or she who has no capital or ground rent
(i.e., the proletarian) is not engaged in a productive or reproductive activity.

Yet, we have seen that this time is also paradoxically present during the labor
process. It is present there as the ontological void that sustains production; as

such it fills the process of production with a potentially infinite number of empty times which constitute capital's principle of ruin and destruction. In fact, capital could not be destroyed by an assimilated or subsumed living labor which valorizes it, not, in other words, by productive labor; rather, capital can be destroyed by a living labor that is present and absent at the same time, *hidden* like the God of Pascal—a labor that is inside and yet outside the production process: not by living labor as labor-power, but by the subjective power of labor, of which labor-power represents the saleable, market form. The time in which the worker is not working is the time of a paradox. However, precisely now the negation of the organic dimension of labor as human sensuous activity, as free and creative practice, that is, as *poiesis,* also becomes apparent. The return of labor to its organic dimension, that is, to a labor that is not a wage-earning activity, requires the crossing back of the territory of the totality of capital, that is, capital in its structural and superstructural forms, the factory and the state, productivity and its disciplinary preparation, the economy and culture. This is a totality that hinges on nothing and has nothing beyond; or so at least it appears. The crossing back is a going beyond that those who are less impeded by the totality of capital are closer to, because have rejected it or have been denied by it. Even though in the time of total subsumption everybody, whether employed or unemployed or, as is more often the case, employed and not-employed at the same time, whether productive or unproductive, is affected by the rules of capital, yet there still remains, there must remain, a space for rebellion and revolt.

At the paradoxical time when the worker is no longer a worker, yet a proletarian who antagonistically confronts and challenges the entire ensemble of capitalist categories and relations, the commodity paradigm enters its deepest crisis. Marx says, "Labour not only produces commodities; it also produces itself and the workers as a *commodity* and it does so in the same proportion in which it produces commodities in general" (p. 324). There could be no clearer statement against the logic of productivism. Indeed, in Marx we find a critique, not an upholding, of this logic. Here it becomes clear that it is not the economic power of production that will change things, but a subtraction from that power—itself a power. The origin of alienation lies precisely in this form of labor: economic (or external) labor. The return of labor to itself, to its organic and creative nature, the return from political economy to ontology, can only be accomplished through the ruin of the system of estrangement and alienation. For this ruin to obtain, capitalist production, economic production, must end; and it can end by simply being left to itself. Capitalist production is in fact the production of labor as its double, its negation, and as an alien power. It produces for the worker a "*loss of reality*" (ibid.). It is only by withdrawing, by subtracting themselves from this logic that the workers will be able to effect a change, and that means, by stopping being workers.[4] Through the power of subtraction, the workers lose the loss itself and may, at the same time, recuperate a sense of reality. We saw in fact that the production of commodities is also the production of labor and of the workers as a commodity. It is this process that attaches and chains the workers to the loss

of their being, to nothingness. And yet this attachment, qualitatively different from the one experienced by the medieval serf, gives at the same time the
illusion of freedom—for freedom there is, to either accept the conditions of
a new form of enslavement or disappear. Marx adds that "the more objects
the worker produces the fewer can he possess and the more he falls under the
domination of his product, of capital" (ibid.). The truth of domination is
then production itself. Domination cannot cease unless production, as the
production of capital, also ceases. *(this could mean no Surplus value – but who knows?)*

The Logic of Neither/Nor and the Means of Life

This domination presents two fundamental moments. They are both moments
of negation, whose co-presence yields a double negation; the same double
negation that, in *Capital,* Marx identifies as the "double freedom" of the
workers. This double negation can be understood as a logic of *neither/nor,*
which essentially defines the condition of workers under capitalism. However, the logic of neither/nor should not be understood only in a negative
sense. On the one hand, it serves as a descriptive term. As such, it describes
the condition of those who no longer belong, or whose belonging is a nonbe-
longing, those who are attached to nothing but themselves; for instance, the
condition of migration and exodus, of those whose traditional ways of life
have been disrupted or destroyed by the emergence and constant expansion
of capital. In this sense, it represents a tragic condition. Yet, on the other
hand, it also has a programmatic, thus fully positive, dimension to it. It is, in
fact, the logic of resistance and desertion, the necessary condition for the constitution of an alternative.

This is not to say that the alternative is easily constituted. The logic of
neither/nor allows us to avoid both a too pessimistic and a too optimistic
view of revolutionary praxis. Marx says, "The more the worker *appropriates*
the external world, sensuous nature, through his labour, the more he deprives
himself of the *means of life* of his labour; and secondly, it becomes less and
less a *means of life* in the immediate sense, a means for the physical subsistence of the worker" (p. 325). A paradoxical situation: "The culmination of
this slavery is that it is only as a *worker* that he can maintain himself as a *physical subject* and only as a *physical subject* that he is a worker" (ibid.). The
worker produces himself as a worker; he uses his power to bring about his own
powerlessness. Under the subsumption of all labor under capital, there seems
to be no escape from this situation; it becomes more and more difficult, virtually impossible, for the proletarian (i.e., he or she who has neither capital
nor ground rent) to make a living unless the logic of capital, with all its threatening offers, is accepted and entered into. Work becomes a necessity—and a
necessity posited by capital. This double condition of negation is seen in the
first volume of *Capital* as the "process which operates two transformations,
whereby the social means of subsistence and production are turned into capital, and the immediate producers are turned into wage-labourers" (1977: 874).

Workers are then free "in the double sense that they *neither* form part of the means of production themselves, as would be the case with slaves, serfs, etc., *nor* do they own the means of production, as would be the case with self-employed peasant proprietors" (ibid.; emphasis added). In order to find a *means of life*, they have to become workers; but they can become workers only because they can dispose of labor as a *means of life*.

The twofold meaning of the expression "means of life" is related to the two senses of the concept of labor: organic (or creative) and estranged (or external or alienated) labor. The latter is forced labor, labor as a wage-earning activity, thus productive labor. The former is not unproductive labor, or better unproductive labor is neither the determinate opposite of productive labor nor is it really different from it, for both of them have productiveness as their measure; rather, this labor that we call *organic* is labor in its totality (a true totality) as against the fictitious totality of capital;[5] it is labor that returns to itself, a labor that also will be referred to as *neither-productive-nor-unproductive*. It is not merely opposed to external labor; it is, rather, in a Spinozian sense, different from it. And the difference must be understood here as essential and radical.

Labor is a *means* whether we consider it as a category of ontology or political economy. It is a means because it is a measure[6] and a mediation; it is a dialogue between one part of nature (man) and nature itself (man's inorganic body). However, this mediation can have a universal character or not. When it has a universal character, man appears, says Marx, as a *species-being*, that is, "a being which treats the species as its own essential being" (1975: 329). This is different from the animals, which "produce only for their immediate needs or those of their young; [and thus] one-sidedly,... man produces universally" (ibid.). This universality has the form of freedom, for "man produces only in freedom from such need" (ibid.).

Fundamentally, this shows that labor can be conceived of as forced or free labor; that free labor is a real possibility. This would of course be a real freedom, not the one posited by capital as a double freedom. It is also the freedom that accounts for artistic production. In this sense, labor becomes a fundamental category of esthetics, and esthetics, rather than being a complement to the general modality of doing characteristic of everyday life, can be equated with practical ontology.[7] Indeed, "man is capable of producing according to the standards of every species;... [and] in accordance with laws of beauty" (ibid.). For Marx it is in the nature of man (also a problematic concept) to treat the species "as its own essential being or itself as a species-being" (ibid.). It is also in his nature to produce *in freedom from* physical needs and thus reproduce, as culture, the whole of nature (ibid.).

Of course, Marx's argument is *essentialist* and linked to the philosophy of the Enlightenment. However, in the passage we are reading it is hard to find a justification of the domination of man over nature; rather, we find an indictment of it, and this precisely when the universal character of the concept of labor is lost, being transformed into a merely particular, or particularistic, and individual means of life. Again, the universal character of labor is such that, through it, man appears as a creator: "nature appears as *his* work and his reality" (ibid.). Estranged labor, on the other hand, takes nature away and transforms its product into an alien power. Estranged labor "reduces spontaneous and free activity to a means, [and] it makes man's species-life a means of his physical existence" (ibid.).

When it is considered in its universality, labor is a univocal concept. The concept of labor, in its universality, has in Marx a function similar to that which, in the philosophy of John Duns Scotus, pertains to the univocal concept of being, that is, to the most common concept. In fact, labor *is* being; its mediating activity has the form of the synthetic moment which in Scotus's ontological syllogism unites two otherwise unrelated extremes.[8]

It is in this sense that we can call this labor *organic*, for it mediates between and unites, *instrumentally*, what otherwise would be left in the separateness of its immediacy. Yet, true immediacy belongs, precisely, to labor itself, to its ontological power of affirmation. Without this power, immediacy would be a scattered inorganic presence, and it would never become *life* and *a world*. To be sure, the instrumentality of organic labor has nothing to do with the external concept of instrumentality, typical of estranged labor and geared toward the domination of nature. The immediacy of labor is not the immediacy of the human will, for the human will, with its rational and reflective determinations, distinguishes itself from that immediacy: "The animal is immediately one with its life activity. It is not distinct from that activity, it *is* that activity. Man makes his life activity itself an object of his will and consciousness. He has conscious life activity. It is not a determination with which he directly merges" (Marx 1975: 328). Thus labor is instrumental and conscious life activity. It depends on the effort of the human will to direct this instrumentality toward its fundamental and original organicity, or to let it open to external forms of estrangement and alienation.

LABOR AS NOTHING

Even in its estranged form, however, labor does not lose its fundamental creative power, but this creation has now the character of narrow economic production, that is, production for the sake of profit. This means that ontology still precedes and grounds political economy, or that political economy is an episode in the history of the social, practical ontology of labor. The class struggle itself, which as is made clear at the outset of the *Communist Manifesto*, well precedes the capitalist mode of production, takes on, under capital, a particular and extreme configuration, for the antagonism between labor and capital becomes irreducible. This irreducibility is the direct consequence of the estrangement and alienation to which capital reduces the natural and organic *appropriation* of the fruit of labor. Private property is the form and substance of this reduction: "*Private property* is therefore the product, result and necessary consequence of *alienated labour,* of the external relation of the worker to nature and to himself" (Marx 1975: 331–332). What the workers lose in the labor process is not merely an economic advantage. As Marx says, they lose reality itself. And to lose reality means to lose ontological status and grounding. Yet what labor produces is not without ontological qualities, for labor, however estranged, remains there as a fundamental creative power. This is why Marx asks the question: "If the product of labour is alien to me and confronts me as an alien power, to whom does it belong?" (1975: 330).

Labor and the product of labor belong, says Marx, to "man himself," but this *man* is an "*alien* being" for the worker who, during the whole process of production, has lost his humanity. If the alien being is *man,* the worker is its negation, *nonman.* Labor and the product of labor belong to "*a man other than the worker*" (ibid.). The word "other" here establishes a difference brought to the point of irreducible antagonism. Other than the worker is man himself, for the worker has lost his humanity, or he has transferred it, directly with his labor, to this *other.* It is precisely by and through the appropriation under a regime of estrangement and alienation that this *other,* this *alien* being, acquires the ontological status of *being-man* as such. The ontological power is labor itself; those who can appropriate this labor and the product of this labor enjoy the status of being; those who cannot do that, fall into nonbeing. Fundamentally, the worker, insofar as he is a worker, is not a man. When capital is everything, labor is nothing. At this level, which is ontological and not merely economic, the class struggle becomes a struggle between life and death, between being and nothing. The negation of the humanity of the worker is inherent in the concept of the worker himself. To re-appropriate his humanity, the worker has to stop being a worker; work, production, has to stop. The concept of a direct producer is what Marx envisages as the overcoming of the concept of the worker. The direct producer re-appropriates the full ontology of organic labor. He or she is also a creator, and not at all a producer in the narrow economic sense. His *property* is *organic,* and not "private." Organic property is not sanctioned by the laws of the State; it is, in fact, not sanctioned at all and of the State it can make no use. Organic property is nothing but the truth which is made manifest in the working together of nature and of that part of nature which the human being itself is.

This continuous shaping of the form of organic property is the "*practical, human-sensuous activity*" called for by Marx in his *Theses on Feuerbach.* In the *Economic and Philosophical Manuscripts,* Marx shows that private property is not the cause, but the consequence, of alienated labor (p. 332). Indeed, labor is *activity,* whereas private property is a *situation,* a state. What we find here is the dialectic between living and dead labor, of which more will be said later.[9] Marx says that what from the point of view of the worker, of living labor, is activity, is, from the point of view of the nonworker, of dead labor, a situation. Both activity and situation are estranged and alienated. Furthermore, what is real and practical for the worker, is theoretical for the nonworker (p. 334).[10] Private property is a *theoretical situation,* that is, a formal, external and legal state. Ontologically speaking it is void. From the point of

By this logic, property is determined by its history, not by the (social) form of its current use.

view of the worker it is simply the alienation form of that real, practical and sensuous activity which, left to its immediacy, would constitute organic property. In reality, property itself is the product of labor; its private or organic character depends solely on whether this labor is alienated or itself organic.

LABOR AS THE ESSENCE OF MAN

The ontological nature of the antagonism between labor and capital is further developed by Marx in the second manuscript. He says, "The worker is the subjective manifestation of the fact that capital is man completely lost to himself, just as capital is the objective manifestation of the fact that labour is man lost to himself" (pp. 334–335).

At first sight, man appears as the middle term and the univocal concept common to the two extremes: capital and labor. In reality, the common concept is labor itself, for it is the only concept which is included in all the three terms: labor, capital, and man. Furthermore, the fact that man is completely lost to himself and becomes nonman is a consequence of the alienated nature of labor, and it is also the origin of private property. Finally, we also have to keep in mind that "man" is nothing but labor, provided that labor is understood ontologically, and not economically, as human sensuous activity—but this would be organic, creative labor. Thus, the concept of labor is to practical, social ontology what the concept of being is to pure ontology: the most common and univocal concept. Even in the dead world of capital, we find nothing but labor, albeit labor in its estranged and congealed form. In the above quotation, Marx distinguishes between the subjective and the objective manifestations of this loss of humanity, of this estrangement. But of course here subjective does not mean relative to a particular point of view, for the point of view of the worker is universal. Subjective does not mean partial; it does not mean nonobjective, for man *is* an objective being, and, in reality, a "non-objective being is a *non-being*" (p. 390). We have seen that capital reduces the worker to a nonbeing; however, this is not why the worker and labor have the character of subjectivity. Instead, "subjective" and "objective" are here used by Marx in a different sense. "Subjective" means "living"; "objective" means "dead." The former is an activity; the latter a situation, as we have seen. Moreover, the subjective has, in this case, preeminence over the objective. In the third manuscript, Marx says, "The *subjective essence* of private property, *private property* as activity for itself, as *subject,* as *person,* is *labour*" (p. 341). Thus, living labor does not lose the character of the objective being, defined later, in the section on Hegel, as "a natural being and as a living natural being" (p. 389), which is active and suffering at the same time. What I am saying is that living labor, understood ontologically and thus, fundamentally, as organic labor, is not simply one aspect of a compound nature, or else human beings would be, at one and the same time, and necessarily so, both labor and the negation of labor, that is, capital. But this cannot be the case. Rather, in its nonestranged form labor is the essence of man in its totality, and this is an

action and a passion. But of course this is not the concept of labor understood by political economy.

Political economy obscures the real nature of the ontology of labor by making *appear* the alien character of the relationship between labor and capital "as
something *real*" (p. 335). The power of creation no longer resides in labor *as
labor*, that is, in its immediate and universal form, but only in labor as subsumed
under capital, in productive labor; and creation is mere production: "The worker
produces capital and capital produces him, which means that he produces himself" (p. 335). But the worker is not all labor: "Political economy... does not
recognize the unoccupied worker, the working man insofar as he is *outside* this
work relationship" (ibid.; emphasis added). The totality of actions and passions, of drives and limitations, which we will consider more closely below, is
reduced by political economy to a single dimension: "... as far as political economy is concerned, the requirements of the worker can be narrowed down to
one: *the need to support him while he is working* and prevent the *race of workers* from dying out" (p. 335). The distinction between the worker and the unoccupied worker is fundamental here. It is the same as the distinction between
productive and unproductive labor, that is, both terms of the distinction fall
within the categories of political economy. What escapes political economy is
the empty time in which both the occupied and unoccupied workers enter a
modality of resistance and revolt. In fact, the unoccupied worker, who usually performs some kind of labor outside the formal paradigm established by
capital, receives his/her identity through and by those same categories. The
working person not employed by capital, that is, the proletarian who is not a
worker, does not, by virtue of this fact alone, perform organic labor. He or
she is still within the "general illumination" of capital and of estranged labor.
The categories of "worker" and "jobless working person" are two determinations of the same reality, they belong to the same logic, just as productive and
unproductive labor do. The totality of organic labor, which is in itself neither-
productive-nor-unproductive, but something *different,* has nothing to do with
having or not having a job. For Marx, this totality is *genuine,* that is, not
"crude," *communism.* In genuine communism, the ontology of labor regains
its unhindered powers.

GENUINE COMMUNISM

Marx gives a definition of communism, of genuine communism, in the third
manuscript. This is a rare fact in Marx's writings, but it is important to dwell
on it because it shows that speaking about what communism is, is no mere exercise in "futurology," but a sense of ontological clarity.[11] First of all, Marx calls
communism a *positive supersession* and a *restoration.* He says, "*Communism* is
the *positive* supersession of *private property* as *human self-estrangement,* and
hence the true *appropriation* of the *human* essence through and for man; it is
the complete restoration of man to himself as a *social,* i.e., human, being..."
(p. 348). Both labor and property are seen in their organic character. Property

is nothing but the consequence of appropriation, the direct result of labor. The *positive* character of this supersession is in line with the concept of ontological affirmations of which Marx speaks later in the text (p. 375) and with his critique of Hegel's dialectic at the end of the *Manuscripts.*

One of the most important moments of this critique has to do precisely with Hegel's concept of negation (the negation of the negation), which Hegel presents as the absolute positive, but which Marx calls a *"false* positivism" (p. 393), to which he counterposes Feuerbach's concept of *the positive in itself* (p. 381). Thus, supersession and restoration have the positive character of affirmation, and this affirmation is the sensuous, practical activity of the natural, objective being which man himself is. It is obvious that what brings about communism so conceived cannot be a change in the economic sphere. Of course, the sphere is rather that of politics. But the question arises: Politics of what sort? Or, rather: What is politics? It is the politics (and this is its true concept) based on the antagonism which has itself ontological foundations. It is therefore in the sphere of political, practical, ontology that this change takes place. In its organic character, that is, in its nonestranged form and in its agreement with nature, human sensuous activity defines not only political and social ontology, but ontology *tout court.* This is the meaning of Marx's definition of genuine communism as the identity of humanism and naturalism: "This communism, as fully developed naturalism, equals humanism, and as fully developed humanism equals naturalism" (p. 348). We will see later, how this synthetic moment goes well beyond the critique of political economy into the constitution of an ontology of liberation.[12] In this ontology, when labor appears *positively* as the medium term between economy and culture, it serves as the univocal concept of the identity established here by Marx. The *oikos* of "economy" will then be what Marx calls "man's inorganic body," nature; and economy will in fact be ecology at this point. Culture, on the other hand, is the shaping, the care, the *cultivation* of the *oikos.*[13] In this careful shaping there is no imposition of external forms, that is, forms that are not in agreement with the nature of the *oikos* itself. This, it seems to me, is the organicity of communism, and, in the last analysis, the identity of economy and culture.

But Marx's definition of communism continues: "It is the *genuine* resolution of the conflict between man and nature, and between man and man, the true resolution of the conflict between existence and being, between objectification and self-affirmation, between freedom and necessity, between individual and species. It is the solution of the riddle of history and knows itself to be the solution" (p. 348). This definition posits the question of communism absolutely beyond the narrow limits of political economy, into the realm of philosophy in general, of metaphysics and ontology precisely, and of ethics. There is a strong utopian strand in Marx's thought at this point, and this not because the *Manuscripts* belong to his "early writings," rather, I believe that this is so because it is in the nature of the concept of communism to be *utopian,* not perhaps in the literal sense of the word, but in a sense similar to the one described by Marcuse who, in the introduction to *An Essay on Liberation,* speaking of contemporary societies, says, "what is denounced as 'utopian' is no longer that which has 'no place' and cannot have any place in the historical universe, but rather that which is blocked from coming about by the power of the established societies" (Marcuse 1964: 3–4). It is then a *real* utopia.

In Marx, more than in Marcuse, the universal dimension of this utopia becomes evident. Of course, Marx's is the language of a nineteenth-century philosopher coming from the Hegelian tradition, and of a man arguing against utopianism, so his definition of communism seems more a-historical than one would expect; or rather it is historical in the Hegelian sense of history as the spirit of the world. Thus, he continues: "The entire movement of history is therefore both the *actual* act of creation of communism—the birth of its empirical existence—and, for its thinking consciousness, the *comprehended* and *known* movement of its *becoming*" (ibid.). To this, he counterposes the crude understanding of communism: "whereas the other communism, which is not yet fully developed, seeks in isolated forms opposed to private property a historical proof for itself, a proof drawn from what already exists..." (ibid.). This "other" communism is utopianism proper: "from what already exists" it seeks to advance to what does not yet exist. Genuine communism, by contrast, posits its own potentiality in the concept of history itself, in the *phenomenology* and the *logic* of a spirit turned sensuous and practical. It posits its own potentiality, from which the actuality of the act will come, in the realm of a practical ontology. Political economy is certainly what hinders this movement, but this movement itself—the movement of history—is broader and more various than the episode constructed and narrated by political economy, the episode of capital.

Let us go back to genuine communism as the resolution of a conflict. All the pairs of conflictual relationships considered here by Marx come down to the opposition between object and subject. This opposition is no longer popular today, for, it is true, when considered in itself, that is, without its resolution, it describes a figure of heterogeneity more present in the analytic forms of discourse than in reality itself. But the resolution is the synthesis, life itself, the organic manner in which what seems scattered and separate comes together in its actuality. To be sure, Marx does not leave the opposition to itself, nor does he solve it in a purely dialectical, but mechanical, manner. This means that what pertains to communism is not the concept of the synthesis, for that pertains to all manifestations of the concrete; rather, what pertains to communism is a peculiar mode of the synthesis. For instance, *private property* is one of the modes in which the synthesis occurs, but not, of course the only one; and from the point of view of communism, this is, particularly, a synthesis that can no longer obtain. In the system of private property, the synthesis that makes up the concrete directly unifies the commodity form to the legal subject and the legal superstructure in general.[14] Private property is the expression of the way in which the ontological modality of appropriation becomes estranged and constitutes, while being in turn legalized by, a system of laws. In communism, the concrete is still the "concentration of many determinations" and a "unity in diversity" (Marx 1973: 101), for, as Marx says, this belongs to the very concept of the concrete. Thus, the resolution of the conflict does not bring about a grey and dull sameness. Instead, it allows for the possibility of a nonconflictual actualization of difference. Here, both the process that creates the commodity form and that which creates the legal form (indeed, two aspects of the same process) return to themselves and create difference *as* difference.

COMMUNISM AND PHILOSOPHY

To be sure, in the *Manuscripts* it is not clear whether this conflict is brought about by capitalism alone, whether it belongs essentially to human nature, or whether the two are combined in the sense that an original *metaphysical* conflict is brought by capitalism to its utmost degree. However, given Marx's concept of human nature (as becoming and always in the making), it is safe to exclude what could at times seem to make room for a traditionally metaphysical understanding of his thought. Instead, there *is* metaphysics, but it is of a different, nontraditional, kind; it is rather in line with Vico's *poetic metaphysics,* which emphasizes precisely the sensuous, human and practical activity, the concept of *making* as the measure of human nature and of the social and cultural world. With a metaphysics of this kind, the possibility of change and of resolution of a conflict is left to the human will—but of a concrete will. The concept of the will, central to the German Idealist tradition from which Marx himself starts and that he later criticizes and rejects, is also a common concept in the movement of thought that goes from Vico to Gramsci, and, before Vico, it is a central concept in the philosophy of John Duns Scotus. In Gramsci, the will—the rational and concrete will—is precisely the movement of self-affirmation; it is, Gramsci says, the superstructure (Gramsci 1971: 403), thus what escapes the immediately narrow domain of political economy.

We have many problems here. On the one hand, we are saying that Marx's concept of communism is based on the will. This is necessary if one wants to avoid the mechanical, deterministic, understanding of dialectic and history, that is, the idea that one historical stage necessarily follows another— necessarily, and not in accordance with the idea of freedom. On the other hand, we have to stress Marx's aversion to the idea of the will, especially of the free will. This aversion is particularly clear in *The German Ideology,* in which Marx and Engels attack the German idealist conception of the will. Yet, if the will—and by that I mean to refer to the concept of the rational or concrete will—is understood as subjectivity and the motor of sensuous activity, of action, then this is not what Marx is attacking. He is against the concept of an arbitrary will; but not only that: he is against a whole philosophical method. Thus, in *The German Ideology,* Marx and Engels say: "In direct contrast to German philosophy which descends from heaven to earth, here we ascend from earth to heaven" (1947: 47). This is a metaphorical manner of speaking, but its meaning is very clear: we start from the concrete, the sensuous, not from the abstract or even speculative moment. Marx and Engels make this very clear: "we do not set out from what men say, imagine, conceive, nor from men as narrated, thought of, imagined, conceived, in order to arrive at men in the flesh. We set out from real, active men, and on the basis of their real life-process we demonstrate the development of the ideological reflexes and echoes of this life-process" (ibid.). This passage, together with the famous statement that follows in the same text a few lines below: "Life is not determined by consciousness, but consciousness by life," strongly supports and justifies, at least at first sight, the structure/superstructure distinction central to a large part of Marxist theory. Yet, one wonders if this method is, besides the necessity of contrasting German Idealism at this point, the one really chosen by Marx. In the introduction to the *Grundrisse* we find a completely different statement on method, indeed quite the opposite of what we have just read, for the concrete is, in thought, not the point of departure, but the point of arrival; and the point of departure is, precisely, the abstract.[15] The will, therefore, that is, imagination, conception, but also thoughtful action, the concrete will, cannot be dismissed as a speculative or abstract moment of a philosophy that has lost contact with reality; on the contrary, it is reality itself.

Given the problematic nature of the argument, it is probably good to say immediately what we have in mind: the creation of communism is a philosophical endeavor, and communism itself a philosophical state. In fact, it is only philosophy that can bring about that *totality* of which Marx speaks. What else could be the solution of the riddle of history and the consciousness that communism itself (the communist subject) would have of being that solution? By "philosophical state" I do not mean, of course, to refer to what only pertains to the mind nor to a caste of professional philosophers, for I am here speaking of philosophy as philosophy of praxis. Yet, this truth is no less important, for otherwise nothing is easier that to conceive of communism as a mere alteration of the mode of production in the strictly economist sense. Let us reproduce Marx's thought once again: "The entire movement of history is therefore both the *actual* act of creation of communism—the birth of its empirical existence—and, for its thinking consciousness, the *comprehended* and *known* movement of its *becoming*" (1975: 348). It is easy, at this point, to split again the *organic* and *total* movement into the opposition and the conflict of a subject and an object, of existence and being, of freedom and necessity, and so on. Indeed, this has been the unhappy history of most socialist thought so far. The failed attempt to build socialism (if not communism) in the Soviet Union, for instance, is the history of the missed resolution of these conflicts. As if communism could be built under the pressure of compulsory laws that only have behind an abstract and irrational will—the will criticized by Marx. This can be done in the spirit of the transition to communism from within a paradigm of strict historical determinism, a concept now criticized by many.

However, from the point of view of the construction of genuine communism, it is untenable. The communist subject posits itself beyond the legal superstructure as well as beyond the economic base; it posits itself in the immediacy of nonideological, nonfetishistic, human and social relations, or better in the neutrality of labor and the law.

E. B. PASHUKANIS

Certainly, under capital and for political economy, the conflict is presented as a logical continuum that does not require a resolution, but must be accepted for what it is, as a metaphysical given. In this sense, it is admirable the way in which Pashukanis draws a parallel discourse between political economy and the law, the concept of value and the will, the subject and the commodity. In *Law and Marxism,* Pashukanis says, "After he has become slavishly dependent on economic relations, which arise behind his back in the shape of the law of value, the economically active subject—now a legal subject—acquires, in compensation as it were, a rare gift: a will, juridically constituted, which makes him absolutely free and equal to other owners of commodities like himself" (1978: 114). This (juridical) will is an ideological construct, and so are all the categories of the legal superstructure, of the subjective sphere. Yet, Pashukanis says, an ideological construct is not nothing, it is not an unreal, *merely* psychological, *merely* subjective, and thus illusory thing; rather, it represents the way in which a given society understands and interprets the material relations taking place within it.

In fact, the categories of political economy are not different: "The categories commodity, value and exchange value are indubitably ideological constructs, distorted, mystified mental images (as Marx put it), by means of which the society based on the exchange of commodities conceives of the labour relations between individual producers" (p. 73). Thus, ideological is not merely what pertains to the superstructure. Rather, ideological is the totality of social determinations that presents the conflict as a logical continuum and as a metaphysical reality. As Pashukanis says in the Preface to the second Russian edition of his book, "the principle of legal subjectivity and the model it implies—which appears to bourgeois jurisprudence as the *a priori* model of the human will—follows with absolute inevitability from the conditions of the economy based on the commodity and on money" (p. 42). And, furthermore, "there is an indissoluble internal connection between the categories of the economy based on the commodity and on money, and the legal form itself" (ibid.). The juridical will is an ideological construct just as the commodity is. Yet, behind its ideological nature, all determinations are based on material relations. Speaking of the categories of political economy, Pashukanis says, "The ideological nature of these forms is proven by the fact that, no sooner do we come to other forms of production than the categories of the commodity, value and so on cease to have any validity whatsoever" (p. 73).

SOCIAL ONTOLOGY

Departing now from Pashukanis, who is interested in the question as to whether the law can be conceived of as social relation, just as capital is, we can draw from what precedes some consequences for our own discourse, that is, our reading of Marx's definition of communism. Communism certainly represents a different mode of production, different from capitalism, and under communism the categories of political economy: commodity, value, exchange value, and so on, cease, as Pashukanis says, to have any validity. They are no longer ideological constructs because the social relations that create them are eliminated, or because social relations are now *regulated* in a radically different way.[16] Yet, the product of labor is still something: "a thing which," says Marx at the outset of Volume I of *Capital,* "through its qualities satisfies human needs of whatever kind" (1977: 125).

If this is true of the categories of political economy, that is, if it is true that they cease to have any validity, not because of an ideological change, of a change in their ideological nature, but because the social relations that give them that nature are eliminated, the same must be true of the categories of the superstructure. The change occurs, respectively, not at the level of political economy or the law. Rather, it occurs at the more fundamental level of social ontology; it is in the constitution of their being that the determinations that make up the concrete undergo a substantial change. Yet, at this point, the point of the resolution of the conflict and of the creation of communism, there is no longer a political economy here and a legal structure there, no longer a logical continuum masking a practical conflict; this is the meaning of the supersession of private property, which, to exist, requires precisely that split and that opposition. Human activity, organic labor, is now the totality of those determinations that, estranged under capital, create a new and total social being, whether this is a man or a woman, an object for everyday life, or a work of art.

The ability to resolve the conflict constitutes the measure of society. Communism is for Marx the only *society* worth of this name, notwithstanding the fact that it belongs to the essence of man to be a social being. The question then does not have to do with whether or not there is a society, but it has to do with its modality. This means that society is not an abstraction, nor is it the negation of the individual: "The individual *is* the *social being*" (Marx 1975: 350). Marx says, "*Society* is therefore the perfected unity in essence of man with nature, the true resurrection of nature, the realized naturalism of man and the realized humanism of nature" (pp. 349–350). It is difficult today to dwell on these thoughts, particularly when one's intention is not to criticize and ridicule them (an intention always based on ignorance or bad faith), but to endorse them as pointers for an alternative. After the so-called collapse of communism, to do this means to be part of a laughable minority. For the vast majority, the word "communism" has the meaning given to it by people like Bastiat, whose ideology has come back today in the dominant and malignant form of neoliberalism. In this sense, communism, far from being a "perfected unity," is *plunder*.[17] For Bastiat, "*Exchange,* like *property,* is a natural right" (1964: 197), and the exercise of this natural right is the essence of freedom (p. 210). Today, neoliberalism is showing to what degree of perfection and freedom are free exchange and free trade able to bring society! Yet, the historical experiments based on the philosophy of communism have done very little (and at times nothing) to break and do away with the logic of productivism, which defines capital. For this reason, the "unity in essence of man with nature," that is, the total and organic conception of life, has more and more given way to fragmentation and estrangement. The concept of, and the desire for, totality continues to live in holistic ways of thinking and practices of a religious nature. What Marx calls "the return of man from religion, the family, the state, etc., to his *human,* i.e. *social* existence" (1975: 349), that is, the construction of that *secular and earthly plenitude* that Gramsci calls "absolute historicism," is seen, paradoxically, as a dehumanization of the human being, as an infringement on the liberty of the individual. Thus, men and women return instead *to* religion, the family, and the state, in search of an identity— as it is happening now in the republics of the former Soviet Union and elsewhere—an identity able only to foment chauvinistic divisions and ideologies.

If one looks for instance at the European twentieth century in the light of Marx's *Manuscripts of 1844,* one realizes that what was missed (and is even now being missed) is not something that lies within the sphere of economics and political economy, but rather within the sphere of philosophy and culture. The rapid industrialization of the Soviet Union and the economy of growth in postwar Western Europe and on a global scale show very well that, economically (*and* technologically) speaking, "man" has the ability to reach and pass the limit. This indeed does not appear to be a problem. It is from the political and social point of view that even those elements of progress, such as the welfare state, soon enter a phase of regression. The *integral* and *total* way in which man could, according to Marx, reappropriate his essence, has become something of a rhetorical figure for the great majority of people. Marx says, "Man appropriates his integral essence in an integral way, as a total man" (p. 351). But what is a "total man"? Of course, for Marx this totality is given, first and foremost, by the "unity in essence of man with nature," thus by society itself. The total man is certainly not the man defined by the one-sidedness of having and possession, but rather the unity of action and passion, *effectiveness* and *suffering.* Marx says, "Private property has made us so stupid and one-sided that an object is only *ours* when we have it, when it exists for us as capital or when we directly possess, eat, drink, wear, inhabit it, etc, in short, when we *use* it" (ibid.). Marx's prescient attack against the society of consumption does not intend to describe the society of the future as a society of scarcity and misery; in other words, communism is not a system that promises "bread and onions" to everybody, as is often thought by those who partake in the social idiocy of the dominant ideology. However, what here seems problematic is Marx's use of the word "use," for the positive meaning of "use-value" as opposed to "exchange value" is well known. In general, we think of estrangement and alienation not when and because we use something, but when and because this something is raised to a level that is not, precisely, that of immediate and direct use, the level of abstraction and exchange. Thus, the fact that Marx speaks negatively here of the concept of "use" is explained by his attempt to redefine this concept at the philosophical, ontological, level. It is precisely *in use* that the analytic gap between subject and object disappears and *praxis* arises as the synthetic involvement of the two terms. But this *use* can go into different directions; it can become *ab-use,* as is often the case under the logic of productivism of our societies, or it can be what Marx calls "*human* use." It is in this latter sense of "use" that the organicity of the relationship between humans and nature is recuperated. In this sense, "use" is the same as "labor." If it is true that consumption is part of production, and production of consumption,[18] then the redefinition of the concept of use redefines the way in which we conceive of the process of production as a whole. Under attack is the concept of thoughtless use, not of use as such. Human use does not start, within the whole cycle of production, at the end of the moment of production proper, nor does labor end when consumption proper begins. This is why I said that labor and use are in reality the same. Marx provides a very deep understanding of this question—and one that proves fertile for today's ecological concerns as well—when he grounds the possibility of the future society, not in a thoughtless transformation of the object of utility: nature, but in the simultaneous transformation of nature *and* the human subject.[19] The human subject changes subjectively and objectively. It is "*all* the physical and intellectual senses" (Marx 1975: 342), estranged under the system of private property and within the modality of "having," that are radically transformed.[20] Marx says, "The supersession of private property is therefore the complete *emancipation* of all human senses and attributes, but it is this emancipation precisely because these senses and attributes have become *human,* subjectively as well as objectively" (p. 352). Here Marx appears as a visionary and, in the positive sense of the word, utopian thinker; as a thinker of the possible, of what-could-be.

THE EMANCIPATION OF THE SENSES

To say that the senses are emancipated can be a very obscure thought, and even more obscure can be what follows: "The *senses* have therefore become *theoreticians* in their immediate praxis" (p. 352). It is, in reality, another way of asserting the resolution of the conflict. Marx prepares the ground for the above statement by saying: "The eye has become a *human* eye, just as its *object* has become a social, *human* object, made by man for man" (ibid.). Unless one wants to believe that Marx is simply playing with philosophical concepts—a play to be later abandoned to favor a more serious and more "scientific" discussion of economic questions—one has to take very seriously this emphasis on the senses, the apparently paradoxical nature of their *theoretical* ability, and the definition of praxis.

Of course, the emphasis on the sensuous is related to the sensationalism and materialism of the Enlightenment, and it is, moreover, analogous to Nietzsche's emphasis on the same concept, as we shall see in the last chapter of this work. With the Enlightenment, the senses become the place of the primal synthesis, yet these are not blind senses, but the senses already endowed with certain rational powers. From them, all experience and all knowledge follow. Thus, in his *Traité des sensations*, Condillac says, "... la sensation enveloppe toutes les facultés de l'âme" (1984: 58). And he concludes his work: "... toutes nos connoissances viennent des senses, et particulièrement du toucher, parce que c'est lui qui instruit les autres" (p. 265). The senses, and particularly touching (thus handling, using, manipulating), inform each other and, ultimately, they also inform judgment. Certainly, the first synthesis of the senses is, just like Marx's concept of the concrete, enmeshed in confusion; hence, analysis and abstraction become necessary. Yet it is the senses themselves that open up the space for thought. The senses, Marx says, become *theoreticians in their immediate praxis:* it is not a simple doing, nor is it a simple recording of sensations; rather, it is the identity of theory and praxis which is based on this understanding of the senses. The act is not the pure act of those philosophies that continue the tradition of German Idealism; it is, rather, the act that knows itself as *this* act and is itself its own theory. With Nietzsche, the sensuous is what remains after the destruction of metaphysics and the demise of the supersensuous as a true world of ideas. The sensuous is *this world,* and the world is the will to power that "imposes[s] upon becoming the character of being" (Nietzsche 1968: #617). By following the senses, with their "subtlety, plenitude, and power" (#820), the world and life become art, a work of art, or work as art. The doer and the doing go back into the deed (#675), that is, to bring together Nietzsche and Marx in this respect, to *their immediate praxis.* In this praxis, and this is also true from a Nietzschean point of view, knowledge is not external and merely overimposed to the act. It is rather the act itself.

It seems obvious that at this point Marx is not simply dealing with the theory of communism; or rather he understands communism as the condition for the overcoming of the separation and relation of externality between thought and being. This does not mean that thought and being become one and the same thing. Rather, they are distinct, and yet united in essence. As Marx says, "It is true that thought and being are *distinct,* but at the same time they are in *unity* with one another" (1975: 351). Here one cannot avoid thinking of Parmenides's position. Parmenides, "the father of materialism" according to Burnet (1957: 182), says in his philosophical poem: "... for it is the same thing that can be thought and that can be" (in Burnet 1957: 173); and again: "The thing that can be thought and that for the sake of which the thought exists is the same" (p. 176).[21]

Is then communism—the solution of the riddle of history—also the solution of the riddle of philosophy, that is, of the question of the relationship between thinking and being? I think that the answer is positive, which means that communism is not simply a way in which society can be organized at the level, first and foremost, of its economy. Communism implies much more than that: the radical transformation of the social subject, and Marx is often explicit and emphatic about this. As he says in another of the "early writings": "To be radical is to grasp things by the root. But for man the root is man himself."[22] This may sound apocalyptic and, after what some have interpreted as the rise and fall of radicalism, no longer tenable.

However, if we go past the ideological and philosophical confusion of the present, we may be able to look at this question with some freshness of thought and perhaps realize that the world needs this radicality much more than it needs the philosophically weak and yet violent inertia of what has usurped the name of democracy. It may very well be that the world needs to recuperate a lost totality, or build it once again, find the solution to a riddle, the resolution of a conflict, the unity in distinction of thinking and being. Probably, one of Marx's most interesting and deepest contributions is, precisely, the emphasis on the senses, on the radical transformation of the social subject—and this is also what, as Murray Bookchin points out, the Marxist tradition has in general completely overlooked.[23]

Of course, there have been exceptions, notably, Che Guevara's concept of the "new man," as well as others; but in general the question of the subject has been seen as not scientific and even not revolutionary (not proletarian) enough. The subject, the subjectivity of the subject, has often been seen as the element holding back the revolutionary process, as the petit-bourgeois, liberal unreadiness lagging behind the ripeness of the objective struggle. Thus, in communist parties around the world, subjectivity was to be castigated as deviant, and no effort was made to understand, at the level of philosophy as well as of everyday life, its meaning and truly revolutionary potential. The communist movement, in the institutional forms it acquired in the so-called socialist or communist countries and elsewhere, became the opposite of what it intended to be. However, the general tendency of a process that turns into a fixed situation is very often at variance with the true substance and motor of ideas. In addition to the notable exception I have mentioned, an emphasis on subjectivity can be found in Gramsci[24] and in readers of the *Grundrisse.* Antonio Negri, for instance, in an interesting reply to Norberto Bobbio's "Is There a Marxist Doctrine of the State?"—as well as in virtually all of his work—gives to subjectivity an explosive content. In the reply to Bobbio, he says, "The 'how' and the 'who' of the revolutionary process are the same" (in Bobbio 1987: 131), which means that the subject and the process are the same.[25] However, the question remains open as to *how* is the *who* of the revolutionary process—a question which finds elements of an answer in the pages of Marx we are presently reading and later, as we shall see, in the *Grundrisse.* In fact, the subject itself is absolute openness looking for a modality of radical and essential difference. This subject is the *proletarian* as defined by Marx at the outset of the *Manuscripts,* not the worker *as a worker.*[26] This means that the subject cannot revolutionize itself (its "how") by continuing to produce capital; rather, it revolutionizes itself by withdrawing from that modality of production. Within the logic of production (or more precisely, productivism), the proletarian who is a worker is completely enslaved. Free at the beginning—actually, the tragic bearer of a "double freedom"—the worker, insofar as he or she is a worker, loses any genuine revolutionary agency. This agency becomes the prerogative of self-designated and self-styled "revolutionaries" who, very often (but not, of course, in all cases), have a very narrow understanding of the concept of revolution and change.[27]

TOTALITY AND THE TOTAL MAN

With the definition of genuine communism, Marx also offers his concept of the *total man*. As we have seen, this is the man who "appropriates his integral essence in an integral way" (Marx 1975: 351). Today, because of the ideological confusion and philosophical bad faith, all talk of totality (and essence) immediately calls forth the concept of totalitarianism. Thinking about totality is equated with totalitarian thinking.[28] In fact, this totality is nothing but the plenitude of being—a redefinition of the old Parmenidean concept as it entered into, and actually grounded, the materialist tradition. Yet, what is it exactly that we mean when we speak of "plenitude of being"? Of course, in the most original sense (that is, according to Parmenides), we mean that being is and nothing is not. For Parmenides, "everything is full of what is" (in Burnet 1957: 175).

This fullness, or plenitude, is not the absolute and abstract positive that, in Hegel's dialectic, follows, and is synonymous with, the negation of the negation, that is, the concept from which Hegel starts and to which he returns. It is rather, in Marx's evaluation of Feuerbach's achievement, "the positive which is based upon itself and positively grounded in itself" (Marx 1975: 381). In Parmenides, this is the concept of the same: "It is the same, and it rests in the self-same place, abiding in itself" (in Burnet 1957: 175). This concept of the positive, which, to put it in an extremely schematic way, goes from Parmenides to Duns Scotus to Spinoza and beyond (notably, Deleuze), constitutes the only alternative to the either/or logic of essentialism and relativism alike, as well as to the logic of fragmentation criticized by philosophers such as Marx and later celebrated in postmodern thought. The totality (or plenitude) that follows from, and is included in, this concept is not such that it denies difference and singularity. To the contrary, it makes them possible, for each expression of being is then total and fully positive. Excluded is not one part of being, but exclusion itself. Thus, a radical transformation of the world is not a reshuffling of the balance of power, nor is it an inversion of the modalities of inclusion and exclusion. Rather, it is a liberation of the fully positive into everything to which it can belong. The idea of the dissolution of power is simply this: not an impossible elimination of power in all its forms, for that would reduce being to nothing, and nothing cannot be; but rather its dispersion and equal presence everywhere. If the "totalistic imagination" has been, as Martin Jay says, a feature of the revolutionary intellectuals (Jay 1984: 13), this cannot be ascribed to their desire for the elimination of difference, as it is usually understood when "totality" is assimilated and equated to "totalitarianism." To the contrary, the desire that sustains this imagination tends toward the constitution of a totality full of totalities, a plenitude full of plenitudes, a world full of worlds.[29]

In Marx, this totality announces itself in many ways. But the most fundamental aspect of it lies, at least in the *Manuscripts,* in its anthropological dimension. In this sense, Marx is neither an essentialist in the traditional, metaphysical sense (that is, a metaphysics that posits essence as preceding existence), nor is he someone using the idea of totality with a nostalgic, romantic look back at the past. Furthermore, his critique of the loss of totality does not rest on moral, or moralistic, ground. In a way which sounds somewhat Nietzschean, Marx says, "The idea of *one* basis for life and another for *science* is from the very outset a lie" (1975: 355). This has to do with science in general, but also with that particular social science that goes under the name of political economy. The question is not whether a science is right or wrong, but how this science (this knowing) relates to life. From this we can see to which extent Marx remains linked to the ideas of the Enlightenment, especially the idea of *progress.* From the correct interpretation of this admittedly problematic concept also follows an interpretation of the concept of reality and technology. For Marx, it is clear that, first and foremost, this world is man-made. In this respect, Marx follows the general direction of thought set by Vico (himself a figure of the Enlightenment), and he calls attention to Vico's ideas in the first volume of *Capital.* But the world is made through industry, through technology, and in this making the true nature of man comes to the fore—man's true nature, that is, making itself. Marx says, "Nature as it comes into being in human history—is the *true* nature of man; hence nature as it comes into being through industry, though in an *estranged* form, is true *anthropological* nature" (p. 355).

THE TRUTH OF HISTORY

Let us stop for a moment and consider this modifying phrase: "though in an *estranged* form." What Marx is saying here is that there is nothing false or mistaken in history. A Hegelian position, and Marx is here criticizing Hegel. What appears to be false, for it de-humanizes human nature, is still part of the true nature of the human being. This is the meaning of Marx's essentialism: estranged labor is not labor as such, certainly not the true and original organic labor, yet through it the latter is also expended and comes to sad fruition. This is why, fundamentally, that is, ontologically prior than economically, capital depends on labor, private property on the sensuous and universal modality of appropriation; rather than the other way around.

Yet, at the same time, estrangement destroys organic totality. The latter still remains as a sort of hidden, and thus restorable, base; however, its actuality is taken away. As Marx says, "It is inherent in the very nature of estrangement that each sphere imposes upon me a different and contrary standard:

one standard for morality, one for political economy, and so on" (p. 362). We are at the origin of the structure/superstructure distinction which had, at one point, become a dogma of a certain brand of Marxism. In reality, the delimitation of spheres is itself a product of estrangement. Once the organic totality is recuperated, even the economic activity of human beings—what constitutes the base—becomes part of their general sensuous activity only. Again, this does not mean that economic concerns will cease; rather, the concept of economy itself is by this completely modified.

The fact that true human nature becomes historical even under a regime of estrangement can be certainly looked at as a metaphysical truth, but such that it proves the solidity of the ontology of labor. This is indeed the central point in Marx's work, both in the *Manuscripts* and subsequently, that is, the centrality and the essential nature of labor. In the *Manuscripts* he says, "To say that the *division of labor* and *exchange* are based on *private property* is simply to say that *labour* is the essence of private property—an assertion that the political economist is incapable of proving and which we intend to prove for him" (p. 374). All of Marx's subsequent work can be seen as an attempt to prove this, and it constitutes precisely his *critique* of political economy. His later emphasis on the industrial working class, which contradicts his definition of the proletarian at the time of the *Manuscripts* and which has created so many problems with respect to the way in which his thought is to be interpreted and applied, may simply be due to the fact that when he was writing (but the situation has changed in the course of the twentieth century),[30] industrial labor (especially heavy industry) was in its rise and its antagonism to capital was at its sharpest and least reducible form. But after the Great Depression, during which capitalism threatened to collapse, and after its salvaging through the Keynesian doctrine of state intervention, the condition and destiny of the industrial working class (particularly in so-called Western societies) completely changed. Yet, what has not changed is the fundamental truth enunciated by Marx that labor is the essence of private property (under a regime of private property) and of the constituted social world in general; that is, in other words, the ontological power that makes and sustains this "world of nations." Labor can be displaced, deterritorialized, and reterritorialized (to use the expression of Deleuze and Guattari), and this is what is happening nowadays under the regime of global capital (a regime that, to be sure, is an historical development of a tendency that pertains to the logic of capital proper). But this displacement, this new international division of labor, does not change the basic truths defining capital and its opposite: labor. The maquiladoras of the U.S./Mexican border, to make a relevant example, do not say that labor is over, and the transformation of the Mexican state of Quintana Roo into a Riviera Maya still has labor (and estranged labor at that) as its essence and truth. It also can be noted that, in Mexico, the development of Quintana Roo (besides the economic and social disparity present within it) is symmetrical to the exclusion and poverty of the state of Chiapas. *Antagonism itself has not disappeared; it, too, has been displaced.*

Certainly, private property and estrangement are not exclusive features of the regime of capital. With the coming of agriculture, during the passage to the Neolithic (or rather, what Lewis Mumford calls the "Paleolithic-Neolithic Union"),[31] the forms—more or less idealized—of primitive communal production and wealth see the beginning of the end. Or in any case, to take a literary example from the classics, they end with the last stage of humanity, the age of hard iron, and its *amor sceleratus habendi* (Ovid, *Metamorphoses,* Book I). What is peculiar to capital, then, is not that labor is estranged and exploited; peculiar are rather the forms of this estrangement and exploitation. Above all the fact that the proletarian enters "freely" in the act of exchange whereby he or she becomes a worker, and hence the reduction of his or her living labor to abstract labor in the form of labor-power, that is, the commodity form of labor. This is an important observation because it says that organic labor and thus communism do not lie at the level of history (as past history), but at the level of ontology, of poetry and the imagination: at the level of the possible. In fact, communism is, precisely, a utopia. Of course, this is not Marx's explicit thought, for he was absolutely against the utopian idea of communism. Yet, as we have seen, he was not against (rather, he was for) the *poetry from the future* only capable of bringing about the radical change of communism: not a "really existing socialism," but a form of social organization that could not be looked for in a golden age that preceded, and not immediately, the age of hard iron.

Thus, true anthropological nature manifests itself through industry, through technology, and *in* history. It *is* history; it makes history. But what is anthropological, and thus historical, is not itself the ground. It is rather what stands above the ground and makes it anthropologically and historically meaningful. Yet the possibility of this standing (thus, its essential moment), the making of the world, lies at the ontological level. Herein lies the radicality of Marx's thought; in its desire not merely to substitute one stage of history with another, one mode of production with another, but to subvert the universal and material conditions of human existence.

ONTOLOGY, MONEY, AND THE LIMITS OF PRODUCTION

The section on money in the *Manuscripts,* begins precisely with this idea, accepted at this point as axiomatic, namely, with the idea of the ontological foundations of anthropology and history. It is actually interesting that the section on money starts with a reiteration and a summing-up of the ontological argument Marx has been making, now rendered explicit. Marx now posits as a condition the fact that "man's *feelings,* passions, etc. are not merely anthropological characteristics in the narrow sense, but are truly *ontological* affirmations of his essence (nature), and... they only really affirm themselves in so far as their *object* exists *sensuously* for them" (1975: 375). On the basis of this condition, Marx draws the concepts of difference (i.e., the fact that there are different modes of affirmation), of praxis (as the involvement of the object in the sensuous activity of a subject), and of the universality of history. History, the science of man, is "itself a product of the self-formation of man through practical activity" (ibid.). Here, "through developed industry, i.e., through the mediation of private property... the ontological essence of human passion come[s] into being, both in its totality and in its humanity" (ibid.). Of course, Marx is not defending the modern concept of private property. In fact, he qualifies this private property as "freed from estrangement": "The meaning of private property, freed from its estrangement, is the *existence* of *essential objects* for man, both as objects of enjoyment and of activity" (ibid.).

Marx is saying this to show how the ontological power of labor—in the broad sense of sensuous, practical activity—is expressed, under a regime of estrangement, in the form of money. On the basis of the universality (and univocity) of this power—which has the form of property as appropriation—money is then "regarded as an omnipotent being" (ibid.). This is similar to the way in which, in Nietzsche's account of the genealogy of truth, one perspectival truth becomes the only, absolute, divine truth (whose eminent form of expression is not money, but God). In this sense, money takes on a real ontological power, for it is essentially appropriation and thus labor. Labor itself, in its estranged form, has to rely on a negated organicity. This organicity, even if it does not manifest itself as such, is still there, and thus it can be restored. Under the regime of capital, money becomes the essential mediation, or, as Marx says, "the *pimp* between need and object, between life and man's means of life" (ibid.). Money expresses all modalities of ontological affirmation as one; yet all ontological affirmations do not have—if understood as to what belongs essentially to their concept—an economic foundation and meaning.

The critique of money, and of the form of value expressed by and through money, is the center of Marx's critique of political economy, in the *Manuscripts* and later in the *Grundrisse*. It is true that Marx (and Engels) accepted the concept of production as developed by the classical political economists and thus opened the way for a Marxist version of the logic of productivism. They did this on the basis of the idea of progress and of the optimism inherent in their concept of history. Yet it is also true that in the cessation of estranged labor and the coming of communal production they saw a way out of this logic—through the concept of the development of the full, total individual. This concept entails the overcoming of the division of labor and thus a completely different idea of production. It is difficult to find unambiguous justifications for the logic of productivism in the work of Marx. It is, I believe, impossible to think that Marx would have seen the forced industrialization of the Soviet Union under Stalin as a correct way of proceeding on the road to socialism and communism. The fact that he saw the possibility of revolution in the industrialized countries of his time unequivocally says that for him the task of industrialization, and the regime of the factory, pertained to the concept of capitalism, not of socialism or communism.

To the concept of communism pertains the liberation of time, not its framing in the factory system.

It is the concept of communism itself that cannot be reduced to economic categories. Its essential meaning transcends those categories; yet, the discourse on communism starts from within a modern market society and on the basis of a long history of the idea that nature can be dominated by human beings (and thus—as part of nature—some human beings by others.) Marx absolutely denounces the idea of the free market, but, regarding domination, he only criticizes the fact that some human beings dominate others (and particularly through the market system), not the idea—to which Francis Bacon gave a modern form—of the human domination of nature. Thus, from an ecological point of view Marx can be, and has been, criticized in turn. Nor is our task that of providing an absolute defense of Marx's philosophy and, especially, of Marxism. Yet, when one accuses Marx of considering labor as the only creator of value, in disregard of nature—as the ecologist historian Clive Ponting does—one forgets that in the *Critique of the Gotha Programme* it is precisely the opposite view that Marx holds (Cf. Ponting 1991: 157). Moreover, the idea that labor is *not* the only creator of value, stated explicitly in the *Critique of the Gotha Programme,* has its roots in the *Manuscripts.* Here Marx, speaking of externalization [*Entäusserung*] of the human corporeal power, says that the establishing [*Setzen*] of this subjective power is itself objective: "In the act of establishing [corporeal man] does not descend from its "pure activity" to the *creation* of *objects;* on the contrary, its *objective* product simply confirms its *objective* activity as the activity of an objective, natural being" (p. 389). Yet Ponting is correct in pointing out the Eurocentric (he does not use this word) and anthropocentric nature of Marxism, which, he says, belongs to a metaphysics of domination rooted in Greek and Roman thought. This metaphysics invests and is strengthened by Judaism and Christianity where, with the notable exceptions of Maimonides and Francis of Assisi, who deny the centrality of man and his primacy over other beings (Ponting, pp. 145–146), the concept of human domination over nature takes on the form of a right and passes as such into modern science and modernity. Ponting also reminds us that in the Taoist and Buddhist traditions, as well as in the traditions of pre-Columbian America, things stand differently, so much so that some economists (notably, E. F. Schumacher in his *Small is Beautiful*) have opposed the Eurocentric tradition with a "Buddhist Economics" (Ponting, pp. 152–153, 159).

These are very serious problems, which I cannot treat exhaustively here. I can only say that they can be narrowed down to one: that of the quest for an alternative. This is, after all, Marx's main concern. But with the celebrated "fall of communism" and end of the possibility of revolution, the question of the alternative becomes not simpler, but more complex. It is clear that the possibility of revolution has not ended; certainly, its axis has moved, and most of the revolutions of this past century have had very little in common with Marxist orthodoxy. Yet, central remains the question of labor, often conceived again in solely economic, and thus self-defeating, terms.

THE ONTOLOGICAL PLANE OF IMMANENCE: SOCIAL PRACTICE AND THE *COULD* MODALITY

Philosophically, the centrality of labor calls forth the concept of the organic. In this sense, labor reconstitutes the whole world, which includes the economic sphere, but it is not reducible to it. The concept of the organic becomes central in Lukács's social ontology. With Lukács, the concept of the organic comes about through the *distancing* operated by man. But it is this same *distancing* that dialectically creates man as man. In Volume III of *The Ontology of Social Being: Labour,* Lukács calls this distancing the "freeing of man from his environment" (1980: 26). The basis of this distancing or separation is labor, and it is through the distancing itself that labor passes from a rudimentary to a sophisticated form and becomes the "model of all social practice" (p. 46), that is, of *praxis.*

Lukács defends a very unpopular theory: the subject/object dualism. He says that this dualism is necessary, yet "deliberately made." This seems like a paradox, but in reality it is a move toward the synthetic mode of practical activity trying to escape the reductions of both determinism and voluntarism. He says, "This deliberately made separation between subject and object is a necessary product of the labour process, and at the same time the basis of the specifically human mode of existence" (p. 24). In reality the subject/object distinction is not the only unpopular concept Lukács recuperates from the tradition. In fact, his entire argument rests on the concept of teleology that for him is inherent in the concept of labor ontologically understood. Thus, he does not speak of a general and generic teleology, but, with Marx, of a teleology of labor that is "ontologically established as a real moment of material actuality" (p. 8). Here we see that by teleology Lukács means nothing but the concept of becoming, a rational becoming. Teleology is then the motor of the dialectical movement through which a "new objectivity" arises (p. 3). It is good to understand this teleology in terms of a rational becoming because present within it are the moments of reflection and consciousness: "If the subject, separated from the object world as it is in consciousness, were unable to consider this object world and reproduce it in its inherent being, the positing of goals that underlies even the most primitive labour could not come about at all" (p. 24). Yet, the most important moment is not consciousness, which to some degree is also present in the life of animals. Rather, the most important moment is what tears man away (or frees him) from the biological sphere (within which the animals remain): this is the *distancing,* which is not an act of consciousness (or at least not of consciousness alone), but it is rather already human praxis itself.

Instead of a dualism, we find a synthesis, instead of a paradox, a dialectical moment. Lukács is careful enough to say that, although they remain within the realm of the biological, animals also "stand in a certain relationship to their environment" (p. 24). Yet, what distinguishes man's separation from his environment and creates the subject/object relationship denied to animals is the *universality* inherent in the specificity of what Marx understood as a species-being. Marcuse called attention to this problem in his 1932 essay on the *Manuscripts,* saying that the concept of species-being must be understood in terms of universality if one is to avoid dangerous misunderstandings.[32] Yet, it remains a specific (or even singular) universality, that is, it characterizes human activity alone.

For Lukács, it is the "complex of social being" (p. 49), grounded in labor, constituted by and through labor and, at the same time, departing from it in many ways (p. 59). Lukács says, "labour is the underlying and hence the simplest and most elementary form of those complexes whose dynamic interaction is what constitutes the specificity of social practice" (ibid.). Labor is then a univocal concept. Lukács never fully addressed these departures from labor, which were to constitute the subject-matter of the never written *Ethics.* But it is clear that they were to be dealt with according to a method different from the strictly dialectical one (of the identity of identity and nonidentity) which provided the first structural differentiation as a distancing of man from his environment. These more complex forms were to become the object of what we can call a "genealogical" method of study. The passage from a dialectical to a genealogical method is adumbrated in the following passage that I will read in two parts: "The identity of identity and nonidentity in its structural form... is reducible... to the way that labour itself materially realizes the radically new relationship of metabolism with nature..." (p. 59). This means that it is through a dialectical process that the distancing (the new metabolism) takes place and a subject/object relationship arises. Then Lukács continues: "... whereas the overwhelming majority of other more complicated forms of social practice already have this metabolism with nature, the basis of man's reproduction in society, as their insuperable precondition" (ibid.). And this means that the distancing (and thus the new metabolism with nature) constitutes the structural basis for the development of culture. As I have noted, this seems to be a move from a purely dialectical to a genealogical method.

Hints of what the ethical problem is can be found in the pages where Lukács discusses the question of the "ought"—a central question of modern German philosophy, of German Idealism in particular. This is a question that, one way or the other, always brings in a certain determinism. In relation to labor and the philosophy of the future, the "ought" modality should be criticized, rejected and replaced by the modality of the *could.*[33]

Lukács speaks of the "ought" in relation to Kant and Hegel. For him, the "genesis of the 'ought' in the teleological nature of labour" (p. 72) has to do with the first, dialectical passage that radicalizes the opposition between man and nature by creating a new metabolism and a distancing. He says, "The ontological nature of the 'ought' in labour is certainly oriented to the working subject, and determines not only his behavior in labour, but also his behavior towards himself as the subject of the labour process" (p. 72). This is a process that leads to the foundation of a work ethic. For Lukács, however, this process is "the ontological foundation for the metabolism between man and nature" (ibid.). In other words, labor becomes the ontological vector of man's "self-control" (p. 73); the "ought" of labor becomes "the growing command of [man's] insight over his own spontaneous biological inclinations, habits, etc...." (ibid.)—a profound idea of freedom that owes a lot to Kant and post-Kantian German thought.[34]

Giving to this process ontological and objective foundation in terms of the "ought" modality does not mean reducing the fundamental character of human freedom (with its ability to think and will and choose itself as freedom) to a static, biologically determined behavior, which would only have a tragic note appended to it. Looked at from the modality of the "ought," that is, from the more sophisticated and complex forms of its history and genealogy, the first dialectical move of a distancing seems to command the entire history of human labor. Thus, even the most sophisticated and complex forms of this history would be determined by it and little room would be left for human agency and freedom. Those new forms would then be determined by the new metabolism that, on the basis of man's separation from nature, would now create, not the possibility of genuine freedom, but only the conditions of tragedy, to which all history must submit. The objectivity posited by the process of the "ought" is a "regulative principle" (p. 73). Yet, notwithstanding the conceptual limitations of the "ought" and the urgency we experience to replace it with the openness of the "could," in which determinism is completely eliminated without falling into the error of denying all determinations, its regulative function is not external. Just as we saw in the case of teleology, here too there is a potentiality whose actualization depends on the dynamic interaction of those complexes made up by labor and constituting the specificity of social practice (p. 59).

To be sure, Lukács tries to avoid determinism by saying explicitly that the teleological positing of the "ought" does not entail the idea of the past determining the present in an unqualified way, but rather it entails the idea of the future directing the present in a determined way. Thus, he calls the "ought" relations "acts in which it is not the past in its spontaneous causality that determines the present, but in which the teleologically posited future task is the determining principle of practice directed towards it" (p. 74). This is what in phenomenology is known as *pro-ject*. Yet, the question remains as to whether the problem of determinism is really avoided. I think that the answer is negative. The "ought" is not simply teleological; it is also always theological: it belongs to that ontotheology that characterizes Western metaphysics. As I have noted and will show later, it is only through the "could" modality that a genuine sense of freedom can be regained.

It is possible that by means of the "ought" of labor Lukács seeks to overcome the structure/superstructure distinction within Marxism and formulate a unifying ontological principle. He emphasizes in fact the relationship between the "natural foundation of human existence"—which for the "new materialism founded by Marx" is "insurpassable" (p. 74)—and the more complex form of social categories arising in the development of history. For him, the "ought" in labor is grounded in labor's first shaping the metabolism of nature and society. He says, "This relationship is the foundation of both the rise of the "ought" in general, from the human and social type of need satisfaction, and of its specificity, its special quality and its being-determining limits, which are called into existence and determined by this "ought" as the form and expression of real relations" (ibid.). It is easy to see how the "rise of the 'ought' in general," with its undeniable character of necessity, corresponds to the base (or structure), whereas the specific "form and expression of real relations" correspond to the superstructure of the traditional Marxist paradigm. The "ought" is then what unifies them. Yet, although the "ought" may be responsible for the basic system of needs—but there, too, responsible could be any other principle or modality—it is difficult to see what would bring it into operation within a more specific and sophisticated system of social relations. If the problem is making sure that these relations are understood as real and as having a material foundation, the "ought" still remains problematic, for it essentially and necessarily reduces these phenomena (the social relations) to their material foundations by reinscribing the determinism one had sought to avoid or eliminate. If this interpretation is correct, we also can say that by trying to avoid a generic (and in all actuality unavoidable) causality (one for which freedom and contingency operate at the ontological level, whereas at the empirical level events are in a relation of cause and effect), one falls into a necessary, or structural, form of causality, in which it seems that this relation of cause and effect goes back to the ontological, "noumenal," level, preordaining everything that must unfold. In other words, the open modality of the "could" (according to which causality remains open to an infinite series of disjunctions: or... or... or... or...) states a generic causality principle whereby whatever eventually obtains simply denies all other events that could have obtained as well. This rule is characterized by openness, and it avoids strict determinism without impairing the view that, within the contingent, there is still an open relation of cause and effect. To deny this would be to solve the question by suppressing it, which is often what is done. Yet, in order to understand this logic we only have to think of what Duns Scotus says, that events are not contingent, but that they are *caused contingently.* When on the other hand, the difficulty is solved through the modality of the "ought," one enters the realm of strict and necessary (structural) causality, represented by the formula "if A, then B." In this case, "B" obtains because it *must* obtain; in the ethical sphere, one says that it obtains because it "ought" to. And yet, Lukács is aware of this. He says that "the 'ought' in the labor process already contains possibilities of the most diverse kind, both objective and subjective. Which of these become social realities, and how, depends on the concrete development of society and the time, and as we also know, the concrete determinations of this development can only be understood after the event" (pp. 74–75). In reality, by clinging to the concept of the "ought" this is a plain impossibility. As I will show later, it is only through the "could" that Lukács's correct understanding of this important point becomes actual and valid.

We see the consequences that such a discourse has for the Marxist question of base and superstructure. With the "ought" of labor, which solves the question of the metabolism between nature and society, it is not simply the base (that is, the new metabolism) that comes about in such and such a way but also what follows and "ought" to follow from it. Nor does this way of looking at the problem account for why, at different historical stages, this metabolism acquires new modalities and functions. For it is easy to see, for instance, that the distancing of "primitive" societies is absolutely different from the distancing produced by (and at the same time producing) technology, even though the principle may be one and the same. What could then this "ought" in labor be, that works unevenly on the basis of a first selfsame distancing? How does the "ought" (the German *Sollen*) compare, for instance, to the *hau* of the Maori, the spirit of the thing? Here, what moves labor and its "legal superstructure" comes from the forest and to the forest wishes to return. This spirit is productive power itself, and the structural moment here constitutes and pervades the whole (Mauss 1990: 10–13). Notwithstanding the character of obligation that is here present, too, the ontotheological, transcendental dimension typical of the "ought" is completely missing, for the spirit of the thing is absolute immanence.

This criticism of Lukács should not obscure the importance of his discourse on the ontology of labor. The criticism of the concept of the "ought" goes beyond Lukács himself, and we have seen that he actually tries to solve the inherent contradictions only to make them more evident. Thus, this criticism does not have to do with the importance that Lukács gives to the fundamental role of labor in human history. This becomes particularly true when Lukács deals with the concept of freedom, which is, however, weakened by his treatment of the "ought," as we have seen. In relation to freedom, Lukács says, "How fundamental labour is for the humanization of man is also shown in the fact that its ontological constitution forms the genetic point of departure for yet another question of life that has deeply affected men over the entire course of their history, the question of freedom" (p. 112). However, here, too, Lukács reproduces the hidden determinism we have seen in relation to the "ought." This determinism is inherent in the dualistic method he has chosen, which we have interpreted as divided into a dialectical and a genealogical part. He says that, in considering the question of freedom, "we must apply the same method as before. That is, point out the original structure that forms the point of departure for the later forms, and their insurpassable foundation, while simultaneously bringing to view those qualitative distinctions that appear in the course of the later development, spontaneously and unavoidably, and which necessarily modify decisively, even in important respects, the original structure of the phenomenon" (112–113). I have quoted the whole passage because here the method employed in the whole study is stated in its most explicit and clear way. Again, it is not clear how this method would really account for the variety of historical and social phenomena. The "insurpassable foundation," that is, the selfsame distancing, constitutes the basis for a series of realities that appear "spontaneously and unavoidably." But there is no hint as to why these realities can be so different as to develop into different cultures and civilizations. Looked at from this point of view, the modification of the original structure is also a problem. It is true that Lukács has already made clear how it is the teleological positing of the future that conditions any present human activity and thus the development of history; yet, on the basis of the "ought," the question remains as to what makes people posit *this* future rather than *that;* in other words, the relationship between the "ought" and the freedom of this positing remains a nonrelationship, an irreducible gap.

In a sentence that has a Heideggerian flavor, Lukács says, "The particular difficulty for a general methodological investigation of freedom lies precisely in the fact that it belongs to the most manifold, many-sided and scintillating phenomena of social development" (p. 113). Again, Lukács directs the reader to his never written *Ethics.* However, the question of freedom, as it relates to labor, is a central question throughout the book. We have already seen how the first distancing is in itself an act of freedom: it is a project of freedom and it makes, at the same time, this project possible. At that point, dialectics proper is abandoned for an ontological genesis, a genealogy, as we have seen. Lukács's main concern is to distinguish his approach from that of idealism as well as from any systematic, logical and epistemological attempt to build a theory of freedom. In a very straightforward manner, he says that freedom "consists in a concrete decision between different concrete possibilities" (p. 114). And this is freedom "as a moment of reality" (ibid.). We have seen that, although the formulation of the question is correct, it runs into problems when reality is understood in terms of the "ought." In addition to this, freedom is also "ultimately a desire to alter reality" (p. 114). Of course, this desire must maintain itself within the real, and reality itself "must be preserved as the goal of change" (ibid.). So, it is in this sense that the teleological method becomes fundamental as the subterranean link, the substance, of the time of change. The element of determination that remains at this point is a necessary one. We have shown this when speaking of the "could" modality. Lukács emphasizes it, and we are in complete agreement, even though we have criticized his directional "ought." He says, "As a determination of men living and acting in society, freedom is never completely free from determination" (p. 115). Lukács sees this in a very concrete manner. He says that this determination is at work in everyday life in the actual labor process, and then he gives the example of chess where, he says, "situations can arise, brought on in part by one's own moves, in which the only move possible is that to which one is compelled" (ibid.). Yet, notwithstanding the importance of the element of determination, freedom—and this is so particularly in labor (where a certain compulsion must always be present)—is always the possibility of alternatives and of redirecting the course of events by the rational will. Lukács says, "In a first approximation, we can say that freedom is that act of consciousness which has as its result a new being posited by itself" (p. 114).

Lukács's ontology of labor—of a labor that creates only use-values—presents the radicality required by a fundamental social phenomenon aspiring to the character of totality, and it is in this sense that it is, properly speaking, an ontology. There is very little here that could be of any interests for the narrow approach of political economy. Labor is immediately understood as what tears itself away from the opacity of nature thereby starting the development of history, the constitution of cultures: an act of freedom. An interesting move, even though sometimes one wonders if it is not more of a Spenglerian than of a Marxist type.[35] The determination of freedom, or freedom in determination, is posited through the teleological self-positing of labor. Here, however, the modality of the "ought" points to an ethics that risks abandoning the plane of history and immanence.

REMARK: THE PRODUCTIVE POWER OF CAPITAL

The productive power of capital is the productive power of labor wrested from labor. This act, or metamorphosis, reaches a degree of completion in the passage from formal to real subsumption, that is, from the extraction of absolute surplus-value (by lengthening the working day) to the extraction of relative surplus-value (by revolutionizing the labor process itself). But that the productive power of labor becomes the productive power of capital also means that the original ontological power of labor, in which the word "productive" really means "creative," is subsumed under new categories devised by capital and political economy. The fact that these new categories also appropriate and use the original linguistic expressions, that is, "productive," "production," should not make us lose sight of the fact that these expressions no longer correspond to their original concepts. Thus, "productive" for capital does not mean what it meant for labor. In the former case, what is really produced is exchange-value and surplus-value; in the latter, it was use-values to be produced—although forms of exchange always existed, they did not entail the concept of exchange-value in the capitalist sense. The productive power of capital is nothing but labor; however, this is no longer a labor which, itself a use-value, can bring forth other use-values but, rather, one that must be exchanged for a wage and can be exchanged for a wage only insofar as it has the capability of increasing and valorizing capital. It is in this sense that labor becomes *productive for and of capital.* In this sense, it constitutes the *productive power* of capital.

In preparation for the next chapter, in which the distinction between productive labor and living labor is discussed (where "productive" has acquired its economic, capitalist connotation), a chapter that will especially deal with sections of the *Grundrisse,* it may be important to make some preliminary observations as a way of clarifying the passage from ontology to the critique of political economy. What will appear is that there is some continuity between (1) Marx's unveiling of the ontological ground of labor and (2) its entrance into a regime of estrangement and alienation, which we have described by focusing on the *Manuscripts,* and the later developments, particularly described in sections of the *Grundrisse* and in the unpublished section of the first volume of capital on the passage from formal to real subsumption. Even though it is not our intention to trace a philological continuity of any kind, nor to enter the discussion as to whether there is continuity or rupture in Marx's work, it may be important to note that it is precisely the *existential* modality of alienation that reaches full political maturity in a regime of real subsumption and large-scale industry in which the worker is excluded from the newly founded productive power of capital and yet completely included in it. What is reflected at different stages of Marx's work is, on the one hand, a change occurring within society and, on the other, a fuller comprehension of problems and concepts anticipated and later developed. The wresting of the productive power of labor by capital becomes increasingly easier and more difficult at the same time: "easier" because capital acts as if the agency proper to living labor were its own, and in this sense it tends to reduce the input of actually living labor in the production process or exclude it altogether from that process; "more difficult" because capital is not living labor, living labor is not capital, and, although living labor confronts an increasingly enormous alien power, it is still its own original power to appear as capital, a power within which the only real agency ultimately resides.

Anticipated in the *Manuscripts* are the themes of subsumption and machinery, and that means, the theme of the productive power of capital. In other words, in the *Manuscripts* the question is already that of the reduction of living labor to productive labor, although the terms are not used. Productive labor is the theme of the first section on the *Wages of Labour.* After describing the general position of weakness of the worker *vis-à-vis* the capitalist, Marx speaks of wages as *means of reproduction only,* that is, the production of new living labor to be transformed into labor-power and thus into productive power for capital: *"production of men, as of every other commodity"* (1975: 283). The tendency toward total subsumption is present in the idea of "a marked division of labour," which makes it difficult for the worker to "direct his labour elsewhere" (ibid.), also because this is what capital already does in its incessant expansion: it goes elsewhere and so "either drives the worker, who is restricted to one particular branch of employment, into starvation or forces him to submit to all capitalist's demands" (ibid.). This is also a formulation of the "double freedom" we find in Volume I of *Capital* and to which I often refer. It also determines a twofold struggle for the worker who has to fight for his physical subsistence and for work, "i.e. for the possibility and the means of realizing his activity" (p. 284)—an activity that precedes the emergence of capital and which really names living labor itself, that is, creative, organic labor.

The question of subsumption is the question of the machine, and that is the question of total estrangement or alienation: "the worker becomes more and more uniformly dependent on labour, and on a particular, very one-sided and machine-like type of labour." He becomes "an abstract activity and a stomach" (p. 285). In the *Grundrisse,* Marx deepens his discourse on the machine, particularly on the "automated system of machinery," which he sees as the culmination of the different metamorphoses of the means of labor; here "the workers themselves are cast merely as its conscious linkages" (1973: 692). If in the *Manuscripts* the worker is said to become "more and more uniformly dependent... on a... machine-like type of labour," in the *Grundrisse* the worker is directly posited as dependent: "Machinery—as fixed capital—posits him as dependent, posits him as appropriated" (p. 702). However, the fact that the worker is now "appropriated" by the machine only accentuates the existential modality of alienation presented in the *Manuscripts.* The agency faked by the machine is not the agency of the worker, but rather the worker is excluded from participating in it. Still, in the *Grundrisse* we read: "The science which compels the inanimate limbs of the machinery, by their construction, to act purposefully, as an automaton, does not exist in the worker's consciousness, *but rather acts upon him through the machine as an alien power, as the power of the machine itself*" (p. 693). This already poses the question, if only by implication, of communism and revolution—a question to become soon explicit in the same passage. It poses that question because it is obvious that the mere fact that the machine replaces the worker in the labor process cannot have any positive effect on the life of the worker; this time that is liberated by the emergence of automation is still stolen time at the ontological and ethical level. The situation of the worker does not change because this is a mere economic fact, although under the specific capitalist mode of production, that is, under real subsumption, an economic fact can be a total fact. Precisely because of this, the question of communism and revolution is posed here: because for a real change to obtain a whole totality must be dismantled and destroyed. This is already clearly stated in the *Manuscripts:* amelioration and reform of the economic and technological conditions will not bring about a better environment for the worker but, rather, a higher degree of exploitation and misery. In the *Manuscripts* we read that "even in the state of society most favorable to him, the inevitable consequence for the worker is overwork and early death, reduction to a machine, enslavement to capital which piles up in threatening opposition to him, fresh competition and star-vation or beggary for a section of the workers" (1975: 285–286). To be sure, in the developed regime of the machinery, and under real subsumption, we no longer have a mere process of "reduction to a machine" but a virtual replacement of the worker with the machine, yet this latter moment is also present in the *Manuscripts,* where the machine is already seen as a competi-tor for the worker (p. 286). Thus, the situation is only apparently better. What all this does, including also a possible increase in wages for sectors of the working class, is oppose "the product of labour to the worker as some-thing increasingly alien to him" (p. 286). Marx concludes by saying, in an unequivocally antiproductivist voice, that "society's distress is the goal of the economic system" (ibid.). We find something very similar to this in the *Grundrisse* where Marx says that fundamentally, insofar as one remains within the logic of capital, the development of the machinery simply enslaves the worker more than ever: "*The most developed machinery thus forces the worker to work longer than the savage does, or than he himself did with the simplest, crudest tools*" (pp. 708–709).

The inability of the productive power of capital to actually improve the conditions of society must be clearly recognized. This means that radical social changes, those changes inherent in the philosophy of genuine com-munism, cannot take place unless capital is destroyed and the productive power it has usurped returns to labor, as labor returns to itself. In other words, the idea that we can be radical and yet maintain intact the totality imposed by capital—a popular idea nowadays—is absolutely untenable.

Another problem that should be addressed, and this has to do particularly with the theoreticians of "immaterial" labor, is the excessive degree of optimism attached to the new position of leading sectors of the proletariat within the system of automation. If it is true that the machine frees the workers to an extent, true that it certainly reduces manual labor; in other words, if it is true that social knowledge and the science of information (the "general intellect") take on this new and substantive role within the production process as they are objectified in fixed capital,[36] it is not necessarily as true that this process produces the *subjectivities* able to revolutionize themselves and things and thus bring about genuine communism. It does not produce them in a mechanical and automatic fashion, but also, and perhaps more important, these subjectivities (the many forms of living labor) always *exceed* this reduction and this manipulation. "Consciousness," and particularly "class consciousness," is no longer a popular concept; neither is the concept of the will. Yet, left to itself, the productive power of capital, notwithstanding the fact that it creates the general conditions for a future society at the level of the infrastructure if nothing else, will never be able or willing to relent its power and give an "immaterial" living labor jurisdiction over the labor process and the other aspects of life, the economy and culture, the totality of life.[37] Moreover, those theories usually leave untouched the most fundamental issue, namely, productivity. To be sure, of those who have analyzed the "Fragment on Machines" in the *Grundrisse,* some are cautious in this respect. Paolo Virno, in particular, has pointed out that there may be a difficulty inherent in the "Fragment" itself. He says, "In order to reactivate political energy, it is important to undertake a fundamental critique of the "Fragment": Marx completely identified the general intellect (or, knowledge as the principal productive force) with fixed capital, thus neglecting the instance when that same general intellect manifests itself on the contrary as *living labor.* This is precisely the decisive aspect today" (1996: 270). It is, indeed. Speaking then of *mass intellectuality,* he says that "an important part of knowledge cannot be deposited in machines" (ibid.), but remains available as living labor.

The most fundamental distinction is then not whether the labor process involves a tool or a highly sophisticated system of machinery, whether it is manual or "immaterial," but, rather, most fundamental is whether it is geared toward the production and valorization of capital or toward social and communal welfare, toward the production of surplus-value or use-values. It is, in other words, a political, not a technological, issue, though technology in the use of politics also has great consequences. In the *Manuscripts,* this distinction, which really describes the gap between labor's ontological nature and its alienated dimension, is radically posed: "... labour itself—not only under present conditions but in general *in so far as its goal is restricted to the increase of wealth*—is harmful and destructive" (Marx 1975: 288). Yet, this is not so when labor is a life activity. That this life activity becomes an "economic fact" (p. 323), which means that labor becomes alienated labor, does not exhaust its ontological and historical potentialities. That labor produces itself, the possibility of its renewal, and thus strengthens its productive power is not a property bestowed on it by capital but, rather, it belongs to the concept of a life activity. Capital exploits this potentiality, but it does not create it. In reality, under capital alienation and estrangement acquire a twofold meaning. Not only is there estrangement in the worker's relationship to the products of his labor (which one experiences even in the case of creative labor) but also "in the *act of production,* within *the activity of production itself*" (pp. 326, 327). It is this second form of alienation, the alienation of an activity, this "activity directed against [oneself]" (p. 327), when labor produces itself (and the worker) as a commodity which is peculiar to the capitalist mode of production, for the first form of alienation is generic and common to all modes.[38] It is here that the discourse developed in the "Fragment on Machines" in the *Grundrisse* inserts itself: under conditions set by capital, labor's *autopoiesis* is the production of alienation, not at all of a liberating and liberated activity, not at all of free subjectivity. It is only the labor that resists entering the logic of capitalist production, at all levels of the socioeconomic spectrum, which retains the possibility of giving a new and radical directionality to its power; the labor which refuses the comfortableness of the general intellect and *lives* in *mass intellectuality* positions itself *politically* in a revolutionary sense within the antagonism of labor and capital. This does not mean that the unemployed are necessarily in a better position than the employed and productive workers to act politically. Rather, the question has to do with the way in which people (whether they are employed or unemployed, "productive" or "unproductive") are able to shape their subjectivity, or, in other words, their consciousness and political agency.

Indeed, labor as life activity is not a problem at all. And Marx asks: "... for what is life but activity?" (p. 327). It is here that the universal aspiration of human activity is recognized by Marx. What is now important to stress is that the ambiguity of the term "productive" is here introduced. Marx speaks, ontologically, of *productive life* as *life activity.* This concept would belong to an esthetic dimension of labor as much as it does, in a disguised and aberrant form, to the will to produce which defines economic production. In a nonestranged form, this activity would be *"life-producing life"* (p. 328; emphasis added). Outside of the reversal of ends proper to alienated labor, this life that produces life, and, what is more, produces it *as a free and conscious activity,* simply defines "human nature"—that is, what takes place within and in the course of the human adventure, human experience, as a result of being in the world with modalities and capabilities which are themselves not of human choosing. What is free and conscious in this activity is its directionality and purpose, certainly not the fundamental capacity or potentiality which may or may not be activated and which, once activated, can be directed in a plurality of senses. Alienation means that "each man is estranged from the others and that all are estranged from man's essence" (p. 328). Arguing against Marx on the basis of the inadequacy, from our present point of view, of his language (namely, the use of words such as "man" or "essence") would really be missing the important point he is making. When "man's essence" is transferred *as knowledge and agency* to the machine and the machine itself is the *situation* in which a certain activity has ended (the Being, which has incorporated a process of Becoming); in other words, when the machine has the legal status of private property, then it confronts the human being as its own estranged essence, as this alien power.

The contradiction inherent in the concept of private property says precisely this: that capital, particularly fixed capital as machinery, is "objective labour *as exclusion of labour*" (p. 345; emphasis added). This is also the meaning of real subsumption: if all labor is subsumed under capital (in the form of either productive or unproductive labor), it is because all labor, as free and independent life activity, is excluded from it; that is, in a form of society that is itself subsumed, labor is excluded from *authentically* and *creatively* participating in what in the *Grundrisse* Marx calls "real wealth"—unless of course radical changes in the political organization of that society take place. And the question of communism is posed again: "The more this contradiction develops," says Marx in concluding the section on machines in the *Grundrisse,* "the more does it become evident that the growth of the forces of production can no longer be bound up with the appropriation of alien labour, but that the mass of workers must themselves appropriate their own surplus labour" (1973: 708).

Marx formulates the sense of this contradiction in a very clear manner, and in a way that provides a link between the *Manuscripts* and the sections on subsumption in *Capital* and on the machine in the *Grundrisse.* It is in the section on machines that we read: "The production process has ceased to be a labour process in the sense of a process dominated by labour as its governing unity. Labour appears, rather, merely as a conscious organ, scattered among the individual living workers at numerous points of the mechanical system; *subsumed under the total process of the machinery itself,* as itself only a link of the system, whose unity exists not in the living workers, but, rather, in the living (active) machinery, which confronts his individual, insignificant doings as a mighty organism" (p. 693; emphasis added). The productive power of labor, assimilated into fixed capital, is "posited as external to labour and as existing independently of it"—now "all powers of labour are transposed into powers of capital" (p. 701). The exclusion of labor is here very clear. Labor becomes "productive" in a strictly and specifically economic sense by and through this act of transposition, which is historically prepared by the act of exchange whereby its (ontological) powers are sold in the form of labor-power.

This is not what merely happens under a regime of machinery and real subsumption; rather, under that regime the original contradiction develops to its utmost degree. In fact, it also belongs to the concept of formal subsumption that the process of production becomes the process of capital itself (Marx 1977: 1020). Not only that, but there is not a clear-cut distinction between the two regimes of formal and real subsumption: the former "can be found as a *particular* form alongside the *specifically capitalist mode of production* [i.e., real subsumption] in its developed form" (p. 1019; brackets added). What already begins with formal subsumption, and that is with the first emergence of capitalist production, is a mystification which is bound to have unimaginable consequences for the proletarian: "The value-sustaining power of labour appears as the self-supporting power of capital; the value-creating power of labour as the self-valorizing power of capital and, in general, in accordance with its concept, *living* labour appears to be put to work by *objectified* labour" (pp. 1020–1021). The expressions "value-sustaining" and "value-creating" power of labor name labor's ontological power; and "value" refers to use-value. When capital appropriates this activity, it defines its own self-sufficiency and autonomy.

What distinguishes formal from real subsumption, namely, the extraction of absolute surplus-value from the extraction of relative surplus-value, is precisely the development of machinery and the fact that the powers of labor now unequivocally appear as the *productive power of capital:* "This entire development of the productive forces of *socialized labour* (in contrast to the more or less isolated labour of individuals), and together with it the *use of science* (the general product of social development [the general intellect]), in the *immediate process of production,* takes the form of the *productive power of capital*" (p. 1024; brackets added). This productive power of capital appears as something absolutely other than the productive power of labor, as if it were capital's actual power, as if capital had actuated some potentiality hidden within its constitution. In fact, capital has no constitution other than the one given to it by labor itself, and it is in this sense that a part of labor becomes identical with it. Yet, the meaning of real subsumption is precisely that even that part of labor which is "identical with capital" (p. 1024) will not appear *as labor* when the productive power of capital has reached full development and is therefore able to impose its own mystified image over the whole spectrum of social life. That does not mean that the productive power of labor, whether in its original and fundamental ontological form or in its identity with capital (that is, as "productive" in the strictly and specifically economic sense), is annihilated; rather, it becomes *invisible.* This invisibility comes to it by way of being excluded and not excluded at the same time, by way of the *confusion* of levels and functions operated by capital. The idea of "confusion" is elaborated by Marx in the section on productive and unproductive labor, which follows the section on formal and real subsumption in "Results of the Immediate Process of Production" (1977: 1038–1049). There, Marx says again that capital is able to make the productive power of labor appear as its own productive power, the agency of living labor as its own agency, *and the productive worker as a service worker* (p. 1042). Fundamentally, capital's ideal, that is, production for production's sake, production as an end in itself, is present also under formal subsumption, but it is only with the regime of real subsumption that it becomes "*adequately realized*" or "*indispensable*" (p. 1037).

The appropriation of the ontological power of labor, of living labor as a value-creating activity, in fixed capital existing as machinery, makes it possible for objectified labor to appear "in the form of the force of production itself" (1973: 694). However, this does not mean that the labor so appropriated and objectified still has the agency of living labor itself. When knowledge and skill are absorbed into capital, they appear as "an attribute of capital," of fixed capital, and in this sense they are "opposed to labour" (ibid.). The paradox of simultaneous exclusion and nonexclusion is again evident: "In machinery, knowledge appears as alien, external to [the worker]; and living labour [as] subsumed under self-activating objectified labour" (p. 695; second brackets in the text). This "self-activating objectified labour," the system of automation, lacks a fundamental aspect which belonged to living labor, and that is, *life*. The agency it shows is a pseudo-agency. Lacking life (conscious life), it lacks a sense of choosing its directionality and a sense of creation. This is so obvious as to be almost trivial. Yet it is important to stress this point because it is only by so doing that living labor can return from its invisibility and show that, notwithstanding the totality created by capital, it is still in charge of the most fundamental aspects of the ontology of the social world, still determining the movement faked by the machine as its own, still capable of formulating and delivering ontologies of liberation; for an objectified and dead world can only have limited autonomy and self-sufficiency. It is in this sense that exclusion and nonexclusion are both necessary to capital and the relative invisibility of labor a requirement for the continuation of its exploitation. This also may help make sense of the contradiction presented by Marx between the foundation of the capitalist mode of production and its development, which is not easy to make sense of, for there seems to be an abrupt change in tone from the form of a critique of the machinery to an optimistic view of its possible employment as real and social wealth. I will return to this later.

The opposition of fixed capital as a machine to labor is clear. Yet, this means that now labor has, at least apparently, two enemies: fixed capital and capital proper. Before the development of the machinery, the instrument of labor was not in opposition to the worker. Without mentioning other modes of production, even with the emergence of capital and under formal subsumption, when the labor activity itself began to undergo a process of estrangement and alienation, the instrument of labor was still a complement and an extension of the human body, the human hand. In fact, it does not belong to the concept of the machine to be any different from any other instrument of labor, but only to the concept of the machine as fixed capital. This in turn means that the machinery could also be used in a mode of production other than the capitalist mode (Marx 1973: 699–700), for the machine is nothing but "universal labour" (Marx 1981: 199). However, insofar as capitalist relations of production remain, the machinery is the privileged locus of manifestation of what appears as capital's own productive power. For one question could be asked: What is a machine? It certainly is not a dead assemblage of mechanical parts, for a machine that does not function would still be that assemblage and yet count nothing as a machine. What makes the machine relevant, what activates it as a machine, is a principle of agency implanted into it from the outside: living labor. Yet, that the machine is assimilated into fixed capital does not mean that it *is* fixed capital. This implies that the destruction of the capitalist relations of production would unveil the machine as a product of labor. As a concentration of social knowledge, the machine, in addition to being capital's privileged locus for the manifestation of its power, is also what may bring about its "dissolution as the form dominating production" (Marx 1973: 700); and fixed capital would then be this accumulated social knowledge as man himself (p. 712). What here becomes extremely clear is, again, the necessity of posing the question of communism, and that means the question of the destruction of capital and of the constitution of an "essential difference."[39] If this is not done, the machine as fixed capital remains inevitably linked to the logic of productivism. As Marx says, "It is therefore a highly absurd bourgeois assertion that the worker shares with the capitalist, because the latter, with fixed capital (which is, as far as that goes, itself a product of labour, and of *alien labour* merely appropriated by capital) makes labour easier for him (rather, he robs it of all independence and attractive character, by means of the machine), or makes his labour shorter" (p. 701). Marx warns against considering fixed capital as "an independent source of value, independent of labour time" (p. 702). And he adds: "It is such a source only in so far as it is itself objectified labour time, and in so far as it posits surplus labour time" (ibid.). However, living labor always remains external to the machine as fixed capital and in opposition to it, although posited as dependent and appropriated. Again, the machine is not fixed capital, but it appears as, and is assimilated in, fixed capital: it is "cast into the role of fixed capital" (ibid.). Only insofar as it assimilates the machine can fixed capital appear as an independent source of value, but the machine can be "cast into the role of fixed capital... only because the worker relates to it as wage-worker [i.e., productive labor], and the active individual generally [i.e., the proletarian, living labor], as mere worker" (ibid.; brackets added).[40] The categories of exclusion and nonexclusion are here present again. The productive worker, the wage-worker, is not excluded from the production process centered on the machine but completely assimilated in it. It is his living labor that is transferred into capital by means of the machine. Yet he is excluded from choosing the directionality and purpose of the machine. His work is (or should be) as mechanical as that of any "inanimate limbs of machinery" itself. The mere worker is also excluded insofar as his activity is useless, or unproductive, if not attached to the system of the machinery as fixed capital; and yet he is not excluded because at least potentially his productive power must remain generally available for exploitation and in any case, under real subsumption, his life is also assimilated within the "general illumination," the social factory.

After the critique of the machine as fixed capital, Marx describes the contradiction between the foundation of capital and its development, that is, the machinery mode itself. As I said earlier, there is a change in his discourse at this point, which makes sense only if we take it as a description of the future society, or of the conditions thereof. The radical changes brought about by large-scale industry, or the machinery mode, have to do with the marginality (reduction or exclusion) of the role of the worker, of living labor, within the labor process. This means that direct labor is no longer the "great well-spring of wealth," labor time no longer its measure, exchange value no longer the measure of use-value. Of course, this is not a description of a "late" stage of capitalism, but already of communism, or at least of the conceptual and practical infrastructure necessary to a communal mode of production and indeed present within the machinery mode. In the passage that follows, Marx's grammar (the use of the present perfect and then of the modal "must") makes it clear: "As soon as labour in the direct form *has ceased* to be the great well-spring of wealth, labour time ceases and *must cease* to be its measure, and hence exchange value [must cease to be the measure] of use-value" (p. 705; emphasis added). Thus, even the structure of the class struggle, the structure of political antagonism is readjusted in favor of the exploited class: "The *surplus labour of the mass* has ceased to be the condition for the development of general wealth, just as the *nonlabour of the few,* for the development of the general powers of the human head" (ibid.). General social knowledge, the general intellect, becomes a direct force of production (p. 706). I do not see here a description of "immaterial" labor,[41] but rather the description of redistribution throughout society of labor activities.[42] In any case, it is of a tendency that Marx is speaking (p. 707). But a tendency is a real concept or structure, not a mere fantasy.[43] What replaces labor time as a measure of value is disposable, free, time, and this is a theme already announced in *The German Ideology.* Disposable time, or not-labor time, is already present under the regime of capital, but it is there present only "for a few," and, hence, it has an "*antithetical* existence" (p. 708). However, capital is, "despite itself, instrumental in creating the means of social disposable time, in order to reduce labour time for the whole society to a diminishing minimum, and thus to free everyone's time for their own development" (ibid.). It may be worth noticing that the labor that is so reduced is wage-earning labor, or, with the abolition of wages, socially necessary labor. But we may recall Marx's question in the *Manuscripts:* For what is life but activity? This of course entails the truth that the reduction of the labor that, no longer productive of capital, is productive of general social wealth does not erase the more fundamental dimension of labor as creative power and life activity, for what would one's development be without this dimension? However, returning to

Marx's last quoted passage, it must also be said that the tendency of capital to reduce labor time remains, as long as capital itself is not abandoned or destroyed, only in the form of a contradiction: on the one hand, capital creates disposable time; on the other, it always tries to convert it into surplus-value. The exit from this situation lies with the revolutionary movement and in the real positing of the possibility of communism. It lies with the *subjective* appropriation of what remains otherwise objective and alien. Once this is done, disposable time "ceases to have an *antithetical* existence" and becomes the measure of wealth, of *real* wealth, that is, "the developed productive power of all individuals" (ibid.). "The measure of wealth is then not any longer, in any way, labour time, but rather disposable time" (ibid.).

In this transitional section, we have seen how the fundamental ontology of labor is obscured by political economy and capital. The productive power of labor, productive in its original ontological meaning, appears as the productive power of capital. This is the same as saying that labor becomes productive labor in a strictly and specifically economic sense, productive of capital. It also produces capital as a productive and self-producing power. Yet, productive labor subsumed under capital, under fixed capital, is still a form of living labor, though objectified and soon no longer "living." But it has its roots in the univocal substance which living labor as such is—a substance that is never subsumable in its entirety, for it has no limits, or rather its limits are those of life and activity, of life activity. It has no limits—if we confine ourselves to the human world—insofar as the human adventure continues. Thus, even under real and total subsumption, living labor is never completely subsumed. For along with surplus value and capital, machinery also creates new, regenerating substance of labor.[44] Living labor, which is both excluded and nonexcluded, enters the machine, but it also exceeds and encompasses it. It becomes visible as productive labor, but, within the machinery mode, less visible than it should be, and in fact almost invisible—as invisible as the living labor that is not accounted for by political economy. We should now look more closely at the difference between productive labor and living labor.

2 On the Difference between Productive Labor and Living Labor

Labour is the living, form-giving fire; it is the transitoriness of
things, their temporality, as their formation by living time.
—Karl Marx *Grundrisse*

THE CONCEPT OF PRODUCTIVE LABOR

In studying the question of productive labor and of its relation to unproductive labor, we have to keep in mind that, for Marx, it is precisely because labor, in and for itself, is *neither-productive-nor-unproductive,* but *creative* (a concept that includes that of economic production, but is not limited to it), that it becomes productive or unproductive under capital in a specifically capitalist sense. Yet, in dealing with this question, we find some analytical difficulties, which may (and in fact do) create some confusion. To avoid this confusion, it is fundamental to distinguish clearly between two levels of discourse and two categories. The two categories are productive labor and living labor (or the subjective, productive, power of labor); productive labor pertains to the discourse of political economy; living labor is an ontological category—although it represents the same force that political economy turns into productive labor. The point is that, under capital, productive labor is only that which produces and valorizes capital. However, the subjective power of labor is a productive power only insofar as the word "productive" is taken in its broadest and most original sense, as *poiesis*—then, it is the same as the word "creative" (see later; also cf. Marx 1973: 711).[1]

Because Marx is analyzing the specificity of the capitalist mode of production, there are times when these two categories—productive labor and living labor—appear as identical. This is so because the concept of capital cannot be grasped outside of the form of value, and productive labor is, precisely, the value form of labor. It is in the exchange process that the use-value of labor abandons its creative freedom and is ready to become *productive.*[2] Indeed, this happens when the worker "surrenders its [i.e., labor's] *creative power*" (1973: 307; brackets added). Thus, when in the *Grundrisse* Marx speaks of the development of the concept of capital, he warns that he cannot start with labor, but with value, "precisely, with exchange value," although labor remains the presupposition of the process as a whole (p. 259). He says that capital, "the communal substance of all commodities" (p. 271) is "objectified labour" (p. 272), which can only be countered by nonobjectified labor. This nonobjectified labor is labor as subjectivity, living labor, the living subject, the worker; yet, it is not labor as such, that is, as unrelated to capital: it is labor already employed by capital *as the subjectivity capital needs*. Marx concludes: "The only *use-value*, therefore, which can form the opposite pole to capital is *labour (to be exact, value-creating, productive labor)*" (p. 272). Here productive labor and living labor appear as identical. However, they are not, and do not need to be. A few pages below, Marx says, "Labour, such as it exists *for itself* in the worker in opposition to capital, that is, labour in its *immediate being*, separated from capital, is *not productive*" (p. 308). However, and I want to stress this point, this does not mean that it is *unproductive*. Not to be productive, or better to be *not productive*, is not to be "unproductive" (which is still a category of political economy); rather, it is to be *neither-productive-nor-unproductive* (an ontological category). *Neither-productive-nor-unproductive* labor is the form of labor before its descent into the realm of exchange, production, and circulation, before its division into and by the categories of capital whereby it becomes *either* productive *or* unproductive. That the concept of capital should not be developed from labor but from value does not take away the ontological priority of labor over capital. In other words, labor is a common element of all production, and it has the form of time; capital is an essential difference, whose destruction or passing away entails the liberation of time, the return of labor to its immediacy.

In *Marx beyond Marx,* Antonio Negri calls Marx's definition of productive labor a "*heavily reductive definition*" (Negri 1991a: 64). However, he goes on to say that it is not "impossible to free Marx, in this case, from the weight of historical conditions, which led him, in order to exalt workers' labor, to restrict in such a miserable way the conception of productive labor" (p. 65). Negri also says that, in its literal formulation—productive labor as capital producing labor[3]—Marx's definition has the merit of insisting on the "workers' opposition as a political opposition, on the political irreducibility of the force of workers and of proletarian revolution" (pp. 64–65). He thus looks at the question of productive labor from the fundamental viewpoint of antagonism—of difference that becomes antagonism (Negri 1991a: 52)—[4] and from that point of view, which is the point of view of the worker and the proletarian, productive labor appears in its other aspect, as the worker's and the proletarian's use-value (Negri 1991a: 65). Productive labor is, yes, that which produces its opposite, surplus value, capital. But it is also, first and foremost, itself, (that is, living labor) as a use-value. However, this does not solve the problem, for unproductive labor, which does not produce capital, is also a use-value.

It is in the exchange process that the difference which living labor is (the difference which living labor is *in its immediacy*) develops into the form of antagonism. Negri very clearly says that antagonism "consists in the fact that capital must reduce to an exchange value that which for the worker is a use-value" (1991a: 67–68). This use-value is subjective labor, the productive power of labor in its ontological character, subjective power, *potenza*. Against the reduction of productive labor, but determined by it, subjective labor, defined by Negri as a "general abstraction," turns into a "general power (potenza)" and a radical opposition" (p. 70). Indeed, in the face of the power of capital, and under the real subsumption of all labor, the radical opposition, the sub-version of capital, cannot come from unproductive labor. Yet, it cannot come from productive labor either; at least not from productive labor *as* productive labor, that is, as the labor which produces and valorizes capital, for the radical opposition—to be political—must be that which stops producing capital, which brings capitalist production to ruin. The abstraction from productive labor also must be an abstraction from unproductive labor, for this latter too receives its definition not in virtue of its quality, but, rather, because of its exclusion from exchange. Yet, this exclusion does not change its nature; unproductive labor does not cease to be a use-value, to be labor and fire. The abstraction, and this is the concept I would like to present here, must take the form of a double negation, a *neither/nor* of resistance and refusal, of withdrawal and desertion, a negation of the logic of *either/or,* but also a negation of the logic of *both/and,* an exaltation of the broken dialectic, which is immediately the absolute affirmation of a radical difference: a new "essential difference," to use a wonderful expression of Marx's, which displaces, and does away with, the logic of capital. This essential difference, the moment of determinateness and affirmation of a self-identity, would make no sense without the negative structure of "indifferent difference" (Hegel), which constitutes the *universality* or *mediated simplicity* as the ontological ground of the particular, singular, and historical. What I refer to as *neither/nor* is this universal, what Hegel calls a not-This in the Sense-Certainty section of the *Phenomenology of Spirit:* "A simple thing of this kind which *is* through negation, which is neither This nor That, a *not- This* [cf. Marx's category of labor which is *not productive*], and is with equal indifference This as well as That—such a thing we call a *universal*" (Hegel 1977: 60).

Neither-productive-nor-unproductive labor is labor which returns to itself as to its immediacy. It is difference that, yes, becomes antagonism, but only to return to itself as difference and be able (that is, have the power as *potenza*) to be what it is and what it wants to be, rather than being posited by capital as capital's disguised necessity. Antagonism itself is nothing but difference that returns to itself, to its freedom and power, after a dreadful journey into the realm of alienation and death; difference that becomes *political* difference. It is a subjective power because it rejects the objectivity and objectification inscribed in the capitalist organization of work. The destruction of the form of exchange—the form whereby labor becomes either productive or unproductive—is the destruction of productive *and* unproductive labor alike. The *neither/nor* configuration of the irreducibly oppositional struggle that labor wages against capital simply says that this labor is *all* labor, the absolute power of labor, a positive power. It is not labor as productive labor but labor that withdraws from the narrow categories of productivity and unproductivity alike. The *neither/nor* configuration says that this labor rejects capital's categories and presents itself in its other aspect, the aspect that (ontologically speaking) most essentially and fundamentally defines it: it presents itself as a use-value. As such, labor is *neither-productive-nor-unproductive.* As I have

Central Q's – but are they answered here?

No!)

noted, Marx calls it *"not productive"* (1973: 398), which is not—I need to stress again—the same as saying *unproductive*. It is *creative* labor, whereas productive labor is merely *created,* or posited, by capital. After all, the *neither/nor* configuration is already inscribed in the condition of the workers who, in their "double freedom"—as Marx calls it—"neither form part of the means of production themselves..., nor do they own the means of production" (Marx 1977: 874). In our own days, in the age of globalization, this double freedom, or double negation, becomes deeper and broader, for it now constitutes the tragic structure of the South of the world, the South of every North. But the *neither/nor* of antagonistic struggle is only apparently a negative construct. In reality, it is the utmost of positivity and affirmation seeking the constitution of its own absolute difference.

How can we otherwise understand the use-value *for the worker* of living labor if not outside the categories of productivity and unproductivity? And how can living labor find itself if it doesn't tear itself away from the logic that either enslaves or annihilates it? And yet, once it has torn itself away from it, what space and time does it find, under real subsumption, to initiate and accomplish its affirmation? In fact, there still exists a time and place for revolution, whose concept must be seen as the univocal ground where living labor, in its difference, lies and moves; as the subterranean fire that links the most abstract to the most concrete. The time of difference, which under capital marks only the passage from M to M' (money that becomes more money: the general formula of capital), is here the time in which difference goes back to its plenitude.

What otherwise is this use-value? Certainly not my craftsmanship. Nor is it a generalized possibility of autarkic production. As Negri says, "Here use-value is nothing other that the radicality of the labor opposition..., the source of all human possibility." And he continues: "Capital sucks this force through surplus value" (1991a: 70).

Labor remains creative even when its creativeness is taken away, changed into mere productiveness, constrained within an alienated form. Negri says, "... the tendency of profit to expand goes hand in hand with a living labor directly exploited but creative nonetheless" (p. 91). This is so because the creative aspect of labor (its ontological dimension) precedes its productive aspect. Labor cannot be productive without being creative. Yet, it can be creative and not be productive. This means that there can be labor without capital, but that there cannot be capital without labor (that is, without the expenditure of some kind of useful labor.)

For Negri, the concept of productive labor must be completely displaced in order to let labor as use-value appear and in order to enter into a definition of the revolutionary class. The revolutionary class is the class for which labor must return to its immediacy and freedom. It is the class that intends to bring about the abolition of work (that is, of wage and productive labor). Negri says, "Work which is liberated is liberation from work. The creativity of communist work has no relation with the capitalist organization of labor.

Living labor—by liberating itself, by reconquering *its use-value,* against exchange value—opens a universe of needs of which work can become a part only eventually. And in this case, it is a question of work as essential, collective, nonmystified, communist work: instead of work as capitalist construction" (1991a: 165).

PRODUCTIVE LABOR AND THE PRODUCTIVE POWER OF LABOR

So far, we have seen what productive labor is: a category of political economy and capital. In this sense, productive labor does not produce use-values but surplus value and capital. Of course, in order to produce surplus value, it also has to produce exchange values and thus ultimately use-values for others, for consumption. This is indeed inscribed in the twofold nature of the commodity. But the production of use-values is not productive labor's main goal. The substance of productive labor is all contained in the formula M–M'—a formula that points to a time of difference, the time in which difference itself is forced into a position of antagonism, as we have seen. What actually comes back to itself is labor in its antagonistic form. There is here a moment very similar to that described by Hegel when he speaks of self-consciousness in the "Lordship and Bondage" section of his *Phenomenology of Spirit.* Here Hegel says, "... as a consciousness forced back into itself, it will withdraw into itself and be transformed into a truly independent consciousness" (1977: 117). It is the same with the independence and autonomy of living labor in its aspect as a use-value. In this use-value, that is, in the living labor that precedes and determines exchange, there lies the ontological power of labor itself, its creativeness and freedom.

We also have seen that Negri criticizes Marx's definition of productive labor, and rightly so. The sections on productive labor are probably the most ambiguous in Marx's work, and, given the importance of this concept, it is necessary to be aware of this fact. In the *Grundrisse,* for instance, Marx often shifts his discourse from living labor to productive labor (which is *a form of* living labor, yet not the only possible form), giving the impression, at times that they are the same thing. Of course, they are not. But this initial confusion may generate a greater confusion when one leaves Marx's texts. This confusion is then used to legitimize that logic of productivism, which is one of the main causes of the failure of revolutionary theory and practice.

Even in Mario Tronti's nonproductivist analysis of productive labor the confusion remains to a degree. In *Operai e capitale* (Workers and Capital), Tronti says, "... one and the same productive force can truly be counted twice: at one time as a force that *produces* capital, and at another time as a force that *refuses* to produce it; at one time *inside* capital, and at another time *against* capital" (1977: 180). However, the truth is that the force *against* capital is not a productive force in the sense in which the force *inside* capital is; the force that *refuses* to create capital is by definition *nonproductive.* And I should like here to remind the reader that "nonproductive" (or "not productive") does not mean "unproductive," but, rather, *neither-productive-nor-unproductive.* In other words, the force *inside* capital is not the *double* of the force *against* (and we should add, *outside*) capital. The impression is that there is a tendency (certainly in some cases involuntary) to accept the logic of *either/or* created by capital, the logic of productivism: thus if a force is not productive it must be *unproductive* in the sense established by capital. Yet, in order to think *against and outside* this logic and get a glimpse of a new horizon, we have to look at this force in its indifference and neutrality vis-à-vis the categories of capital, in its *neither/nor* modality. In this sense, it is already a radically different and subversive force. The withdrawal from these two categories of capitalist production (productive and unproductive labor) reveals the univocal ground of labor as it is *for* itself, and for the worker. Even so-called unproductive labor is then understood as unproductive only of and for capital, from the point of view of capital. In reality, it is obvious that this "unproductive" labor often relates to essential social needs.

In Marx, the question of productive labor is only seen in relation to the critique of political economy, that is, of capital. Marx does not elaborate on the new, radically different, ontology of communal production; an ontology which liberates time as its own substance[5] by overcoming, not of course the common element of production, but the essential difference of productive labor and capital. However, there remain, in the *Grundrisse* and elsewhere, important indications of what production and the relations of production could be like when labor is able to return to itself. In the chapter on money, Marx says, "On the basis of communal production, the determination of time remains, of course, essential. The less time the society requires to produce wheat, cattle etc., the more time it wins for other production, material or mental" (1973: 172). And, as we have seen, toward the end of the *Grundrisse,* in the last notebook (Notebook VII), in the so-called "Fragment on Machines," he sees in *disposable* and *free time,* the time of *not-labor,* rather than in labor time, the new measure of wealth for a society based on communal production (p. 708). He also says that this disposable, or free, time, is the "time for the full development of the individual, which in turn reacts upon the productive power of labour as itself the greatest productive power" (p. 711). Marx distinguishes, although this is a distinction blurred by analytical difficulties that he does not resolve, between *productive labor* as a category of capital, and the *productive power of labor* as the ontological foundation, which is enhanced by liberated time. The free disposition of this power remains productive, in the original, etymological, sense of the word, only insofar as its production turns into action, liberating action, and its fundamental ontology into an ontology of liberation. Here productive means creative, a poetic and practical activity. It is an instance of that *poiesis,* which, as Giorgio Agamben points out in *The Man without Content,* comes from the Greek verb *poiein,* which means "to produce" in the sense of bringing something into being. In Marx, this sense of *poiesis* coincides with that of *praxis,* or human production, which comes from the Greek verb *prattein,* "to do" in the sense of acting (Agamben 1999: 68). This identity of *poiesis* and *praxis* in Marx is called a "revolutionary thesis" by Etienne Balibar in his *The Philosophy of Marx* (1995: 41). Indeed, speaking of *The German Ideology,* Balibar says that: "... Marx removed one of philosophy's most ancient taboos: the radical distinction between *praxis* and *poiesis*" (p. 40). The identity of poiesis and praxis is kept throughout the *Grundrisse,* and this is why it becomes more difficult to understand Marx's reductive definition of productive labor. It is because this concept has nothing to do with the constant passing over of *praxis* into *poiesis* and of *poiesis* into *praxis* with which Balibar characterizes Marx's revolutionary thesis. Rather, productive labor, posited as doubly free is in actual fact doubly negated: negated to the worker as an immediate means of life, and negated with respect to the production of surplus value, for capital appropriates it in such a way that it soon appears as capital's own productive power. In reality, this productive labor is nothing other than necessary labor, which does not pass over into the freedom of praxis, but rather falls into the abyss of its own negation. It becomes, in fact, surplus labor. It reproduces itself, but only in order to continue producing and valorizing capital. Productive labor is then nothing but the form that the productive power of labor (its subjective power) is compelled to take on as soon as it enters into an exchange relation with capital. It is the value form of labor, or the form in which the productive power of labor is known to, and recognized by, political economy. As Marx says at the end of the *Grundrisse,* "Use-value falls within the realm of political economy as soon as it becomes modified by the modern relations of productions, or as it, in turn, intervenes to modify them" (1973: 881). This is, of course, particularly true of living labor as a use-value. The end of productive labor is the liberation of the productive power of labor as living labor and as time.

THE END OF LABOR

If the concept of productive labor is not clearly defined, it is difficult and dangerous to speak about the end of labor, the abolition of work, or even the refusal to work. For, as Guy Debord very lucidly saw, "what is referred to as 'liberation from work,' that is, increased leisure time, is a liberation neither within labor itself nor from the world labor has brought into being" (Debord 1995: 22). The liberation of labor is, yes, labor liberated from itself, but this holds only insofar as it is understood that this "itself" of labor is posited by capital as necessary and surplus labor; otherwise, the mere use of the machine, in its ability to reduce necessary labor, would have liberated us from work. However, under capital, labor is posited as necessary only insofar as it gives way to surplus labor. Indeed, capital's real intention is not that of positing necessary labor, but surplus labor. As Negri says, "... *the relation between surplus labor and necessary labor is... the relation between the two classes*" (1991a: 97). Moreover, Marx says, "Labour may be necessary without being productive" (1973: 533). It is evident that capital would not be interested in positing *this*

No!

necessary labor, for only labor which becomes productive is useful and necessary to capital. Here we also see that unproductive labor may be (as often is) necessary.

In the last decades, automation and globalization have favored the growth of ideologies predicting or describing the end of labor (or work). These ideologies have often worked on the basis of a misunderstanding of the Marxist analysis that, starting with Marx himself, has repeatedly called attention to the abolition of labor in a future society. Studies such as Herbert Marcuse's *One-Dimensional Man,* Serge Mallet's *The New Working Class,* Mario Tronti's *Operai e capitale* (Workers and Capital), and Guy Debord's *The Society of the Spectacle,* among others, stressed the necessity of ending a certain regime of labor (or work), the concept of the abolition of labor, the strategy of refusal in order to impede the functioning of capitalist production (Tronti 1977). Of course, from within the Marxist discourse it was understood that what must end is capital, not labor. Or, rather, labor also must end insofar as it increases and valorizes capital, that is, productive labor, wage labor, necessary and surplus labor, labor subsumed under capital; but the theory did not affect labor as a fundamental ontological power, neither-productive-nor-unproductive, creative labor. Today, the passage from the theory of a new working class to the assumption that there is no longer a working class, no longer a proletariat, from the abolition of labor in its productive form to the abolition of labor *tout court* is often easily made.[6] It is then necessary to reassert some theoretical and practical boundaries. It is also necessary to ask again a fundamental question: What is the subject of labor today? And that also means asking the question as to what the subject of praxis, of social change and revolution is. It seems that this subject is labor itself, the many labors or subjectivities returning to themselves over and beyond, *against and outside,* the determinations of capital and its science. This is a *structural* argument, insofar as labor is here looked at as a structure, a socially and historically determined structure that, however, only accidentally takes on the form of appearance of productive labor. The ideologies of the end of labor (or work) base themselves on the fact that the social presence of labor—in the so-called advanced world at least—is now less visible. They further operate on the general and false assumption that the antagonism between labor and capital is now either reduced or has altogether disappeared. It is then necessary to call attention, from the point of view of labor, to the social and political movements that reestablish, at a global scale, the presence of this seemingly disappearing antagonism. According to those theorists who equated society with the factory system (notably Tronti, Negri, and in general the Italian Autonomy Movement), the irreducible antagonism between labor and capital could only be overcome through a revolution brought about by a labor able to organize itself inside and against capital, as well as against itself *as labor power,* yet always at the level of production. Today, the ideologies of the end of labor rule out *a priori* this theoretical and political line. By contrast, the theoretical effort that still sees in the antagonism between labor and capital the basic contradiction of the present is a development of those same theories, but in a mutated world. This mutation is not simply economic but is social and cultural as well. As *material* production is more and more shifted to the world's South, the North experiences the novelty of that mutation of labor, "immaterial" labor, which is sometimes constructed as *nonlabor,* other times as not merely an economic but also a cultural shift into the production of knowledge with the notion of the liberation of time that comes with it. In reality, as I have suggested, the concept of *invisible* labor might better render the concrete substance of this new state of affairs.

We must then clearly distinguish between productive labor (a category of political economy) and the productive power of labor (a category of ontology). The former is what must be rejected as another name for the workers' alienation, the death of their subjective and collective power. Productive labor is precisely what produces surplus value and profit, and reproduces the workers' use-value only insofar as it can become an exchange value again, the "alienated presupposition" (Negri 1991a: 52) of the new cycle of production. Productive labor is then the substance of exploitation, for only insofar as it is productive will labor yield its living power to the objectifying power of capital. The latter category, however, the productive power of labor, is living labor itself, which has the form of time, and whose revolt against capital implies its ability to posit itself as necessary, not as a step toward its transformation into surplus labor, but as the ground of its own activity and freedom. In this sense, as Balibar suggests, the necessity of *poiesis* becomes the freedom of *praxis.* The end of productive labor is not, of course, the end of production. It is, however, the end of production as an end in itself: the end of the anarchy of production, of capitalist production. Production becomes then a means to the possibility of free action, the objective ground of subjectivity. The expansion of capital (capital's and productive labor's only end) gives way to the true concept of development (which is based on the freedom of praxis).[7]

Once this distinction is clearly made, it is evident that the ontological critique of productive labor does not tend toward a destruction of the concept of labor as such; rather, it clears the ground for the return of the subject of labor to itself, to its *ethos* and its immediacy, and to its identity with the object (cf. Marx 1973: 85). However, if the ontological return occurs with one single voice, it is a multiplicity of labors that fill it with substance and impart movement to it. It is they that end the regime of wage labor. Revolutionary is then not the abolition of labor as such but the abolition of surplus labor and of necessary labor *as a necessity posited by capital.* This covers the spectrum of what productive labor is. We are left with *this* labor, or, rather, with *these labors,* with the *thisness* of labor, the *thisness* of time and production. Destroyed is the value form of labor. The labor that remains is not a curse, but the liberation of a plurality of possibilities. Nowhere is Marx clearer about this than when he makes fun of Adam Smith for whom, Marx says, labor is precisely this, a curse. But for Marx, and this precisely because for him production is not synonymous with capitalist production, labor is "in

Genesis ⁄⁄

itself a liberating activity" (1973: 611). The curse is not labor, but the sub-sumption of labor under capital. Claiming the superfluous when maintaining intact the structure of capital is not and cannot be revolutionary. Instead, labor remains. And this labor that remains is praxis: the action of freedom, the self-realization of the subject, its coming back (from assimilation and antagonism) to a destiny of difference. Speaking of Smith, Marx says, "Certainly, labour obtains its measure from the outside, through the aim to be attained and the obstacles to be overcome in attaining it. But Smith has no inkling whatever that this overcoming of obstacles is in itself a liberating activity—and that, further, the external aims become stripped of the semblance of merely external natural urgencies, and become posited as aims which the individual himself posits—hence as self-realization, objectification of the subject, hence real freedom, whose action is, precisely, labor" (1973: 611).

THE *THISNESS* OF TIME AND PRODUCTION

The *Grundrisse* is a work about time, and it is so in a fundamental sense. This means that time is the most fundamental category of the *Grundrisse*. Again, it means that time is the *subject* of Marx's critique of political economy—subject in the double sense of subject-matter (or object) and of ground (or foundation). This becomes evident as soon as one opens the *Grundrisse:* "The object before us, to begin with, *material production*" (Marx 1973: 83). This is how *Notebook M* starts. But *material production* is time, both as objectified and as subjective labor. The *tense* of this time which is immediately labor is alternately the perfect and present tense: "The difference between previous, objectified labour and living, present labour here [i.e., in the accumulation of capital] appears as a merely formal difference between the different tense of labour, at one time in the perfect and at another in the present" (pp. 465–466; brackets added). Material production is, then, time as *having been produced* and as *producing,* as *having become* and as *becoming.* The difference between these two modalities is the difference between the substantial form of capital and living labor, between the capitalist and the worker. It is a difference that presents itself immediately as antagonism and opposition. It is, in fact, the structural constitution of the class struggle.

But Marx also says, "Economy of time, to this all economy ultimately reduces itself" (p. 173). This means, again, that time is the irreducible subject of political economy as a science as well as of the critique of political economy. But time as being is also the subject of metaphysics. And if time itself, as Kant says, does not change when everything else changes in time,[8]—if, in other words, time remains (in substance) identical with itself—yet, at the same time and in a certain respect, it changes, for *this* time is different from *that* time, and there is no time over and beyond each *this* of its individuation. This means that each moment contracts all time within itself, and that the present—as Benjamin stressed—is always in transition (Benjamin 1969: 262). In terms of what Marx says in the *Grundrisse,* this means that, even though each mode of production is precisely only *a* mode, the individuating modality is not simply an external addition. If all time is contracted in *this* moment and all production in *this* mode of production, the modality itself, far from being extrinsic and general, is essential and singular.

The problem of production is then the problem of time, for production is time. Now, it is as absurd to speak of *time in general* as it is to speak of *production in general:* "Wherever we speak of production, then, what is meant is always production at a definite stage of social development—production by social individuals" (Marx 1973: 85). The *principium individuationis* is here stated in all its meaningfulness. And so is the reality of history. There is no production beyond *this* production: "Production is always a *particular* branch of production... or it is a totality" (p. 86). Whether it is considered in its particularity or in its totality, production is a concrete whole, and this is what *material production* stands for: a sort of Aristotelian composite of matter (material) and form (production), a *formed matter.* Of course, "production in general" can be used as a "rational abstraction," for—as Marx says—"it really brings out and fixes the *common element* [of all production] and thus saves us repetition" (p. 85; brackets added). But that it saves us repetition does not mean that production in general or general production is actually found as either a concrete or abstract reality. As an abstraction, it is only rational, that is, purely formal and empty. It is not the *determinate abstraction* (cf. Negri 1991a: 47) Marx speaks of when he deals with abstract labor or with the question of method. In fact, in these latter two cases—of which more will be said later—the abstraction is still historically determined and it fully and exclusively belongs to the capitalist mode of production. But this is not the case with production in general or general production, where it is not yet a question of "the relationship between scientific presentation [*Darstellung*] and the real movement" (Marx 1973: 86). Indeed, the aim of those economists who start with general production (with "the *general preconditions* of all production") is in actuality "to present production... as distinct from distribution etc., as encased in eternal natural laws independent of history, at which opportunity *bourgeois* relations are then quietly smuggled in as the inviolable natural laws on which society in the abstract is founded" (p. 87). This is an eminently political aim.

It is very important not to confuse the empty, merely formal and rational abstraction, which may nonetheless have some usefulness in discourse and method, with the determinate abstraction, which has a massive socio-ontological and historical status of its own. In other words, it is important not to confuse the empty formula of the thing with the thing's actual structure and power, the level of predication with that of reality.

THE CONCEPT OF ESSENTIAL DIFFERENCE

All of the above does not cancel the truth that "all epochs of production have certain *common traits, common characteristics* [*Bestimmungen*]" (p. 85; emphasis added). This commonality is certainly very important. However, even more important are the different determinations, the *essential difference,* without which a mode of production would not be *this* mode. Indeed, the word "mode" in the expression "mode of production' is fundamental. If one spoke about production in general, one would be speaking about a *what* without knowing *which what* it was, without knowing the *how* of the *what.* But that would amount to speaking about something very indefinite and vague. Furthermore, the *how* that constitutes a *what* as *this what* is not an accidental one. Rather, it is essential. Yet, by being essential, it is not eternal, immutable, and common. It is essential, and yet it is a difference. It is, in fact, an *essential difference:* "... the elements which are not general and common, must be separated out from the determinations valid for production as such, so that in their unity—which arises already from the identity of the subject, humanity, and of the object, nature—their *essential difference* is not forgotten" (p. 85; emphasis added).

The importance of distinguishing between the *essential difference* and the *common element* of production cannot be stressed enough. In fact, by confusing the two, bourgeois political economy is able to prove, *logically,* that capital is a necessary and common element of production. The syllogism of political economy is as follows: as no production is possible without an instrument of production or past labor, and as capital is also an instrument of production and past labor, then capital is "a general, eternal relation of nature" (pp. 85–86). Of course, Marx adds, "that is, if I leave out just the *specific quality* which *alone* makes this 'instrument of production' and 'stored-up labour' into 'capital'" (p. 86; emphasis added).[9] The logic of bourgeois political economy makes capital into a common element of all modes of production because it does not isolate the specific determinations from the common determinations of production. Both kinds of determinations are essential, but they are not essential in the same way. Of course, all epochs have both specific and common determinations, but whereas the latter are always the same, the former are each time different. That the specific determinations are also essential only means that production is not conceivable without a *mode of* production. That they are different means that this mode always changes (and yet *a* mode must be there). The capitalist mode of production is not production proper, that is, production as immediate subjective creation, though the concept of production proper is subsumed within it. Fundamentally, the capitalist mode of production requires the conversion of use-value into exchange value, the reduction of the labor capacity to a commodity (labor power), and the creation of surplus value. By contrast, the common element of production is nothing but the "already" of "the identity of the subject, humanity, and of the object, nature" (p. 85), namely, living labor. However, in the *already* of this identity, living labor is always useful labor.[10] It is, of course, time, but time as quality, not as quantity. With the emergence of a market economy—and particularly with the specificity of capital—living labor is split into two different aspects or properties: useful (or concrete) and abstract labor—"different in their very essence" (Marx 1977: 309). Abstract labor, which at first could seem to be the common element, represents, in reality, a specific quality of the logic of exchange value. In fact, abstract labor is the creator of value, which is the substance of exchange value and thus of money. However, this does not mean that abstract labor is a pure invention of capital. Rather, it is that aspect of living labor which capital is able to isolate and extract, to reproduce, and be produced by.[11] At first sight, abstract labor appears as the most common element of all useful labor. Indeed, this seems to be correct from a logical and ontological point of view. However, this view would entail the presence of abstract labor before and beyond capital—a view that would be the opposite of what Marx says, for capital would be, again, necessary and eternal. Both Rubin (1972) and Lukács (1971), among other writers, see abstract labor as pertaining exclusively to capital. In fact, abstract labor is the value-creating or value-increasing property of labor. Yet, precisely because of this, the following can be said: As a creator of value, abstract labor becomes the middle term in the dialectic between human beings and nature. It becomes the vanishing mediation between the object of capital and capital, and it appears as a power of capital. Outside capital, abstract labor would vanish in the return of labor to its immediacy. This does not mean that the logical possibility of abstract labor would disappear, for labor *can* become abstract. It only means that, for abstract labor to actually appear, certain historical and social conditions must obtain. Of course, this does not mean that capital is always possible. What I want to say is that, if abstract labor is—in Harvey's apt expression—"a *distillation*... out of a seemingly infinite variety of concrete labour activities" (Harvey 1989: 15; emphasis added), then it must somehow be there from the beginning. The point is that, under noncommodity production (production of use-values)—and this would restore the correct historical perspective—there is simply no separation between the two aspects or properties of labor in question.[12] The common element is then living labor before its division into useful and abstract labor. Consequently, the *essential difference* of capital is not simply abstract labor, but the separation of living labor into its two properties and the negation of its immediacy. In the Introduction to the *Grundrisse,* Marx says that "although the simpler category may have existed historically before the more concrete, it can achieve its full (intensive and extensive) development precisely in a combined form of society, while the more concrete category was more fully developed in a less developed form of society." And he goes further: "Labour seems a quite simple category. The conception of labour in this general form—as labour as such—is also immeasurably old. Nevertheless, when it is economically conceived in this simplicity, 'labour' is a modern category as are the relations which create this simple abstraction" (1973: 103). This abstraction is *indifference* "towards any specific kind of labour" (p. 104).[13] Yet, this indifference "presupposes a very developed totality of real kinds of labour, of which no single one is any longer predominant" (ibid.). In practice, this indifference, or neutrality, "corresponds to a form of society in which individuals can with ease transfer from one labour to another, and where the specific kind is a matter of chance for them, hence of indifference" (ibid.). It is capital that, by confronting labor as a totality, creates the indifference of abstract labor; yet, by doing so, it also posits the conditions of its own ruin, for the indifference of abstract labor will, in turn, confront capital as a totality. Inscribed within the form of abstract labor there is, therefore, the political antagonism of the class struggle. Moreover, abstract labor describes, not only the historical reality of capital but also the relation of this reality to the communal mode of production able to supersede it, for the indifference of labor—as abstract labor—makes the return of labor to itself all the more possible. But labor will return to itself in the original unity of its nature—a unity that capital has tried to tear apart. In this unity, the subjective power of labor regains its original and undeniable force. The implication is not that abstract labor is in complete opposition to useful labor. In fact, there can be no expenditure of the former without expenditure of the latter. Thus, even though capital's only interest is time as quantity, it cannot avoid the quality of time as a plurality of subjective practices. The latter is capital's problem and principle of ruin.

REMARK 1: DIALECTIC AND METAPHYSICS

To speak about time is, in general, to speak about metaphysics or ontology. Now, this can seem strange, for Marx is certainly an antimetaphysical thinker. Indeed, insofar as Marx's philosophy is based on dialectic, it is an antimetaphysical philosophy. In fact, dialectical thinking represents one of the ways in which Western philosophy has tried to overcome metaphysics. Hence, dialectic and metaphysics have often been contrasted as opposite. The opposition between dialectic and metaphysics can be reduced to the opposition, within Presocratic philosophy, between Heraclitus and Parmenides. Supposedly, the former says that everything constantly changes, everything is in flux; the latter that nothing ever changes, that everything remains the same. The former presents a philosophy of becoming; the latter a philosophy of permanence. However, this view is not necessarily correct. Both Hegel and Heidegger have shown the fundamental agreement of Heraclitus and Parmenides. Moreover, reality itself shows—as soon as one thinks a little about it—that becoming and permanence cannot be in a position of mutual exclusion, but, rather, that the one cannot be without the other. The correct view would then be that things change and yet do not change; or rather, according to Aristotle's solution to the Presocratic challenge, they change in some respects but do not change in others.[14]

The Italian Marxist philosopher Antonio Labriola, who corresponded with Engels in the course of a few years, explains how the opposition between dialectic and metaphysics only holds insofar as one uses "metaphysics" in a pejorative sense; but this is then only vulgar metaphysics. Yet, this is the sense given to it by Engels himself who extended Hegel's characterization of the ontologies of Wolff and other German philosophers (Labriola 1965: 190–191). Thus, in his *Antidüring,* Engels used "metaphysics" to characterize a modality of thinking that opposes the genetic and dialectic understanding of the order of things (Labriola 1965: 222). It is this sense of metaphysics that one understands even with respect to fundamental Marxian categories such as commodity fetishism, money, and money as capital, as well as others. Yet, Labriola says, this is not the only meaning of metaphysics. This opposition, made fundamental in the dogmatic and false Marxism of Stalin,[15] is really without any philosophical foundation and only generates a dangerous distortion—a distortion not only of Marxism but also of philosophy and thinking. The belief that by rejecting metaphysics and only embracing dialectic one finds the ultimate and most enduring truth, only turns dialectic itself into a metaphysics of the worst kind.

ON THE DIFFERENCE BETWEEN THE *GRUNDRISSE* AND *CAPITAL*

The question of dialectic raises the question of the relation of Marx to Hegel, as well as the question of the relation of the *Grundrisse* to *Capital*. According to Negri (1991a), these questions are resolved by denying anything which is more than a terminological and conceptual resemblance between Hegel and Marx and by establishing the *Grundrisse* as autonomous from *Capital*. For Negri, the *Grundrisse* is not a rough draft to be used for philological purposes, but a *political text* in its own right. Indeed, the *Grundrisse* is for him superior to *Capital,* for the *openness* of the former makes possible what the *objectified categories* of the latter impede: the action by revolutionary subjectivity (Negri 1991a: 8–9).[16] At the end of his book, Negri denies the dialectic, "that eternal formula of Judeo-Christian thought, that circumlocution for saying—in the Western world—rationality" (p. 189).

Rosdolsky—by contrast, and before Negri—sees what he constantly calls the *Rough Draft* as "a massive reference to Hegel, in particular to his *Logic*" (Rosdolsky 1977: xiii) and considers superficial the view that Marx's relation to Hegel is only terminological and external. Furthermore, as the title of his book explicitly says, the *Grundrisse* is for Rosdolsky a preparation to *Capital*. However, he warns that one "should not... exaggerate the similarity of the two works" (p. 51). And pointing to the transformation of money into capital as an important moment of this similarity, he concludes: "Both are the product of Marx's dialectical method... *The difference lies only in the method of presentation*" (pp. 189–190; emphasis added).

It is evident that the views of Rosdolsky and Negri are diametrically opposed, yet their opposition does not require that readers of the *Grundrisse* or of Marx in general take sides with either one or the other. As Rosdolsky's reference to Schumpeter shows,[17] his interpretation tends toward an appraisal of the dialectic against a background which seems to reduce the hermeneutical options to either metaphysics[18] or positive science. Rosdolsky's further references, to Lenin and Lukács, make it clear that the question of the dialectic and of the passage from Hegel to Marx—notwithstanding the latter's radical and materialist inversion of it—has to remain central within Marxism, against both vulgar metaphysics and its offspring, positivism. "The publication of the *Grundrisse* means that academic critics of Marx will no longer be able to write without first having studied his method and its relation to Hegel" (Rosdolsky 1977: xiii).

Negri, however, starts from different theoretical and practical premises. His reading, which stems from the experience of the Autonomy Movement in Italy and is in accordance with the Althusserian and Deleuzian destruction of Hegelianism, is also an attack against the orthodoxy of Marxism and of the traditional communist party. Furthermore, by abandoning the dialectic, Negri is not concerned with the question as to whether Marxism is a metaphysics or a positive science. He has, in fact—at the time of *Marx beyond*

Marx and subsequently—a different conception of metaphysics, namely, metaphysics as an antagonistic and alternative political ontology, a constitutive practice, which seems to have little or no use of the categories of traditional dialectic. In this sense, the dialectic also falls within the vulgar metaphysics it tried to combat.

The question of the relation of the *Grundrisse* to *Capital* and of Marx to Hegel becomes a hermeneutical and a political question. To be sure, hermeneutics itself is always political, yet it is not so in a dogmatic way. I cannot elaborate on this problem here, but I will try to present a few suggestions. On the one hand, Rosdolsky's view is hermeneutically correct insofar as it considers the dialectic as intrinsic to the real movement *and* to the mode of presentation in the *Grundrisse*. In this sense, it is also fair to say that the *Grundrisse* can illuminate the reading of *Capital*. On the other hand, it is also important to recognize the *openness* of Marx's dialectic against the circularity of the dialectic of Hegel. Thus, Hegel goes to pieces when the form of capital proves unable to return to itself, when what seemed to be a circle turns out to be a spiral. "Exchange value posited as the unity of commodity and money is *capital*, and this positing itself appears as the circulation of capital. (*Which is, however, a spiral, an expanding curve, not a simple circle*)" (Marx 1973: 266; emphasis added). But circularity is, for Hegel, the *essential requirement* of dialectical logic: "The essential requirement for the science of logic is... that the whole of the science be within itself a circle in which the first is also the last and the last is also the first" (Hegel 1989: 71). Like Nietzsche's Zarathustra to the dwarf who said that "time itself is a circle," Marx is saying to an ideal Hegel (for instance, to Proudhon): "do not make things too easy for yourself!" (Nietzsche 1978: 158). However, the spiral movement is not a denial of the dialectic; it is rather a denial of the circularity that lies more in the movement of the concept than in the real movement.[19] The dialectic remains as the motor of a movement that breaks free of the circle into a spiral. At this point, the question must be posed as to why the dialectic is unable to perform the circular movement prescribed by Hegel and why what was supposed to be the end and coincide with the beginning is displaced and thrown into the open.

The answer to these questions can be found in the concepts and *in the reality* of crisis and catastrophe.[20] The dialectic is broken because reality is broken. The former remains open because openness characterizes the real movement. Thus, politically, Negri's reading of the *Grundrisse* is very convincing even though I do not see the reason for denying the dialectic *tout court*.[21]

REMARK 2: VULGAR METAPHYSICS AND POETIC METAPHYSICS

In the history of philosophy, it is possible to distinguish between a metaphysics of transcendence and a metaphysics of immanence. The former can also be called *vulgar* metaphysics. Its main tenet is the principle of "the ontotheological One" (Alliez 1996: 200). The latter is a *poetic* (or *poietic*) metaphysics whose presupposition and result are ethical, practical, and whose inner motor is political to the core. Marx's metaphysics of time is of the latter type, and it is, as Negri says, a "cursed" metaphysics (Negri 1992: 151). It is a cursed metaphysics because it is a materialist one, and because it carries within its womb the tools for a radical transformation of the world.

Critical metaphysics, which starts with Kant, still falls within a vulgar type of metaphysics, even though, by denying access to the thing-in-itself, it keeps reason from deluding itself. But to criticize vulgar—in Kant's case, dogmatic—metaphysics without building a metaphysics of immanence is equal to remaining caught within it. This is also the case with Heidegger, the school of deconstruction, and analytic philosophy in general. It is not the case with Nietzsche and Marx.

It is true that today one cannot overlook Heidegger's fundamental contribution to the question of time. Yet, as Negri says, one does not need to compare Marx to Heidegger in order to understand Marx's concept of time. In fact, "Marx has a metaphysics of time as, indeed, more radical than Heidegger's" (Negri 1992: 41). With Marx, "... temporality can be rooted in man's productive capacity, in the ontology of his becoming—an open temporality, absolutely constitutive, which does not reveal Being but produces beings" (ibid.). The difference between "revealing" and "producing" is fundamental. The Heideggerian modality of revealing (and this is also true of the later Heidegger on language and technology) still retains something of the *beyond* typical of vulgar metaphysics.[22] For Marx, by contrast, the metaphysics of time does not reveal anything. If there is a hidden subject, it affirms itself in and through production (as the identity of doing and making). If there is a subterranean fire, it breaks itself open through its incessant labor. Negri continues: "... Marx liberates what Heidegger ties up; Marx lights up with praxis what Heidegger brings back to the mystical. Heideggerian time is the form of Being, it is the indistinctness of an absolute ground; Marxian temporality is the key through which a subject which is formally predisposed to the adequacy with an absolute procedure becomes materially able to enter such a process, to define itself as constituent power" (p. 42).[23] The substance of this constituent power is time. Marx's metaphysics of time is the open dialectic of living labor *set free* by the inability of capital to reconstitute its own identity.

Identical is only that concept which, without being a *one,* is contracted into an infinite series of possible differences. In the history of Western metaphysics, this concept was established by Duns Scotus in an objective fashion. This means that the concept is not an empty abstraction but a real, objective being. The self-identity of this concept, namely, its neutral immediacy, which is also absolute difference, allows for its univocal expansion and inclusion into everything that is.[24] This concept can be given different names: being, time, power (as *potential,* i.e., not as *constituted,* but as *constituent* power).[25] It is the principle of that which is and is not, which can be and not be. In Marxian terms, moving from pure ontology to political ontology, this concept is nothing but living labor itself. It is then the principle that demystifies the view of bourgeois philosophy and political economy according to which the laws governing the capitalist mode of production are immutable and eternal. In fact, the capitalist mode of production is *this essential difference* that, as long as it is, totalizes itself and works toward the subsumption of everything else under itself. But precisely by so doing, precisely by this act of subsuming and totalizing, of turning itself into a *positive whole,* of leaving *nothing* outside itself, it reaches its concept and vanishes and withers away. *The concept of the end so much talked about in these recent years, is nothing but the coming to completion of an essential difference.* It is true that this essential difference (the capitalist mode of production) is such that it has subsumed everything under itself and has left (actually, created) *nothing* outside. Yet it would be useful to ask, in a Heideggerian fashion: is this nothing really nothing or is it something after all? The answer is that the nothing which lies outside the positive whole in which our essential difference has transformed itself is time as the constituent power of being, time that either becomes completely subsumed under capital and constitutes the substance of the latter's valorization or exceeds the capacity of capital and is seen by the latter as waste time.[26] If it is nothing, that is only because capital has no use for it. Capital has in fact already become, it has accomplished—through the appropriation without exchange of one part of its own negation: surplus labor—its M–M' movement, it has tried to rejoin itself a step ahead of itself. Yet this nothing—which is capital's own creation—is caught within the spiral movement of capital as the force that breaks the circle open into a spiral, for, in its constant drive to go beyond itself, to expand and yet desperately try to maintain a stable identity, capital steps into the very nothing it needs to use or disregard (cf. Negri 1991a: 91, 100; Marx 1973: 462).[27] Yet capital cannot avoid stepping outside itself, for this movement belongs to its concept. The nothing outside capital, the *not-capital* is *labor, living labor,* regardless of whether it is *productive* (i.e., actually employed by capital for its own valorization) or not. I will return to this point later.

THE PROBLEM OF METHOD

In "The Method of Political Economy," Marx deals with the relationship between the method of presentation and the real movement. He says that "the method of rising from the abstract to the concrete is only the way in which thought appropriates the concrete, reproduces it as the concrete in the mind. But this is by no means the process by which the concrete itself comes into being" (1973: 101).

One will not be able to think the concrete as concrete if one does not grasp its elemental structure. And one cannot grasp the latter on the basis of *Vorstellung,* representation. In thought, the concrete comes at the end of a process of analysis and synthesis, though in reality it comes at the beginning. In the process of thinking, the concrete appears "as a result, not as a point of departure, even though it is the point of departure for observation [*Anschauung*] and conception" (p. 101). If thought stops at the level of concretion, it will only reach a confused representation of reality and an abstraction; the latter, however, will not be a meaningful, determinate abstraction, but an empty one.

Of course, Marx's abstraction is not the empty abstraction of the logician, but it is a *determinate abstraction,* that is, "the abstraction which seeks the real in the concrete" (Negri 1991a: 48).[28] It is the internal structure of the concrete divided into its constitutive elements: division of labor, money, value, commodity, and so on. Ascending from these abstractions to the concrete makes it possible for the latter to be reconstituted in thought as it really is: a "concentration of many determinations," a "unity of the diverse" (Marx 1973: 101), without having the obscurity and confusion of representational, pictorial thinking. As Marx himself says, making the example of labor, "even the most abstract categories, despite their validity—precisely because of their abstractness—for all epochs, are nevertheless, in the specific character of this abstraction, themselves likewise a product of historic relations, and possess their full validity only for and within these relations" (p. 105). This means that these abstractions are not timeless, but always rooted in time and in history.

The method that goes from the abstract to the concrete is the one that takes into consideration the common element of production and the specificity of each mode of production. The common element is not something determined *a priori,* on the basis of thinking alone: "As a rule, the most general abstractions arise only in the midst of the richest possible concrete development, where one thing appears as common to many, to all" (p. 104). However, the most important determination is not the common element—with which, however, one needs to start—but the specificity of production: "In all forms of society there is one specific kind of production which predominates over the rest, whose relations thus assign rank and influence to the others" (pp. 106–107). Marx continues with a poetic metaphor full of philosophical and political significance: "It is a general illumination which bathes all the other colours and *modifies their particularity.* It is a particular ether which determines the specific gravity of every being which has materialized within it" (p. 107). Then, in a way that brings to mind the unpublished chapter of *Capital* on the formal and real subsumption, Marx says, "Capital is the all-dominating economic power of bourgeois society" (ibid.).[29] The concept of capital is not, as it was for political economy, an abstraction of commonality and a general relation of nature, but it is the most fundamental of the categories "which make up the inner structure of bourgeois society" (p. 108). At this level of analysis—as well as in reality—another fundamental category—one without which capital would not be capital—is wage labor. The end of this process of analysis, which brings to the reconstitution of the concrete in its totality and specificity, is the world market and the crisis of capital. The concept of crisis, however, is one that runs throughout the whole development of capital, and it becomes the concept of the class struggle or—for capital—of the history of bourgeois society. It is the concept of time itself, for, under capital, time is the time of crisis.

Money

The time of capital is the time of crisis. It is the difference between M and M'. This difference is a constitutive and, thus, a positive one. It is in fact the process of realization of capital and the condition of its development.[30] But that which constitutes it, living labor, is the negation of that which is constituted by it, capital. Living labor constitutes itself as its own negation: "It posits itself objectively, but it posits this, its objectivity, as its own not-being or as the being of its not-being—of capital" (Marx 1973: 454).

The time of difference is that which changes becoming into a having become.[31] The latter moment is not simply the end of the process, but it is also the beginning of a new process. It is a repetition, but one that—in the process of realization—occurs in a time of difference. Money is the subject of this time: a subject that does not have a reality of its own. In fact, money is only the form of value, whose reality, or substance, is labor time that "exists only subjectively, only in the form of activity" (p. 171). In this sense, labor, as the time of expenditure of its power, is the real subject. Yet, under capital, living labor is expended only if alienated by the worker to the capitalist in an act of *free* exchange whose vanishing mediation is money.[32] Living labor is then wage labor. This means that money, in one of its various functions, appears as the link between the subjectivity of becoming, of living labor, and its objectification into a having become. But money is only the form of appearance of exchange value. Thus, the *Grundrisse,* in its aspect of being a huge pamphlet against Darimon and the Proudhonians, speaks of the necessity of abolishing not simply money but exchange value, that is, the specificity of the capitalist mode of production: "… it is impossible to abolish money itself as long as exchange value remains the social form of product" (p. 145).

Yet the having become of becoming is not fully capital until money has changed into more money. The dialectic between becoming and having become is not proper to capital, but it belongs to the *already* of the identity of human beings and nature (p. 85). This is why the concept of subsumption becomes fundamental. If money becomes the form of being[33] and being is time, money's transition to capital is accomplished by subsuming the whole being of the worker—through the appropriation without exchange of a portion of the labor time and the reduction of the other portion to a "consumption fund" (p. 594) for the satisfaction of needs. Although the opposition between labor and capital becomes explicit only in a developed form of production (namely, with the production of surplus value), it is already, though latently, contained in the "simple forms of exchange value and money" (p. 248), the commodity form.

THE FORM OF THE THING

In section 1 of "The Chapter on Capital" of the *Grundrisse*—"The Production Process of Capital"—Marx goes from the phenomenology of the concept of capital to the production of surplus value and profit. It is not my intention to deal systematically with the whole section. Rather, I will try to underline passages of it that are important to the understanding of the concepts of labor and time.

Let me start with the concept of capital. The first thing I want to say is that capital is labor *and yet* it is not labor. It is not labor, for labor is the not-capital: "the real *not-capital* is *labour*" (Marx 1973: 274). What is meant here by labor is *living labor,* labor as subjectivity, activity, as the "form-giving fire" (p. 361), which economically and philosophically constitutes a much more general, universal, and fundamental category than capital. Capital, in fact, only pertains to the capitalist mode of production, but it pertains to it in an essential way, as its *essential difference* or specificity. Living labor, by contrast, pertains to production as such; it is a *common element* of production. I am not talking here of productive or valorizing labor, which is the form in which labor is subsumed under capital, but of living labor as—I repeat—the fire that gives form to all beings that come out of the relationship between humans and nature or humans and technology.

This living labor is, perhaps at times only as possibility, the horizon of capital. Even though capital tries—out of a necessity inherent in its concept—to subsume all labor under itself, living labor always and potentially exceeds the capacity of capital, and this is why a revolution is possible. The necessity inherent in the concept of capital is that which leads capital to employ and not employ as much living labor as it can; it is, in other words, the fundamental contradiction of capital that manifests itself in a special way in the law of the tendency of the rate of profit to decline.[34]

It is also true that, however, capital is labor. But as such, it is only accumulated, objectified, dead labor. In this sense, capital is understood as a thing, not as a relation or process (Marx 1973: 258); thus, the most important aspect of capital is lost. To say that capital is accumulated labor—Marx argues against

Adam Smith—is to refer to "the simple material of capital, without regard to the formal character without which it is not capital" (p. 257). Marx's argument here repeats what he has already said in the introduction when he was speaking of the difference between the element common to all production and the essential difference of each mode of production" (pp. 85–86).[35] Because capital is an essential difference and not a common element, it cannot be understood simply as labor.

This is not only true from the point of view of the most general abstraction, namely, the point of view that abstracts what is common out of the concrete and thus points to what in the concrete is essentially different. As I have noted, capital is not labor because labor is the not-capital. The labor that is objectified as capital (in the means of production, for instance) needs to be *resurrected from the dead* by living labor (p. 364). Furthermore, capital cannot be a thing because what characterizes it—insofar as it is the representative of money as the general form of wealth—is "the constant drive to go beyond its quantitative limit" (p. 270; see also p. 334). This drive also constitutes the source of capital's main contradiction, one that leads it into crises.

What this tells us is that capital is nothing but time (not time in general, not time *as time,* but a specific modality of time) striving continuously to go beyond itself. It is the time of production as the time of exploitation, the time of total subsumption; it is the urge to make value out of value, surplus value, and profit. It is, in this sense, time as lack of time.

It is because capital is not labor, or not labor *as labor,* that Marx says, "To develop the concept of capital it is necessary to begin not with labour but with value, and precisely, with exchange value in an already developed movement of circulation" (p. 259). In fact, labor as such, not productive or valorizing labor, is, in the last analysis—notwithstanding the fact that labor is always socially determined—a relation of nature. As Marx says in *Capital,* "Labour is, first of all, a process between man and nature, a process by which man, through his own actions, mediates, regulates and controls the metabolism between himself and nature" (Marx 1977: 283). But capital, by contrast, is an exclusively social category. To go back to the *Grundrisse,* Marx adds: "It is just as impossible to make the transition directly from labour to capital as it is to go from the different human races directly to the banker, or from nature to the steam engine" (Marx 1973: 259).

Thus, the beginning is made with value, exchange value. But what is value? Exchange value, "the substance of money" (p. 221), is nothing but a given amount of labor time contained in a commodity. The substance of value is labor, but the form of appearance of this substance is exchange value and money. From the point of view of the genesis of capital, money is to be considered as the medium of circulation and at the same time, and in addition to that, as what suspends itself from circulation. In this sense, money *is and is not* in circulation, and this constitutes its transition to capital.[36] The full form of capital—as productive capital—is M–M'. However, the form of circulation

M–C–C–M (which presupposes the simple form C–M–M–C) is the first appearance of capital, precisely, of commercial capital. "As soon as money is posited as an exchange value which not only becomes independent of circulation, but which also maintains itself through it, then it is no longer money,... but is *capital*" (p. 259).[37]   *Social relation ≠ process*

As we have seen, capital is *not a thing* but a *process*. This is so because money as capital is not a thing but a process. Although the concept of capital cannot be developed from labor, it is labor that remains the substance of things and that also gives form to things. Even the transition from thing to process is something accomplished by labor. In fact, when money returns to itself from circulation and becomes capital (a return that can be seen as a broken identity), labor also returns to itself. "But the nature of the return is this, that the labour objectified in the exchange value posits living labor as a means of reproducing it, whereas, originally, exchange value appeared merely as a product of labour" (p. 263). What is here clearly indicated is the passage from value to surplus value, for living labor will be necessary and surplus labor. The return is a violent attempt at attaining an impossible identity, and it is in reality not a return, for M *has become* M'. But what is M–M'? In the words of Éric Alliez: "It is the convulsive movement of what does not come back to itself, the specter of what does not come back into itself, thereby breaking the natural motion of need that had bodied forth in the notion of reciprocity that led to exchange, and from exchange to the polis—thereby drawing the entire astrologies of the Same into an abyss of dissimilarity" (Alliez 1996: 2). M–M' is this abyss. It is not time as time, but the specific modality of a time that is unable to return to itself. The question is here that of the separation between use-value and exchange value and of the fetishism that comes with it. The impossibility of the return is not the positive one due to consumption, for in this case a return of sort would still obtain. Rather, it is the totally negative lack of a return that, as Marx says, "becomes *madness*" (p. 296)—a madness that, however, constitutes the inner logic of capital.

THE LABOR OF FIRE

If capital is not labor, or if it is (and this only from the point of view of substance) only objectified labor, then what is labor? Labor as the *not-capital* is fundamentally two things. It is living labor and productive labor. It is very important to distinguish between these two concepts, for productive labor is always living labor, but living labor is not always and not necessarily productive labor. This distinction constitutes one of the main themes of the present work.

As Marx says in the already cited unpublished sixth chapter of *Capital,* "when we speak of *productive labour* we mean *socially determined* labour" (Marx 1977: 1043). Yet, productive labor remains the most problematic concept in Marx's critique of political economy. Marx equates living labor with productive labor. Of course, he does so because, according to the method of

Not: He refers to v (variable capital) as living labor (as distinct from c = congealed labor)

immanent critique, he looks at these categories from the point of view of capital in order to correct some mistakes of socialist writers, and, most importantly, because he wants to attack the uncritical view of some bourgeois political economists who say that all labor is productive (see, for instance, Marx 1973: 272–273). However, he himself creates some confusion because, at times, one gets the impression that there is no living labor over and beyond productive labor, whereas this is only the case under capital; and this impression is dangerous because it is easily convertible into a dogma: the dogma of productivism. Then it is difficult to understand how productive labor (as productive of capital) must end and living labor become the power and substance of a future society. For this reason, it is important to repeat a fundamental point, namely that labor, in and of itself, is *not productive* (or better *neither-productive-nor-unproductive*), but *creative,* and that it only becomes productive or unproductive under capital.[38] In other words, it is important to keep in mind that the category of productivity itself is a category of capital. Capital itself is "productive" (p. 325); in its ability to go beyond its limit, it is a revolutionary agent: "its production moves in contradictions which are constantly overcome but just as constantly posited" (p. 410). Yet, Marx says, "The universality towards which it irresistibly strives encounters barriers in its own nature, which will, at a certain stage of its development, allow it to be recognized as being itself the greatest barrier to this tendency, and hence will drive towards its own suspension" (ibid.). The end of productive and unproductive labor is the beginning of real creative labor, of real freedom; it is the lighting of a communal fire, not the self-conceited absorption into a solipsistic desire.

But productive labor is not creative labor; rather, it is *created* labor, namely, it is posited by capital as necessary and surplus labor. Productive labor is value-preserving and value-increasing labor, and it is opposed to unproductive labor, which is, however, also living labor. Marx introduces the concept of productive labor as he analyzes the relation of capital to labor. Starting from the idea that the opposite of capital cannot be one particular commodity, for the substance of capital itself is the communal substance of all commodities, that is, objectified labor, Marx says that the opposite of capital is then "labour which is still objectifying itself, *labour* as subjectivity" (Marx 1973: 272). The difference between objectified and subjective labor, which we have already seen in the *Manuscripts,* is also expressed by Marx as the difference between labor, which is *present in space* and labor which is *present in time.* "If it is to be present in time, alive, then it can be present only as the *living subject,* in which it exists as capacity, as possibility; hence as *worker*" (p. 272). Of course, this is living labor, which is also said to be productive insofar as it is used by capital for its expansion or valorization. But it seems to me that the difference between productive and unproductive labor cannot be made on the basis of the description of labor as subjectivity or as presence in time. Thus, productive labor is only that labor which produces surplus value, that is, unpaid labor; it is a form of living labor, but not the only one.

It is then important to see living labor as a category, not of political economy or capital, but of ontology. In fact, living labor is the "creative power," which, however, under capital, "comes to confront the worker as an *alien power*" (p. 307). It is the subjectivity of which the worker *divests* himself. But living labor—and this needs to be stressed again—is not only and not necessarily productive labor. The two coincide only when, as the result of the exchange between capital and labor, labor is transformed into capital (p. 308). Marx also says, "The specific relationship between *objectified* and *living* labour that converts the former into capital also turns the latter into productive labour" (Marx 1977: 1043). Living labor is then called *productive* because it is in the production process that this transformation occurs. But labor becomes *productive*—in capital's sense of the word—only because, fundamentally, it *can* produce—in the common sense of the word. In other words, labor is not an ontological, creative power because it is *productive;* rather, it becomes *productive*—and this is the only reason capital wants it—because it is *in itself* an ontological, creative power. Without labor, capital would be nothing. But the opposite does not hold true. Without capital, labor would not be productive, and yet it would not be nothing, either. Then, what would it be?

For a logic (that of capital) that posits labor as either productive or unproductive, it seems that if it is not productive it must be unproductive. This is, at first sight, a logic of either/or that works quite well as far as the rhetoric of capital is concerned. However, at a closer examination, it reveals itself to be a logic of *both/and* generated by the contradictions of capital itself: "Capital, as the positing of surplus labour, is equally and in the same moment the positing and not-positing of necessary labour; it exists only in so far as necessary labour both exists and does not exist" (Marx 1973: 401). But the positing and not-positing of necessary labor has nothing positive in it, for its positing is exploitation and its not-positing is annihilation. It is the *double freedom* that characterizes the worker's existence (see Marx 1977: 272, 874). Hence, contrary to those writers who tend to resolve difficulties by means of this logic,[39] *both/and* is not an alternative. In reality, the *both/and* modality enjoyed by the few is the condition for the *neither/nor* modality of a growing majority; *both/and* is a paradise whose presupposition and result is the tragedy of a *neither/nor. Chiapas* is an example of this. The possibility of a change does not reside in the acceptance of the *both/and* mentality but in the creation, out of a double negation, of a new radicality, one in which the having become of becoming is resurrected again to return to the immediacy of its subject. The logic that breaks that of capital is a logic of *neither/nor,* a logic of double negation, or, again, a logic of double resistance and absolute affirmation.[40] Through this logic, labor returns to itself, not posited by capital as valorizing labor but posited by itself as *neither-productive-nor-unproductive labor,* as an immanent and real structure, as living labor or form-giving fire. Productive labor, in fact, in its double aspect of value-preserving and value-creating labor, only makes sense within the logic of exchange value and money. In its first aspect, productive labor reproduces use-value. As a form of living labor, it still gives form to things. But in its second aspect—that for which alone it is productive—it only creates exchange value, and the only thing to which it gives form is capital.

THE ABOLITION OF PRODUCTIVE LABOR

The abolition of productive labor is not simply the abolition of its second aspect, surplus labor. Even its first aspect, necessary labor, would cease to have to be conceived of in the way established by the logic of exchange value and capital. In the same way in which Nietzsche's abolition of the true world of ideas is also the abolition of this world as a world of appearances and thus the abolition of vulgar metaphysics as a whole, Marx's theory of revolution entails the abolition not only of valorizing labor but also of the necessity of necessary labor *as a necessity posited by capital.* It is, in other words, the abolition of the concept of productive labor as a whole and of its counterpart, unproductive labor. It is also the abolition of the concept of waste labor. Neither-productive-nor-unproductive labor is labor that returns to itself as to its "*immediate being*" (Marx 1973: 308).[41]

It is, however, important to note that labor in its immediacy is not the *in itself* but the *for itself* of labor. The fact that under capital labor is not able to return to its immediacy is due to its being posited by capital as the essential moment in the mediation through which alone capital relates to its object. This object is, in the last analysis, the form of capital itself as more money and profit. It is the *for itself* of capital in search of independence, power, and identity. The power of capital is labor, which becomes a power *for* capital only by ceasing to be a power for itself. In this sense labor too becomes the object of capital but only, of course, as labor alienated from the worker and confronting him as an alien power, indeed, as the productive power of capital itself.

The ability of capital to posit the necessity of labor as necessary labor, so that this positing is at the same time the positing of surplus labor, rests on its ability to create—through the circularity of production and consumption—a relentless system of need. Need is, in fact, "subsumable"[42] and subsumed under capital. It is the vanishing mediation between production and consumption, that which posits both and is, in turn, posited by both. Living labor that returns to itself as to its *immediate being* is the exit from a system of need.[43] In fact, the immediacy of labor is its freedom—not its *double freedom,* that is, the freedom of the modern workers who "neither form part of the means of production themselves..., nor do they own the means of production" (Marx 1977: 874)—but that which rests on the univocal disposition of its being. It is the freedom that destroys the *both/and* logic of capital to affirm itself as a new, absolute and radical essential difference.

As the negation of capital, this new essential difference is the abolition of money and exchange value. It is not the abolition of labor, but the triumph of living, creative labor over a system of alienation and death. Labor that returns to its immediacy is labor that escapes the abyss and madness of capital. No longer divided into useful and abstract labor, no longer a vanishing mediation in the M–M' process, this labor becomes the subject (i.e., the ground and agent) of a new determination of the concrete. It is in this sense that the *Grundrisse* is, as Negri says, a political work, for it presents a theory of radical subversion and revolution. As we have seen in the section on method in particular, there is, in the *Grundrisse,* a destruction of the logic of bourgeois political economy whereby capital is surreptitiously presented as an eternal element of production and relation of nature; but there is also a constructive dimension in it. This latter has to do with a new experience of time and labor—a time whose perfect tense is no longer the presupposition for the mortification of its becoming, but, rather, the ground from which becoming itself can attain the full recognition and status of being; and a labor that, freed from the law of value, is able to recuperate its self-identity and produce difference as difference, that is, not the difference that is measured by the universal equivalent form (the form of money), not, in other words, the quantitative difference yielding only the price of the thing. It is, rather, the difference of each individuating expenditure of useful, creative labor: the moment that contracts all fire within itself, all being and all power. In this sense, labor, in its self-identity and in its capacity to run throughout *whatever* is socially and culturally constituted, without however losing track of itself, is difference that creates difference. This labor comes into a direct, organic contact with the world, whose power it is. It destroys the old forms of time, the lines of history able only to cherish a dream and a destiny of death, to establish itself as the living, immediate form of freedom.

THE CRITIQUE OF LABOR IN CAPITALISM

Often the critique of productivism becomes an outright critique of labor; the critique of capitalist production, a critique of production as such. In reality, what this does is shift the focus of the critique. I think that an example of this is offered by Moishe Postone's book *Time, Labor, and Social Domination.* Here one gets the impression that Postone wants to get rid of the concept of labor altogether. Starting from a critique of a perhaps oversimplified category that he calls "traditional Marxism," he says that, contrary to that tradition, which analyzes and criticizes capitalist production from the standpoint of labor, his own wants to be a critique of labor in capitalism (1996: 16). Whereas traditional Marxism has a transhistorical concept of labor, Postone wants to look at labor historically, as Marx had done. However, this leaves him with a one-sided understanding of the concept of labor; and indeed, with a reductive concept of history. Or at least, it is not clear why the history of labor should be the history of labor in capitalism. Contrary to what Postone says, I would not call *transhistorical* the idea that labor is present in all modes of production (as the substance and most common concept of all modes); and this includes, of course, the communal mode of production of the future. I actually think that this is Marx's idea and that it makes a lot of sense, both logically and historically.

Of course, I completely agree with Postone's view that Marx's critique of political economy entails a radically different and new concept of production itself (Postone 1996: 27). I also agree with his critique of productivism. Yet, the critique of productivism, of production in the capitalist sense, does not imply a critique of labor in all its forms. Nor, I repeat, is it correct to say that by keeping the concept of labor over and beyond capital one falls into a transhistorical understanding of it. Or rather, one has first to define the concept of transhistoricality: if this concept refers to a metaphysical level that transcends all history, then it is not what I am talking about; however, if it refers to the immanent ground of history, regardless of the difference among historical stages and modes of production, then nothing is wrong with it. In other words, it depends on the meaning one attaches to the prefix "trans." In the first case, "trans" means "beyond," but in the second case it means "through, across." In this latter sense, the concept of labor is indeed a transhistorical concept, and it is precisely because of this that capital can be determined as an essential difference; in fact, it is an essential difference of one and the same concept of labor, which is a common concept—common to all modes of production, though different in each of them. If the transhistoricality of the concept of labor is lost (in the second sense defined earlier), labor's ontological critique of political economy becomes impossible.

For Postone, "[a]t the core of all forms of traditional Marxism is a transhistorical conception of labor" (p. 7). But he maintains that "[f]ar from considering labor to be the principle of social constitution and the source of wealth in *all* societies, Marx's theory proposes that what uniquely characterizes capitalism is precisely that its basic social relations are constituted by labor and, hence, ultimately are of a fundamentally different sort than those that characterize noncapitalist societies" (p. 6). But this is patently false. First of all Marx does consider labor to be a general principle of social constitution. When this social constitution takes the form of capital, labor becomes productive in a specific, capitalist sense. Or rather, productive labor is both the cause and the effect, the substance and the outcome of that process of social constitution, but it is so only insofar as labor which is "not productive" (neither-productive-nor-unproductive-labor) is there to begin with. Of course, the basic social relations of capitalism are constituted by labor; yet, this is an essentially different sort of labor from that which constitutes, for instance, the social relations of feudalism. What is different is the *which,* not the *what* of this constitution; in other words, the difference does not lie in whether there is production (and hence labor) or not, but in the *mode* of production.

We do not have to go further into Postone's argument to realize his fundamental (and elementary) error. Basically, the error lies in his reductive understanding of labor. What, if not labor, would characterize the social relations of (past and future) noncapitalist societies? Certainly, not labor subsumed under capital, not productive labor as productive of capital. Yet, it is still a form of labor that constitutes (in its interaction with material resources) the necessary and nonnecessary wealth of all social formations. Unless we think of work as opposed to labor (as in Arendt's confusing distinction),[44] of leisure, or play. But these concepts do not solve any of the real questions faced by the world societies; questions of scarcity, survival, and the search for a decent life. Certainly, labor can be playful rather than draining, free and creative rather than compulsory and dull (and it is really in the synthesis of these opposites, namely, what in labor is necessary and what is free and creative, that one finds the sense of an alternative); yet, it would still be a form of labor.

The above argument is in direct opposition to Postone's, and I believe that Postone has overlooked the difference between the common elements of production and the essential difference of each mode underlined by Marx in the Introduction to the *Grundrisse*. Thus, for Postone the mistake of "traditional Marxism" in general is to believe that a "transhistorical, ontological content takes on various historical forms in various society" (p. 61). We have seen, however, that this transhistoricality, the ontology of labor itself, is conceptually and structurally necessary if one wants to avoid the reduction of labor to productive labor alone. And we have seen that this thought is fundamental in Marx. For Postone, instead, "labor is indeed socially constituting and determining, according to Marx, but *only* in capitalism" (p. 62). The alternative he presents to the traditional critique is what he calls a "social critique of the specific character of labor in capitalism" (p. 67). This critique is "a theory of the determinate structuring and structured forms of social practice that constitute modern society itself" (p. 67). As I will show later, in dealing with the question of the institutionalization of labor, the forms that constitute modern society belong to the logic of capital in a specific way. Yet other forms obtain in other societies that arise from and are in accordance with other modes of production. To limit the social critique of "structuring and structured forms," really of institutional modes and techniques, to capital alone amounts to an erasure of history outside the paradigm of capital. Then it is capital that becomes, not transhistorical, but ahistorical, for it becomes the form of history itself. Indeed, transhistoricality, in the acceptable and necessary sense I pointed out earlier, is the condition for a true concept of history. This is, of course, not simply a Marxian problem, but a more general logical and philosophical one. It is the same problem that Augustine, for instance, addresses in dealing with the question of form (and thus the questions of time and change)—and this can be brought to bear on the question of the mode of production once it is looked at philosophically. For Augustine, transformation is conceivable precisely because between form and form an underlying structure of formlessness resides.[45]

Postone is not very clear as to the nature of the forms of social practice constituting his critique. He speaks of "an abstract, impersonal, structural form of domination underlying the historical dynamic of capitalism" (p. 68). However, it is not clear why a theory of social constitution needs to isolate an historical period, a mode of production, not for the sake of analytical clarity, but, rather, as the synthetic moment, the result, of one's research—a fact that gives the impression that there is perhaps no question of social constitution over and beyond that period or mode. Moreover, positing the question of the abstract in such a fashion, that is, again, not analytically and methodologically, but synthetically, runs into serious philosophical and political problems. In fact, the forms of social domination are no longer understood in terms of *class* domination and antagonism, but according to "abstract, impersonal and structural" modalities the nature of which remains nebulous. Yet, if one reads Marx's subtle exposition of the problem of method in the passage from the abstract to the concrete (Marx 1973: 101), one realizes that a critique that loses sight of the concrete is not tenable.

It is not my intention to deal with all the other arguments in Postone's study, but it may be good to note that, notwithstanding his critique of Habermas, Postone ultimately remains within the same Habermasian paradigm. He criticizes Habermas's misinterpretation of Marx on the same grounds for which he criticizes all theories constituting what he reductively calls "traditional Marxism." For instance, he says, "Habermas... hypostatizes transhistorically the alienated character of labor in capitalism as an attribute of labor per se" (Postone 1996: 238). He also criticizes his theory of intersubjectivity, and that is, the reinterpretation of the dialectic of labor according to a paradigm of interaction, or rather the unduly emphasis put on interaction over labor. Again, he presents his own alternative as a superseding critique of both the traditional dialectic of labor and of Habermas's new paradigm. Speaking of his own reading of Marx's theory he says, "In such an approach, the possibility of emancipation is grounded neither in the progress of 'labor' nor in any evolutionary development of linguistically mediated communication; rather, it is grounded in the contradictory character of the structuring social forms of capitalist society in their historical development" (p. 260).

In reality, by emphasizing the role of these structuring social forms, Postone does nothing but thematize Habermas's concept of *organization,* which, as Stanley Aronowitz says in his critique of Habermas, is seen by the latter as "Marxism's missing link between infrastructure and superstructure" (Aronowitz 1981: 61). Aronowitz continues: "Organizational forms are the key linkage between *communicative* action (interaction) and *instrumental,* or productive action" (ibid.). For Aronowitz, "Habermas wishes to establish a world of harmonious relations, and not on the ground of a transformation of power relations" (p. 62). Although Postone formally underlines the "contradictory character" of the forms of social constitution, a fact that seems to reinscribe within society the antagonisms Habermas discards, his removal of the forces of social domination from the concrete reality of class antagonism and production is the same as that of Habermas. In fact, as Aronowitz says, Habermas "regards the sphere of production to be free of internal antagonism" (ibid.). If, as Aronowitz says, " we must reject [Habermas's] attempt to substitute moral and cognitive learning for class struggle" (p. 63), a substitution facilitated by the structural link of organization, the same holds true of Postone's replacing the class struggle with some vague forms of social domination.

The elimination of the ontological, "transhistorical," dimension of labor and the displacement of the class struggle also yield, in Postone's analysis, a reductive concept of the proletariat. If Postone is right in saying that "the proletariat is not, in Marx's analysis, the social representative of a possible non-capitalist society," for, indeed, the future society of communal production also entails the dissolution of the proletariat as a class, that does not mean that the proletariat (understood in the broadest possible sense, and certainly not simply as the employed working class) is not the "revolutionary Subject" at the present stage of society (Postone 1996: 355). In Postone's reading of the *Grundrisse*'s section on machinery, we find, because of his reduction of all labor to labor in capitalism, that is, because of the nondistinction between living labor and productive labor, a curious emphasis on the potentialities of *dead labor*. This emphasis is indeed close to the most extreme forms of the theory of "immaterial" labor, that is, those forms that give little or no consideration to the fundamental importance still maintained by a living labor outside of the subsumption of accumulated forms of knowledge and power—the General Intellect, as we have seen. Postone considers "quasi-romantic" the notion that "overcoming capitalism entails the victory of 'living labor' over 'dead labor,'" and he adds that "Marx's analysis implies, on the contrary, that the possibility of a qualitatively different future society is rooted in the potential of 'dead labor'" (p. 357, n. 122). What Postone is advocating here is "the possible separation of society from its capitalist form" (p. 360). However, it is not at all clear how this separation could come about. Postone says, "In the traditional interpretation, overcoming capitalism's basic contradiction involves the open realization of labor's centrality to social life. I have argued quite to the contrary that, according to Marx, labor's constitutive centrality to social life characterizes capitalism and forms the ultimate ground of its abstract mode of domination" (p. 361). The separation of society from the forms of capital takes the form, for Postone, of a political public sphere (p. 362), which however seems to suggest that capital remains in place as a structural moment but separated from the political time of society. The elimination of labor's centrality from life introduces the substitute forms of leisure and play (p. 364). However, the question is not whether we work or play, but rather whether the life-activity we perform is determined and posited by us or by the forms and structures of capital, whether our work is a wage-earning activity for the sake of valorizing capital and reproducing productive labor or, to use Foucauldian language, part of the care of the self and the others—a situation in which working is *working on,* shaping one's life and the life of the community not as a means to an end (e.g., productivity) but as an end in itself. The idea that the machinery of dead labor might regulate social life is much more dangerous than any "utopia of labor," which Postone is at pains to avoid. Dead labor *is* capital. Moreover, as we have shown earlier, the autonomy of dead labor is limited in time. To use Foucauldian language again, an ontology of liberation can pave the way for those power relations that entail, and are at the same time entailed by, various practices of freedom (Foucault 1997: 282–284, 299). The liberation of labor from capital, specifically and under real subsumption, even the liberation of dead labor as machinery from the domination of fixed capital, can ground some practices of freedom (perhaps an innumerable series of possible practices).

But these are still practices of labor, that is, of life-activity, of living labor. It would be absurd to think that dead labor itself, the machine itself, became the actual subject and agent of these practices of freedom. The reappropriation of this dead labor on the part of the immediate producers, the proletariat, that is, the actual and not merely analytical separation of fixed capital from the machinery, requires the destruction of fixed capital itself. Then dead labor can be put to use by free living labor rather than by the agency faked by capital as its own, which gives Postone the impression that there is an actual agency in dead labor as such. Although Postone says, quite rightly, that "this society does not, and cannot, evolve in a quasi-automatic fashion into a fundamentally different form of society" (p. 359), his emphasis on the potentialities of dead labor, his elimination of living labor, his marginalization of the importance of the class struggle and of the proletariat as a subject of history, contradict his basic assumption. It seems indeed that because of the technological revolution within the capitalist mode of production, because of the machinery mode, of the accumulation of the knowledge and power of humanity—and without any support of the revolutionary will, the subjective doing of what is excluded and nonexcluded from the logic of domination and alienation thereby constituted—new social forms of life can come into existence, a political public sphere, a world of leisure and play for which the structures of power inherent in the modality of productive labor are nothing but a distant dream. Then, if the victory of living labor over dead labor is a quasi-romantic notion, this gradual evolution into a flat and polite world of political discourse is an attempt at neutralizing the antagonistic nature of the struggle which individuates *beyond the political* the full actuation of the capacities of a living labor freed from the constraints of political economy, capable of setting directionalities to that dead labor that it constantly constitutes and is constantly constituted by—the exit from the regime of productive labor, yet not the death of labor.

THE CRITIQUE OF LABOR AS SUCH

The critique of economism, with an implicit critique of the "ought," sometimes also entails a critique of teleology, but not always. The two concepts are not, in fact, necessarily related. In Lukács, teleology is certainly preserved, and *telos* has the same meaning that *project* has in phenomenology. Instead, problematic in Lukács was the idea of the "ought" whereby teleology reinscribed itself in the order of ontotheology. However, when the concept of labor is looked at from a point of view that intends to be absolutely radical (whether it actually becomes radical is something that remains to be seen), the critique necessarily involves the three aspects of economism, teleology, and the "ought." This is the case with the critique presented by Baudrillard in the book *The Mirror of Production*. The book begins with an attack (dramatically conceived and presented) against productivism. To be sure, the attack is not against productivism in general, but against the place it occupies in (the imaginary of) the revolutionary left: "A specter haunts the revolutionary imagination: the phantom of production" (Baudrillard 1975: 17). He calls this a "romanticism of productivity" (ibid.). It is really an attack against Marxism, that is, against the critique of political economy and of the capitalist mode of production. But Baudrillard says, "The critical theory of the *mode* of production does not touch the *principle* of production" (ibid.). As everyone readily sees, the mode of production defines its "how"; it is perhaps more difficult to see what the *principle* of production is. The principle of production is simply this: *that there is production*.

We will see how Baudrillard actually gets entangled in a series of logical and historical difficulties (not to say absurdities) that, however, do not seem to disturb him in the least. This happens because, by wanting to get rid of the "principle" of production, he really advocates the end of production as such, that is, of all forms of production, the fact *that there is* production: an untenable proposition. He arrives at the concept, so fashionable in the last three or four decades, of the "end"; not only the end of political economy, but of everything else. For him, to maintain the principle of production (as well as *a* mode, *any* mode) means to remain caught within political economy. In this sense, capitalism is no longer the problem; production is. However, it is important to distinguish between production in capitalism, with its principle (where "principle" means "rule" or "requirement") of productivity and growth, that is, the very logic of productivism, *and* the necessary production without which life itself would not be possible.

For Baudrillard, it is not production as the production of capital that must stop, that is, the obsession with productivity and growth. No, for him the question of production is the question of Western metaphysics: "... in order to find a realm beyond economic value (which is in fact the only revolutionary perspective), then the *mirror of production* in which all Western metaphysics is reflected, must be broken" (Baudrillard 1975: 47). This is Baudrillard's main thesis. Yet, for capital the problem of metaphysics mirrored in political economy is already resolved by the fact that exchange value becomes the fundamental, perhaps the only real, use-value. There is no double anymore; the mirror is reality. What does Western metaphysics have to do with this?

But let us follow Baudrillard's argument more carefully. For him, the critique of the (capitalist) mode of production only deals with the *content* of production, not with its *form*. By leaving the form and principle of production untouched, critical theory lets the language of productivity enter, "[t]hrough a strange contagion," the revolutionary discourse (Baudrillard

1975: 17). Yet, Baudrillard does not see that, in reality, not only *a* form, but even *a* content of production must remain. In other words, the critique of the *capitalist* mode of production cannot become a critique of all modes, and this not for ideological reasons, but because production is an essential aspect of human life. Even the distinction between content and form of production made by Baudrillard looks suspicious. In reality, a mode of production is always a unity of content and form, as we have seen in Marx's (Aristotelian) formulation of this: it is a *what* modified by a *which*. The critique of the capitalist mode criticizes both content and form of that mode. Yet, it would be unreasonable to think that no mode of production and no production at all could remain.

But, indeed, Baudrillard is not only arguing against the economic concept of labor; he is against labor as an ontological concept as well. He distinguishes between *form of representation* and *form of production,* which he calls the "two great unanalyzed forms of the imaginary of political economy" (p. 20). Apparently, these two forms limited Marx's own analysis of production. Baudrillard says, "The discourse of production and the discourse of representation are the mirror by which the system of political economy comes to be reflected in the imaginary and reproduced there as the determinant instance" (ibid.). I do not want to deny the relative importance of the dimension of representation and of the imaginary, yet everything does not happen there. There may be mirrors: but determinant is indeed what they reflect.

On this basis, Baudrillard argues for a critique of everything: "In order to achieve a radical critique of political economy... [a]ll the fundamental concepts of Marxist analysis must be questioned, starting from its own requirement of a radical critique and transcendence of political economy" (p. 21). This is circular reasoning: in order to achieve a radical critique of political economy one must question the necessity of this same critique! When Baudrillard points to the confusion, within critical theory, between the liberation of productive forces and the liberation of man, he shows himself to be an acritical reader of Marx. In fact, if it is true that there is in Marx's own writings a source of confusion in relation to the concept of production, readers of Marx should eventually grasp the distinction he draws between the capitalist concept of productive labor and the ontological nature of the productive power of labor. What would otherwise be the liberation of man that Baudrillard counterposes to the liberation of the productive forces if not the subjective appropriation of this productive (*poietic*) power? Otherwise, the phrase "liberation of man" is an empty formula, or rather it is the dissolution of man's most essential features and an attack against all humanism. This is indeed the meaning of Baudrillard's next passage, which is in parentheses in the text: "Why must man's vocation always be to distinguish himself from animals? Humanism is an *idée fixe* which also comes from political economy—but we will leave that for now" (p. 22). In reality, Baudrillard does not explain why this is so. And this makes one wonder what it is exactly that he means by political economy. In a sense, Baudrillard breaks the boundaries between political economy and ontology too early; or, rather, he never sets them. Hence he is able to inflate his critique of everything up to the point that nothing is left that is recognizably human. Toward the end of the book, the concept of universality and the concept of the concept also come under his critique, but it is never clear what alternative he wishes to present.

The concept of labor, here as later in Méda, is understood as a creation of political economy: "... the system of political economy does not produce only the individual as labor power that is sold and exchanged: it produces the very conception of labor power as the fundamental human potential" (p. 31). But here Baudrillard is speaking of one and the same thing. In fact, under capital the fundamental human potential *is* labor power to be sold and exchanged: labor power becomes a commodity. Yet, who can deny that the power of labor, the capacity to work, the possibility to act in such a way as to transform the environment and oneself, precede the subsumption of labor under capital? Baudrillard's view is based on at least two mistaken assumptions. The first is his complete rejection of use-value (which played such an important role in Lukács's ontology). For Baudrillard, "Far from designating a realm beyond political economy, use-value is only the horizon of exchange value" (p. 23). Here analysis becomes mere metaphor, a mistake Baudrillard has earlier reproached Marx for. Besides that, it is difficult to agree with this statement. Use-value, regardless of the role it also plays under capital (where even exchange value is a use-value of some sort), is related to that metabolism between man and nature that both Marx and Lukács describe. Use-value is the reason and the result of labor in its most concrete yet most generic sense, that is, it comes out of concrete labor, yet it does not belong exclusively to any specific mode of production, because it is common to all.

The second mistaken assumption is that in primitive societies there is no production. This means: no use-value, no labor or labor power. It is interesting that, in his critique of everything, Baudrillard accepts the term and concept of "primitive societies" and does not challenge the use of the word "primitive." Essentially, in developing a discourse on labor as an irreducible category of political economy, Baudrillard is compelled to eliminate from the range of possible meanings of its general concept all human activity that has developed according to a separate mode. Yet, it would be far more realistic to say that labor and production are necessary aspects of human activity in general, and that what characterizes political economy is rather the fact that this labor is alienated and this production conceived only in terms of endlessly growing productivity and profit. Instead, Baudrillard (but he is only an example of a more widespread way of thinking) shows that he is interested in manipulating the categories of critical theory rather than understand and explain them. Thus, for him "Marxism assists the cunning of capital. It convinces men that they are alienated by the sale of their labor power, thus censoring the much more radical hypothesis that they might be alienated as labor power, as the 'inalienable' power of creating value by their labor" (p. 31; italics removed).

The emphasis should here be on "creating value," for this is the idea that needs explanation. Baudrillard forgets that it is precisely a sold and bought labor power that creates value, for "value," as Marx says, means "exchange value," and this is creating only by the withholding of part of the worker's remuneration, so that the real value is surplus value. Otherwise, the transformation of matter during the labor process does not by itself create value in this sense. Unless Baudrillard means that the principle of alienation lies in the making of use-value, in the passage of *poiesis* from a subject to an object, in the new, arising synthesis. Yet, if this is the case, the only "radical" alternative would be to stop all doing and all making, not merely production in the capitalist sense. Even though Baudrillard draws a line between Marx and Marxist theory, his argument still presents many problems. For him, under attack must be the "productive potential of every man in every society" (p. 31), not the directionality this potential takes under direct or indirect compulsion, not the use to which that potential is put. Under attack is, in other words, anthropology, for, in the productive power of man, Baudrillard sees a fundamental anthropological postulate. This is not altogether wrong, but one also should remember that this anthropology rests on a more fundamental ontology, as we have seen in Chapter 1.

In reality, Baudrillard criticizes Marx's *ontological* understanding of labor. But when he himself speaks of the "objectification of nature" (p. 34), he is very imprecise. He should rather speak of the "subjectivization of nature" and the "objectification of human activity." It is in this sense that, as we have seen in the *Manuscripts,* humanism and naturalism become for Marx one and the same thing (Marx 1975: 348). By contrast, Baudrillard's phrase "objectification of nature" means nothing, and it is the result of his inability to understand the synthetic moment at work in Marx's dialectic. Finally, for Baudrillard the whole issue becomes one of symbolic exchange. He says, "The real rupture is not between "abstract" labor and "concrete" labor, but between symbolic exchange and work (production, economics)" (Baudrillard 1975: 45). It is in this *mirror of production* that, accordingly, human suffering and misery must be sought. In this mirror, "in which all Western metaphysics is reflected" (p. 47), the universality of the concept separates man from his nature, and it is here that alienation occurs. Concepts—the concept of history being one of the most important in this respect—are universalized and become transhistorical: "As soon as they are constituted as universal they cease to be analytical and the religion of meaning begins" (p. 48). But Baudrillard does not say why a universal concept cannot be analytical. Instead, he continues by giving a deontologized, linguistically and psychologically flattened, version of the concept. Accordingly, concepts "set themselves up as expressing an "objective reality." They become signs: signifiers of a 'real' signified" (ibid.). Yet, Baudrillard does not realize that concepts do not express reality, but they maintain their own reality and their own objectivity. It is not that they *become* "signs"; rather, they constitute the ontology of the form, and as such they are a fundamental part of the structure of reality. Even when taken in the

Saussurian sense, as a part of a sign, they bridge the space between constitution, interpretation, and expression, but they are never, properly speaking, expression. Yet, they are usually so understood by a contemporary French school of thought that works on the basis of a misappropriation of the Saussurian concept of the sign.[46]

On the basis of this misconception, Baudrillard assigns to the concept-sign—rather than to the constitutive social practice of power and control of which the concept is, of course, a part—the responsibility for a reading, an interpretation, of history that prepares the ground for a system of "repressive simulations." He is here dealing with the question of historical and anthropological interpretation through universal concepts. This is an important issue, although I think that the right argument to be made is precisely the opposite of Baudrillard's argument. In fact, the problem does not lie in the fact that universal concepts are used in the attempt to get an understanding of non-Western cultures and peoples, but, generally speaking, the problem lies in the way in which universal concepts are constructed—as peculiarly Western forms for the enhancement of hegemonic practices of assimilation or exclusion. In other words, it is not by saying that the Maori *also* produce that one imposes on them a set of external categories, but by dismissing their mode of production as non-efficient, nonmodern, or unproductive, one understands the Western capitalist concept of production as universal, and indeed as *the* universal. Instead of saying that there is production and production, Baudrillard eliminates the problem altogether: "There is *neither a mode of production nor production in primitive societies*" (p. 49). As I have already noted, in this critique of everything only the concept of the "primitive" seems to be in no need of being questioned. Since at this point Baudrillard is also speaking about psychoanalysis, he continues: "There is *no dialectic* and no *unconscious* in primitive societies. The concepts analyze only our own societies, which are ruled by political economy" (ibid.). Baudrillard's own alternative is to stop exporting Marxism, psychoanalysis and bourgeois ideology and rather "bring all the force and questioning of primitive societies to bear on Marxism and psychoanalysis" (p. 50). However, who will do that? Baudrillard says "we." Yet, because we are not "primitive," how are we going to even get close to this "force" and this "questioning"? This is much more presumptuous and Eurocentric than the sober claim of Marxism to universality.

Let us limit our reading to the concepts of production and mode of production. For Baudrillard, in a way not entirely different from Postone in this respect, "Marx made a radical critique of political economy, but still in the form of political economy" (p. 50). To this completed but insufficient critique, Baudrillard wishes to substitute a vague "critique of the political economy of the sign" (p. 51). Symbolic exchange is what remains after the end of the critique of political economy. Recall that use-value is not what lies beyond exchange value, but it is, rather, exchange value's horizon. The beyond is, as we shall soon see, a romantic interpretation of the forms of exchange in so-called primitive societies.

First of all, Baudrillard gets rid of labor, a concept whose "emergence" is traced back to the eighteenth century (p. 53). Then, he eliminates the concept of totality: "Everything that speaks in terms of totality (and/or 'alienation') under the sign of a Nature or a recovered essence speaks in terms of repression and separation" (pp. 55–56). But again, he does not explain why this is so. Totality seems to bear the same relation to his critique as universality. Yet, there is also a positive understanding of the concept of totality, which comes precisely from anthropology and from issues that Baudrillard also deals with; but he does not see it. I mean to refer to Marcel Mauss's concept of the *total fact*, which describes so-called primitive societies by a universalizing method, precisely.

Baudrillard may be right in criticizing the thoughtless, mechanical application of Marxist categories to "primitive" societies (he makes the case of Godelier), but that does not mean that these societies have no concept and practice of production. Their production does not take place according to the capitalist mode, of course, yet to say that they have no production and no concept of labor is to push theory to the point of the absurd. In order to understand this, there is no better place than Mauss's essay *The Gift*. Baudrillard does refer to Mauss's ideas, without mentioning him: "The exchange-gift, to be exact, operates not according to the evaluation or equivalence of exchanged goods but according to the antagonistic reciprocity of persons" (Baudrillard 1975: 75). This, however, does not take away the importance of a theory of production and the existence of a life economy in those societies.

According to Marcel Mauss, the exchange-gift occurs on the basis of an obligation, and it is the reason and form of this obligation that he sets out to study in *The Gift*. Yet, this is so closely related to a theory and practice of production that one of the most important terms described by Mauss denotes the most fundamental moment, the *raison d'être*, of production itself: consumption. I am here speaking of the word *potlatch*, which means "to feed, to consume" (Mauss 1990: 6). This is not the place to deal extensively with Mauss's great study. I will only say two things. One is that the reason for exchange is not identical with the reason for production proper. By that I mean to say that exchange can be understood from within the system in which it inscribes itself: the system of laws. In this sense, we have to recall the brief discussion of Pashukanis's ideas in order to understand how the forms of exchange relate to, and are regulated by, the material conditions of life that they regulate in turn. The gift is the universal ground bridging the gap between the base and the superstructure, to use Marxist terminology and concepts. It is not simply the thing exchanged. Rather, this thing is nothing but the empirical, phenomenal form of a totality of social relations that include, of course, the productive power of labor. The second thing I want to say has to do precisely with this productive power. In the section of his book entitled "The Force of Things," Mauss says that arguably "in the things exchanged during the potlatch, a power is present that forces gifts to be passed around, to be given, and returned" (p. 43). Here the legal and ethical category of obligation shows its essential constitution and determination. Even though it is mixed with religious and magical moments, this power is productive power, and it is possessed by the thing exchanged (p. 44). Among the Maori, this power or force is called *hau,* the spirit of the thing, which is there "in cases where the law, particularly the obligation to reciprocate, may fail to be observed" (p. 10). Thus, "in Maori law, the legal tie, a tie occurring through things, is one between souls, because the thing itself possesses a soul, is of the soul" (p. 12). Notwithstanding the difference between the Maori and the Western orders of things, one can still see how universal concepts play a role in both. In fact, what makes a culture different from another is the answers it gives to questions that confront humanity in a common way. These *structural* questions are in the order of universality, not because they are abstract, but because they are concretely common; and even the basic answers, for example, the principle of alienation (in the ontological, not in the economic sense), must be similar. This is how the obligation to give, to receive, and to reciprocate (the obligation to reciprocate above all) comes about: "because to accept something from somebody is to accept some part of his spiritual essence, of his soul" (p. 12). But of course this is not the economic alienation typical of capital. It is rather what occurs in the first dialectical moment of the relationship between man and nature as described by Lukács: an unavoidable universal. Yet, as we have seen, this is the central moment of Baudrillard's critique of everything.

THE LIMITS OF THE CRITIQUE OF PRODUCTION

Contrary to what Baudrillard says, Marxism and psychoanalysis (and even "bourgeois ideologies") are tools for understanding, not only Western but also non-Western societies. Marxism, in particular, is informed and sustained by an aspiration to universal emancipation—emancipation from the servitude of labor and from the forms of social domination that come with it, regardless of any given mode of production. To romanticize "primitive" societies is rather backward and reactionary. At the same time, there is bad faith in rejecting all Western accomplishments only on the basis of their provenance. Rather, when one goes a little deeper into the question, one realizes that nothing is indeed purely Western and that the category itself is flawed. To say, particularly, that labor is a product of eighteenth-century Europe, and thus of Western metaphysics, without specifying that one is speaking of productive labor in the capitalist sense, is inadmissible. To oppose this model (and regime) of labor with an imprecise idea of life (economy and culture) in "primitive" societies makes one wonder what happens to the rest of history and of the world.

The great civilizations of the past are certainly not all Western, nor are they "primitive" in any possible meaning of the term. The past construction of cities and other immense and splendid structures in most regions of the world does not support the thesis that labor (when left unqualified) emerged or was invented at one point only in history. Tenochtitlán or Benin City, which left the first European invaders in breathless admiration, is not conceivable without conceiving also an organized and developed system of labor. That this labor is a universal, that it is hidden in the forest of the earth, only says that it provides the univocal ground for all social and cultural formations. The city itself, as Lewis Mumford says, is "a product of the earth" (Mumford 1938: 3) and an "earth form" (p. 316). The substance of this form, which also comes from the earth, is, at least in part, labor itself. The difference between cultures is a function of the dialectical relationship of geography and history, and its unit and measure is, with Mumford again, the region. I am not attempting here to give a clumsy answer to complex questions. What I intend to do is throw some light on the fact that denying the existence and usefulness of universal concepts and realities only brings us to an absolute theory of cultural relativism contradicted by, not only historiography, not only history and anthropology, but also lived experience and common sense. The opposite of this absolute cultural relativism is not, of course, a static essentialism; it is, rather, the awareness that the human condition (with its concepts and practices) is not an invention, but that *inventio* (i.e., labor) is the way in and through which different habitats are shaped and constituted in response, precisely, to those structural and universal questions defining the human condition itself.

Thus, radicalizing the ontology of labor means neither reducing all forms of social life, of human activity, to a restricted concept of labor that in one way or the other always supports the logic of productivity and productivism nor refusing to give labor the universality, which all commonsense inquiry is able to discern and prove. Instead of denouncing the concept of labor as an inherently capitalist or productivist concept, a radical ontology of labor—an ontology of liberation—should focus on the way in which labor is institutionalized. In the institutionalization of labor, one finds the character and meaning, the sign, of a society. In other words, it is the "how" rather than the "what" of labor that needs to be understood and, possibly, dismantled. It is in this sense that Marx focuses on the *mode* of production and actually considers with annoyance the concept of production in general. Yet, this does not mean that he denies that there is production in general, or rather the universality of the concept of production, if by that one means that all modes of production are precisely essential modifications of one and the same activity and concept. Certainly, by being *essential* modifications, essential differences, they must be considered as the only synchronic manifestations of that generality, as the only individuations of that universal; to dwell on the generality and the universality as such would, at this point, only obfuscate the real issue: that of understanding the *thisness* of labor, its historicity. The issue is here difficult. For instance, today we do not deny the global dimension of capitalist production (a dimension that, to be sure, pertains to the concept of capital as such but today manifests itself in the most conspicuous way): on the one hand, we do not justify it by recurring to the idea that production has always existed and that therefore the real issue is production in general; on the other, we do not merely say that production means production in the age of globalization. They are two different things. Properly speaking, production in general does not exist; yet, even overcoming the capitalist specificity of globalization would be impossible if other forms of production were not possible and did not already announce themselves at the interstices or at the horizon of this given and present form. Instead, what we say is that the production of capital must stop so that a new paradigm of production may take shape. But to launch an indiscriminate assault against all forms of production, against production as such, against labor as labor, is the same as losing sight of the specificity of capitalist production as well as deciding to delete the problem rather than try to find a solution to it.

The concept of institution is the key to solving the question of the distinction between living labor and productive labor. As I have repeatedly said, productive labor is *also* living labor, but not all living labor is productive in the capitalist sense of the word, and in the sense in which Marx also uses the concept. Productive labor is living labor institutionalized. In this sense, what constitutes a problem is not the fact that we do some work, but the obligation to work. And not merely this obligation in a generic sense, but that which is posited, institutionalized and normalized by structures of constituted power, which in our age are rooted in the essence and machinery of capital. The factory is the typical example of this obligation under the capitalist/industrial regime. Yet, the obligation itself constitutes a modality that goes beyond the factory, or rather, as many authors have said, the model of the factory becomes, at one point in history, the general model of society as a whole.

A recent survey of the history of the concept of labor and of its status today, as well as the attempt to offer an alternative, can be found in Dominique Méda's *Le travail: Une valeur en voie de disparition* (1995). After describing labor as an "invention" of modernity, which comes in the eighteenth century as an answer to the "great fear" that envelops Europe from the end of the Middle Ages up to the seventeenth century (Méda 1995: 295),[47] Méda—who does not mention Gramsci—calls for a renewed *praxis* able to displace the centrality of labor. This *praxis*, which is, rather, informed by the philosophy of Habermas, consists in the concept of the public sphere, where time is liberated from labor making it possible for the individual to have access to "other modes of sociability, other means of expression, other ways... of acquiring an identity or participating in collective management" (p. 301). This public sphere—the space for action and interaction—is not to replace production and labor, but to be placed alongside them. Of course, it is not difficult to agree with Méda's contention that production does not exhaust all human activity and time. Yet, the problem is that in Méda's view production and action are merely juxtaposed, and one is left to wonder how the articulation between the two spheres will take place. Méda's book, which is good for its historical survey and for its stimulating polemical moments (notably, against liberalism and the philosophy of Rawls), does not seem to consider the question, implicit in its object of study, of the necessity of dissolving the objective nexus between technique and political power. Without the recognition and dissolution of this nexus, which is the same as Marx's doctrine of subsumption, it is difficult to see how the working class can even have access to a public sphere that remains on the other side of the objective nexus itself, related to the interests of the dominant class, and in relation to which the working class cannot but be antagonistic.

In Méda's book, there is no trace of the antagonism of labor to capital, and of labor's quest for autonomy. Labor is seen as an "invention" (in itself a dubious concept) of the economists who "for the first time, give it a homogeneous meaning" (Méda 1995: 65). And this labor is time: "its essence is time" (ibid.). Of course, Méda is aware of the fact that in Smith and the other political economists (including Marx and his critique of political economy, she claims), the concept of labor that prevails is productive labor. Here labor, one should rather say, is not "invented," but it is displaced from its ontological terrain and channeled into the categories of political economy. Thus, political economy, or even mere economics, can become the social science *par excellence.* But in Méda's account, the ontologization of labor is still part of the general invention of its concept, for it is with Hegel and Marx that labor becomes "an ideal of creation and of self-realization," or, in other words, "the essence of man" (pp. 92–129). Thus, even alienation is a consequence of this invention (p. 106). But at the end of her book, without returning to the concept of alienation (which of course impedes the full realization and activity of the individual), Méda finally recognizes that "Marx had perfectly understood, in his time, what is at stake in today's expression of 'full activity'" (p. 309). This *full activity* is the "development, alongside labor, of other activities, whether collective or individual, such that everybody may become, as Marx desired, multi-active" (ibid.). Furthermore, Méda stresses that for Marx—and this is her own position, too—the concept of full activity "must be applied not to society as a whole, but to each individual, who would dispose, at the same time, of laboring time [*un temps d'emploi*] and of time for other activities which would belong neither to employment nor to labor" (ibid.). It is difficult to see how Méda justifies this latter judgment on Marx with her previous one according to which Marx is the most exceptional and rigorous exponent of productivism (p. 166). Her ambivalence in relation to Marx depends on the fact that a critique of labor such as the one she presents is forced to see labor in the light of productivism only, for it wants to deny its univocity and ontological power. Such a critique, instead of finding in Marx a critique of productivism (notwithstanding Marx's own ambiguities, as we have seen), reduces the concept of labor to the economic base and frees the superstructure as the only place of creativity and action. The difference is that now, instead of being in a vertical position, one above the other, superstructure and structure, action and production, are in a horizontal position, one alongside the other; yet they are still far from being united in insurgent and constitutive *praxis.*

Indeed, in the philosophy of praxis, labor is not merely a moment of the base or structure. At the level of production, labor—which is already praxis, that is, engaged in the political movement that tends to transform society as a whole—is the subject that antagonistically confronts the objective ensemble of forces of production and State power. The opening up of a public space of discussion must be, for that which is at the same time included in and excluded from public view, the result of a revolutionary process and of an unrelenting revolutionary will, not the silent companion of production. This means that the question as to what labor is cannot be solved by separating once again, or juxtaposing, production and action, but by seeing production as one of the moments of human creative activity—yet here "production" must not be understood in the capitalist sense. Labor would then be the subject and substance not merely of production, but of all creative activity. Of course, this labor would no longer be productive of capital. But this should not be a problem; it should, rather, be the aim of a theory of revolution.

RUBIN

The overcoming of capital is the overcoming of a determinate and essential difference, not of a general necessity. Therefore, maintaining the notion of the necessity of production is not at all remaining open to a productivist logic. Under capital the end of production is the making of surplus-value and profit, not production proper. In Volume II of *Capital,* we read: "The production process appears simply as an unavoidable middle term, a necessary evil for the purpose of money-making" (Marx 1978: 137). On the other hand, creative production—under the communal mode of production—does not mean that the usefulness of what is produced no longer counts; that is, it is not, nor does it have to be, disinterested production. The creative (or even poetic) aspect of production does not mean that all products of (material or "immaterial") labor are works of art, at least not according to the way we usually understand the concept of a work of art. Rather, what it means is that by operating the split away from objectivity toward subjectivity the gap between work of art and mere production narrows; and the gap between conception and execution may even disappear. The result of subjective labor may very well have, as it should, its usefulness outside itself, outside mere contemplation. But usefulness itself must be redefined. It is this redefinition that does not belong to the field of production, of the economy and of the structure (base); rather, it belongs to the field of action or, which is the same, of praxis.

The confusion in the concept of productive labor is, as Isaak Rubin wrote in 1928, "an unclear idea of Marx's own views" (Rubin 1972: 259). In the section on productive labor in his *Essays,* Rubin quotes from the first volume of *Capital:* "Capitalist production is not merely the production of commodities, it is, in its very essence, the production of surplus-value" (Marx 1977: 644). Rubin, who had not read the *Grundrisse,*[48] quotes from the sections on productive labor in Volume I of *Theories of Surplus Value* where Marx repeats the arguments we find in the *Grundrisse* as well. Fundamentally, productive labor is that which produces capital. According to Marx, "Only bourgeois narrow-mindedness, which regards the capitalist forms of production as absolute forms—hence as eternal, natural forms of production—can confuse the question of what is *productive labour* from the standpoint of capital with the question of what labour is productive in general; and consequently fancy itself very wise in giving the answer that all labour which produces anything at all, which has any kind of result, is by that very fact productive labour" (Marx 2000: 393).[49] Rubin explains that "Marx throws out as useless the question of what kind of labor is productive in general" because "[e]very system of production relations, every economic order has its concept of productive labor" (Rubin 1972: 260). Thus, "Marx confined his analysis to the question of which labor is productive from the standpoint of capital, or in the capitalist system of economy" (ibid.). Then Rubin goes on to speak of the difference between the production and the circulation of capital, which adds confusion to the question of productive labor, and says that, for Marx, only one type of labor "is 'productive' not because it produces material goods, but because it is hired by 'productive' capital, i.e., capital in the phase of production" (p. 269). Thus, "[t]he labor of salesmen is not productive, not because it does not produce changes in material goods, but only because it is hired by capital in the phase of circulation" (ibid.). By contrast, "[t]he labor of the clown [in the service of the circus entrepreneur] is productive because it is employed by capital in the phase of production" (ibid.; brackets added). This analytic distinction seems to leave even Rubin unsatisfied. We enter here a scholastic question, a source of confusion that cannot be clarified but must be left to itself. At the end of his study, Rubin himself says that perhaps the term "productive" was not Marx's best choice to speak of the difference between labor hired by capital in the phase of production and labor hired by capital in the phase of circulation (p. 275).

However, Rubin, whose interest lies more in giving a social and cultural dimension to political economy as against mere economics than in performing a critique of political economy itself, also leaves unsolved the question as to why labor that is not productive (i.e., neither-productive-nor-unproductive, but creative, labor) should not be given philosophical and political consideration. He does not see, therefore, that Marx's definition is one-sided, or, as Negri says, *heavily reductive* (Negri 1991a: 64). It is of course true that if one considers all labor "productive labor" one may—as did the political economists Marx wanted to refute—lose sight of the essential difference and the historical character of capital. But for bourgeois political economy that was not a mistake; it was rather a precise and deliberate political endeavor. Yet, by reducing all living labor to either productive or unproductive labor, one risks reducing the political, insurgent potentiality of subjective labor, the subjective power of labor. Indeed, the confusion Rubin points out in relation to the difference between labor hired by capital in the phase of production and labor hired by capital in the phase of circulation (the latter being unproductive) becomes fruitful only if one looks at the phase of circulation in a broader sense than political economy does and translates it into the superstructural level. In this sense circulating is not capital as capital, but capital as transfigured and segmented into the many manifestations of its own regime. The neither/nor of labor becomes then (is contracted into) a potentially infinite multiplicity of labors, an infinite number of possible *thises,* a *laboring multitude*[50]—of which the *this* of total subsumption, with its essential modifications and specificity, (whether in the realm of materiality or immateriality, visibility or invisibility) shows to be, yes, the dominant one, but of a dominance bent toward the metaphysics of its own ruin. That would be productive labor, which, to an extent, is already capital. Its historicalness cannot be concealed, notwithstanding the efforts in that sense made by political economy and the dominant ideologies. The other labors, the *many* labors, in touch with the negative universal that sustains them, the double negation of inclusion and exclusion, ground the conditions for a political ontology of liberation.

3   Radicalizing the Ontology of Labor
Institution and Utopia

Pauperism, political economy, and the discovery of society were closely
interwoven.
—Karl Polanyi

One sees that philosophy also has its chiliastic vision, but one whose
occurrence can be promoted by its idea, though only from afar, and it is
thus anything but fanciful.
—Immanuel Kant

IN ORDER TO UNDERSTAND the concept of the institution as the clarifying moment of the distinction between living labor and productive labor,
we have to turn to the work of Michel Foucault. Both in *Madness and Civilization* and in *Discipline and Punish*, Foucault addresses the question of labor,
and of productive labor, from the point of view of a constitutive, positive
ontology of the institutional world. Here, the procedures and structures of
rationalization later applied by Taylorism to the labor process in the narrow
and most technical sense, show their historical roots of blood and terror. In
their historicity, these procedures and structures give productive labor (as productive of capital) a rather sinister dimension. The concept of work ethic, used
to justify at some level the idea of productive labor and to produce the immoral
status of unproductive labor by the same stroke, reveals the disfigured traits
of its inner constitution.

Of course, it would be preposterous to say that labor is a new concept and
reality, new with modernity, that before modernity there was no labor or
even no obligation to work. One needs only to think, even in a very schematic
way, about the condition of the medieval serf, of the ancient slave. Think
about the great constructions of antiquity in the civilizations that flourished
before the advent of capital in different areas of the world. One realizes that
their accomplishments could not have been achieved without labor, and compulsory labor at that. So, what was new with modernity might have been a
certain institutionalization of the obligation to work, and this happened for
a variety of reasons. If it belonged to the concept of the serf to do manorial labor, of a slave to perform slave labor, with the coming of modernity a
paradoxical concept of freedom—that Marx called "double freedom"—is
created by new relations of production that will then flourish during the
industrial age. The relationship between the urban and rural areas takes on
a new form, conditioned in particular by the economic, social and political

disenfranchisement that brings about brigandage in the countryside and at the doors of cities and vagabondage within the city itself. Those manifestations of social life that defy any acceptable concept of labor, that cannot be subsumed under any mode of production (for it is their purpose to disrupt production in all its forms), are in fact among the forms which political economy will soon classify as unproductive. And so they are indeed, for, if anything, they are disruptive of the nascent capitalist economy, its social organization, and its ideals of productivity and productive labor. It is this latter concept of labor that can be said to have emerged with modernity, not labor in an unqualified sense.

POVERTY

Poverty became one of the main problems of modern, industrial society, perhaps its most conspicuous pathology,[1] and it was as a remedy to poverty that, as Foucault notes, one resorted to labor: "In the first phase of the industrial world, labor did not seem linked to the problems it was to provoke; it was regarded, on the contrary, as a general solution, an infallible panacea, a remedy to all forms of poverty" (Foucault 1965: 55). Of course, the serf, the slave, the city artisan was also poor. But he did not have to deal with the ambiguities of a double freedom, which begins in the initial phase of modernity and becomes systemic with the Industrial Revolution. He was part of the means of production, the land, or he belonged to a guild and was the owner of his craft and skills. What we understand as modernity arises in a world of crumbling social institutions, labor begins to be set free (and only in this sense can one speak of its emergence), but this was of course a negative, paradoxical, freedom. The disappearance of the old institutions requires that now labor is institutionalized in a new way, along new and productive lines. For, what is the new form of poverty that goes from vagabondage to banditry and brigandage if not wasted labor and wasted productivity, that is, labor and productivity that do not find ways of implementing themselves as such?

As Fernard Braudel says, "Poverty was such in Florence in April, 1650 that it was impossible to hear mass *in pace*, so much was one importuned during the service by wretched people, 'naked and covered with sores,' 'ignudi e pieni di scabbia'" (Braudel 1995: 2, 735). In the same century, but also before and after that, Naples was "the theater of a perpetual social war, something going far beyond the limits of ordinary crime" (p. 737). The cities of Europe, as we shall see more concretely when we go back to Foucault, tried to defend themselves against poverty. Braudel again says, "In Spain, vagrants cluttered the roads, stopping at every town... Along the roads to Madrid moved a steady procession of poor travelers, civil servants without posts, captains without companies, humble folk in search of work, trudging behind a donkey with empty saddle bags, all faint with hunger and hoping that someone, in the capital, would settle their fate" (p. 740). Finally, "[i]nto Seville streamed the hungry crowds of emigrants to America, impoverished gentlemen hoping to make

good, and along with them the dregs of Spanish society, branded thieves, bandits, tramps all hoping to find some lucrative activity overseas..." (ibid.). The
phenomenon, present all over Europe but also in other areas of the world, was
social, economic, and political. Although Braudel is hesitant to call it a class
war, it indeed was such, and it constituted the ground and landscape for the
emergence of modern institutional labor. Indeed, this war anticipated today's
structure, under the regime of a full-fledged global economy, of the international division of labor and of the social movements of resistance to it. Living labor that was not institutionally productive either ended up in the mad-
houses, in the prisons or on the scaffold, or it organized itself along the lines
of banditry and brigandage (or of piracy at sea). The bandits and brigands
formed "states in miniature with the great advantage of mobility" (Braudel
1995: 745). They cut across the territorial states upsetting both national and
international order. Braudel notes that "these tiny forces irritated established
states and in the end wore them down" (ibid.). And he emphasizes the social
and radical dimension of their activities: "Like the guerrilla forces of modern
popular wars, they invariably had the people on their side" (ibid.).

The modern, institutional concept of labor emerges then from a class war
that takes place at different levels of the social sphere: within the city, in the
relationship between the city and the countryside within one and the same territorial state, and at the international or transnational level. The opposition
to its institutionalization is represented by the antagonistic living labor that
remains at the margins of established society and continuously threatens its
order. New forms of institutional order will be required, as we shall see, to
cope with this problem. However, what is characteristic of this 'unproductive'
living labor is its antagonistic relation to established and constituted power.
Braudel says, "Banditry was in the first place a revenge upon established
states, the defenders of a political and even social order" (p. 745).[2]

Yet the established political and social order was not shy in retaliating
against this revenge, but to the method of brute force and sheer cruelty it now
added, and gradually developed, sophisticated techniques of control. By
shifting the original antagonism from the economic base to the moral level,
it was able to have the nascent proletariat carry the burden of that order's
social failure. In this sense, the institutionalization of labor as productive
labor, that is, its normalization and moralization, served the purpose perfectly
well. As Foucault says, "Labor and poverty were located in a simple opposition, in inverse proportion to each other. As for that power, its special characteristic, of abolishing poverty, labor—according to the classical interpretation—possessed it not so much by its productive capacity as by a certain force
of moral enchantment" (Foucault 1965: 55). Here it is Adam Smith, among
others, that Foucault has in mind: labor as a curse—a notion that, as we have
seen, was energetically rejected by Marx. Labor was then used as a remedy
against all forms of rebellion, or what was interpreted as social deviancy or mere
idleness: "Labor in the houses of confinement thus assumed its ethical meaning: since sloth had become the absolute form of rebellion, the idle would be

forced to work, in the endless leisure of a labor without utility or profit" (p. 57). However, notwithstanding the emphasis that Foucault puts on the moral, rather than economic, determination of the concept of labor, the link between the two, or the prefiguration of this link in the following centuries, is already evident. Productive labor—even at this preindustrial stage—acquires a dual nature, and its moral determination seems in fact to be a clumsy justification for its economic use. Thus, if it is true that, as Foucault says, "[t]he prisoner who could and who would work would be released, not so much because he was again useful to society, but because he had again subscribed to the ethical pact of human existence" (pp. 59–60), it is also true that the substance of this pact lay in the promise not to disrupt productivity and economic growth again. The tenuous line separating the working poor from the idle and mad could suddenly disappear, and clinging to a form of productivity was the only way to ensure oneself against falling outside of the ethical, but really social and economic, pact. Thus, a century later in Britain with the enclosure movement, and then particularly with the Poor Law of 1834, the compulsion toward forms of industrial productivity was determined by making other forms of life (particularly in the countryside) "intolerable" (Hobsbawm 1962: 185).[3]

Foucault describes confinement as an "institutional creation peculiar to the seventeenth century" (Foucault 1965: 63). Yet, what is here important is that, when the industrial age comes into its own around and after the time of the French Revolution, that institution is used as a model for the new social and economic order. It is in fact a preconfiguration of the factory world—not simply the factory itself but also the slums around it and, after factories are moved away from the countryside to the new urban centers, the industrial city itself. Of course, this is prefigured in Foucault's work when he says that this new institution "marked a decisive event: the moment when madness was perceived on the social horizon of poverty, of incapacity to work, of inability to integrate with the group; the moment when madness began to rank among the problems of the city" (p. 64). This is another way of stating Marx's concept of the double freedom of the proletariat but for a period slightly earlier than the one Marx deals with. All the same, the poor are left with the choice to either accept the conditions of the new contract, and by doing so subscribe to perennial poverty, or sink into madness and disappear. One or two centuries later, their situation would not be better, but perhaps it was worse; in any case, the institutional form given to labor at this point in history, as either productive or unproductive (either sane or insane) labor, would become a pillar of the new industrial society, and living labor as such (that is, neither-productive-nor-unproductive-labor) would completely disappear.

I now take distance from Foucault's analysis and description, for he sees a rupture where there probably is substantial continuity.[4] Thus, for Foucault there is an overturning of categories such that at the end of the eighteenth century the economic dimension of poverty replaces the previous moral one. He says that "freed from the old moral confusions," poverty now becomes "an economic phenomenon" (1965: 229).[5] And he explains this as follows: "In the mercantilist economy, the Pauper, being neither producer nor consumer, had no place: idle, vagabond, unemployed, he belonged only to confinement, a measure by which he was exiled and as it were abstracted from society. With the nascent industry which needs manpower, he once again plays a part in the body of the nation" (p. 230). Not only does he play a part, but he becomes "the basis and the glory of nations" (ibid.). Yet this view, which was probably held in France even by progressive and enlightened writers, was rather a rhetorical device more than a factual reality. The part the poor played in the body of the nation seems to be more realistically explained by a reference to the Enclosure Acts and the Poor Law of 1834 in Britain than by a verbal, thus once again moral, exaltation of their potential. That this served both moral and economic purposes seems to be as true in the eighteenth (and probably in the nineteenth) century as it was in the seventeenth century, although in the latter the lack of the specificity of the nascent capitalist mode of production gave it a vagueness the former dissolved. What I am saying is that probably the drastic shift from moral to economic ground did not take place in the way described by Foucault, but that the moral and economic aspects of poverty and labor were always pragmatically and ideologically combined and made to serve different purposes. Certainly, during the French Revolution and later in Napoleon's army, the poor acquired opportunities they did not have before. But this precisely does not alter the thesis that the exaltation of poverty was not a merely economic matter. The question has certainly to do with ideology, particularly the ideological construction of the nation, as well as of the nation's identity.

However, what matters here is not establishing whether Foucault was right or wrong; rather, the question is identifying the difference between productive and living labor at the time when the differentiation really took place. As we have seen, the difference lies in the fact that productive labor is living labor *institutionalized*, and this process of institutionalization is the same as, or a necessary element of, the formation of a specifically capitalist economy. In this sense, it is the Foucauldian concept of the *micro-physics* of power, introduced in the first part of *Discipline and Punish*, which deals with torture in the mid-eighteenth century, that provides an answer to our question. Here the institution *produces* a body which is in turn bound to be productive. Foucault presents a "political economy" of the body (the scare quotes are his own) later described as a "political technology of the body." He says that "it is largely as a force of production that the body is invested with relations of power and domination; but, on the other hand, its constitution as labour power is possible only if it is caught up in a system of subjection...; the body becomes a useful force only if it is both a productive body and a subjected body" (1977: 26). This is the body that produces *abstract* labor, certainly a physiological and thus concrete activity, but one that is regulated, normalized, by means of specific and detailed techniques. Here the thesis of *Madness and Civilization* and that of *Discipline and Punish* seem to come together: production in the modern sense is indeed a relatively new concept, modified and enhanced by capitalism;

yet, subjection is a very ancient concept and certainly structural and fundamental in the classical age of absolutism. The institutions work synthetically
in this respect. The micro-physics of power may entail analytic dissection, as
Foucault explains later in this study (Foucault 1977); yet, what it constitutes
is the result of a synthetic activity. Foucault says, "What the apparatuses
and institutions operate is, in a sense, a micro-physics of power, whose field
of validity is situated in a sense between these great functionings [i.e., the
knowledge(s) later characterized by Foucault in various ways as "technopo-
litics," "political anatomy of detail," etc.][6] and the bodies themselves with
their materiality and their forces" (p. 26).

This regulated, disciplined body is a unity of production and subjection.
Constituted as labor power, it marks the difference between productive (or
unproductive) labor and living labor as such. The latter could be characterized as the agile, flexible, and erotic body, which, at least in theory, remains
outside the discipline of production and constitutes itself through a logic of
neither/nor. That this is a quasi-utopian moment, for bodies are always regulated and disciplined one way or the other, does not affect our distinction,
which is not formal, but real. To make this a little more concrete, we can think
about the difference between the body of the soldier, the prisoner, the factory
worker, and that of the bohemian, the hermit, the guerrilla. Insofar as one is
able to stay away from the institutions, the unity of production and subjection is negated; the body, subtracted to that unity, becomes free to formulate
its own self-discipline.[7] Certainly, in this subtraction (which is the same thing
as the logic of neither/nor) there may be, or perhaps there must be, some
forms of simulation and dissimulation. Thus, the body of the *capoeira* is
another good example of this. In the capoeira fight/dance (an Afro-Brazilian
martial art), the subtraction of the body from the microphysics of power and
the constitution of new decentered moments of power/knowledge, are brought
about through simulation and dissimulation. Capoeira, a preparation for slave
rebellion and guerrilla war masked as a dance, is nothing but a disruption of
the production process, in which alternative time and space are constituted as
if out of nothing, out of what is available: the voice, the body (perhaps even
with arms and hands tied up).[8] In these new and masked forms of time and
space, the categories of production (in a slave but already capitalist society)
and subjection are dispersed in the apparently only playful prefiguration of a
liberated future.

THE SEQUESTRATION OF TIME AND BODIES

The work of Foucault provides us with the conceptual and critical tools for
overcoming the confusion between living labor and productive labor. Yet, in
and by itself, Foucault's work remains within the general paradigm created by
that confusion. This happens because, notwithstanding his powerful critique
of the concept of the institution and of specific institutional practices,
Foucault also shares in the prejudice against the concept of labor typical of

twentieth-century French thought. Because of this, when he could clarify the confusion on the basis of his own analysis, he reinscribes it with full force in his discourse. Of course, he does not commit Baudrillard's mistake of saying that labor only pertains to the concept of capital, but he reduces, once again, labor to productive labor. By doing this, he loses sight of the fact that the result of the rise of specific institutions in the modern, industrial age is not the transformation of a generic human activity into labor but, rather, the transformation of labor into productive labor under and in accordance with the specificity of capital.

This confusion reappears in Foucault's work when, in the conclusions to the lectures "Truth and Juridical Forms" of 1973 (Foucault 2000), with which we will deal here, he criticizes the Hegelian and Marxian idea that man's concrete essence is labor. He says that "labor is absolutely not man's concrete essence or man's existence in its concrete form." And he continues: "In order for men to be brought into labor, tied to labor, an operation is necessary, or a complex series of operations, by which men are effectively—not analytically but synthetically—bound to the production apparatus for which they labor. It takes this operation, or this synthesis effected by a political power, for man's essence to appear as being labor" (Foucault 2000: 86). What is meant here by labor is *productive* labor. However, what makes a set of institutions so specifically different from another that human beings can be tied to labor in such different ways as to account for the difference in modes of production and the specificity of historical ages? That human beings are tied to labor is not a novelty of the modern, industrial age; it is not a condition that pertains exclusively, or even only peculiarly, to capital. But the way in which they are tied to it is new and specific to the capitalist mode of production.

The question is, then, how the transformation of a generic making into labor would specifically pertain to the modern world of capital. If it is true that man's essence, his generic making, can be constructed as labor only under a given regime of technopolitical measures, then this is true of all modes of production, all ages of history, and all areas of the world. The labor that went into the construction of the pyramids in different areas of the world must have been of the same nature. Thus, the difference seems to be one between spontaneous activity and an activity organized and structured *as* labor. But then we have a zero-sum discourse, and we still have to explain the specificity of labor under capital, that is, its "productive" nature. Let us keep in mind that for Marx productive labor means capital-producing and valorizing labor. We then understand that it is the ambiguous use of the word "productive" that creates confusion, for, in a generic sense, "productive" also can be used to describe labor in a noncapitalist mode of production. Thus, when Foucault speaks of the "production apparatus," he really refers to a general concept, not one which is historically specific—though that may not be his intention. Notwithstanding Foucault's explicit defense of the adequacy of a nonhistorical approach in this respect,[9] the fact remains that either labor is coterminous with history (i.e., with the human episode in the universe), and thus we have to explain how it goes through different modes without changing in substance, or it is a modern phenomenon only, in which case the construction of the pyramids, and of all premodern history, was not based on labor, which would be an absurd claim to make.

To his credit, Foucault never makes that claim, which—however absurd—has been made, as we have seen. Rather, what happens in Foucault is that the specificity of the capitalist mode of production—perhaps too strongly emphasized at the time of *Madness and Civilization* when the passage from the ethical to the economic understanding of labor was worked out—is shifted into becoming a general paradigm of history. Probably, the reason for this is that Foucault is particularly interested in the compulsory dimension with which labor always seems to present itself. Yet, a generic compulsion is not the same as the obligation to work—to be accepted by the worker on the basis of a free disposition of the will—which becomes systemic, structured and institutional under capital. The solution to the problem is that this labor is now *wage labor*, and wage labor is the result of a "free" exchange on the part of its possessor. The exchange remains "free" because, as opposed to serfdom and slavery, the worker does not become, by and through the act of exchange, someone else's property, but he only sells one portion of his labor time, his labor power. Of course, this is only *formally and not existentially* the case. But this fact alone is sufficient to give the compulsion to labor a nonabsolute character, that is, to make room for the ambiguity inherent in the concept of productive or wage labor that, alone, attaches the worker to nothing. Certainly, no one would deny the high degree of compulsion that, to make an example, went into the construction of the Taj Mahal. Shah Jahan and his bureaucracy were certainly able to structure the Indian labor force in an absolute way. But precisely because it was absolute (or "despotic"), that form of compulsion did not rest on the "free" acceptance of a contract of exchange.[10] More important, whether the labor force was occupied in the construction of buildings and cities or in the traditional textile industry, there was not, in seventeenth century India or in other areas of the world before and outside the specificity of the capitalist mode of production, the concept of productivity that became fundamental with capital. Before capital, notwithstanding its compulsory nature, labor was useful, not productive; at least, not specifically so. Yet, what we see here is precisely the truth that the question of productive labor is a question of political economy, whereas that of living labor is a question of ontology. And we can even liberate Foucault from the responsibility of the confusion, because we see that he is really dealing with a question that goes far beyond the limits of political economy.

There is, in this text by Foucault, an attempt at redefining the old Marxist question of the relationship between structure and superstructure. At the very end of his lectures, Foucault says, "Power and knowledge are thus deeply rooted—they are not just superimposed on the relations of production but, rather, are very deeply rooted in what constitutes them" (Foucault 2000: 87). I believe that this is true. Here we do not find the usual attempt at redefining a relation by simply overturning its terms but a move toward a more immanent way of understanding the relation as a whole. It is certainly not a question of which term has priority over the other, but, rather, a question of grasping their intimate and necessary connection.

In the last lecture of "Truth and Juridical Forms," Foucault starts from the concept of panopticism, which he defines in the previous lecture. Panopticism, or surveillance, is a general modality "peculiar to modern, industrial, capitalist society..." (p. 73). It is a modality of surveillance and control, but also of molding and shaping people's time and bodies.

Foucault gives his audience (and readers) a riddle to solve. He says he will describe the prescribed routine of a French institution of the 1840s: "I'll describe the routine without saying whether it's a factory, a prison, a psychiatric hospital, a convent, a school, or a barracks, and you will guess which institution I have in mind" (p. 73). It turns out that the institution in question is a women's factory. The prescribed routine offers a model of what Foucault here calls "institutional sequestration," really a sequestration of individuals' time and bodies. The sequestration is accomplished through the detailed method of technopolitical control also described by Foucault in *Discipline and Punish*. In this lecture Foucault also goes over the distinction between two kinds of confinement: one which is geared toward *exclusion*, typical of the classical age; the other is characterized by the modality of *attachment* (or sequestration), and it is typical of the industrial age.[11] He says, "In the age we're concerned with, the aim of all these institutions—factories, schools, psychiatric hospitals, hospitals, prisons—is not to exclude but, rather, to attach individuals" (p. 78). This attachment always seeks to produce or to enhance and guarantee production. We are here at the divide present in Foucault's work, but present in history as well. Here production acquires its specifically capitalist sense, no doubts about that. Yet, is it true that such a drastic change from exclusion to attachment occurs? Isn't exclusion also a relatively modern form of control, typical of capitalist societies? Isn't attachment a modality one finds in all premodern history and actually the most fundamental feature of feudal society? If the answer to these questions is positive, as it certainly is, then the change that occurs with the coming of modern industry has nothing to do with a passage from exclusion to attachment and it is not determined by a change in the modalities of control. Rather, exclusion remains, whereas a new (that is, nonfeudal) form of attachment is worked out and implemented. Indeed, exclusion remains as a specter behind attachment. Moreover, it is not that newly devised modalities of control bring about a new form of attachment; rather, the possibility of this new form of attachment calls forth those modalities and makes them possible or, rather, necessary. One could then say that exclusion and attachment (namely, exclusion and inclusion) complement one another. This becomes most evident in what Giorgio Agamben, partly on the basis of Foucault's concept of biopolitics but going beyond Foucault, has called "the hidden paradigm of the political space of modernity," namely, *the camp*, "the pure, absolute, and impassable biopolitical space" (Agamben 1998: 123). For

Agamben this figure is founded on the state of exception, whose topological structure is defined as "Being-outside, and yet, belonging" "*Essere-fuori e, tuttavia, appartenere*" (Agamben 2003: 48). Indeed, it is easy to see that capital, in particular, needs to both attach and exclude: it attaches some of the total living labor and excludes another part of it, and in so doing it wins over both. Here we go back to one of the central points in the *Grundrisse*. I am referring to a sentence we have discussed before, where Marx says, "Capital, as the positing of surplus labour, is equally and in the same moment the positing and not-positing of necessary labour; it exists only in so far as necessary labour both exists and does not exist" (Marx 1973: 401). When translated into Foucault's terms, this great statement of Marx says precisely this: in order for labor to become productive and valorize capital, it must be both attached and excluded.

It is true that attachment has production as its only priority and that, conversely, production has a higher regard for attachment than exclusion. But this is so only in appearance. Without the not-positing of necessary labor, there would probably be no positing of it either; that is, without exclusion (or the specter of it) no attachment. Foucault says, "The factory, the school, the prison, or the hospitals have the object of binding the individual to a process of production, training [*formation*], or correction of the producers. It's a matter of guaranteeing production, or the producers, in terms of a particular norm" (2000: 78). But we have to be very careful and understand what is happening here, for this by itself does not exclude exclusion. The watershed described by Foucault is not between all past history and the modern, industrial age; rather, it is a divide between the eighteenth and the nineteenth centuries. Then, another interpretation is possible, namely, that with the coming of the industrial age the centuries of "confusion" and "anarchy" we have described earlier, the open centuries of geographic discovery and global trade expansion, the centuries that followed the relatively structured order of the Middle Ages, come to an end. A new order and a new structure prevail. In other words, in terms of control and surveillance, institutional power finds a new, viable, and reliable modality, and in a sense, notwithstanding the novelty of the Industrial Revolution, this represents a going back to the "security" of the Middle Ages—through a new and different modality of attachment, to be sure. Individuals will not be attached to the land, but to the factory and to the other institutions, and ultimately, substantially, to nothing. As Foucault says, "The factory doesn't exclude individuals: it attaches them to a production apparatus" (2000: 78). Yet, the process of competition that brings the individual proletarian to be hired or not, attached to the factory or not, is a process of inclusion and exclusion. Moreover, there is now a "voluntary" involvement in this new modality of attachment. One wants to be attached because, in the passage from formal to real subsumption –a passage that, as Jason Read has recently stressed, does not happen once for all but is equivalent with the logic of expansion proper to capital (Read 2003: 103–114)— nonattachment means starvation and death. This may explain why confinement proper appears as no longer necessary, or rather, still necessary but to a lesser degree. But it is helpful to keep in mind that confinement itself is a relatively modern phenomenon, whose usefulness may diminish or disappear with the industrial age, but whose apogee is found neither in antiquity nor in the Middle Ages (though, what can one say of the self-imposed form of confinement represented by monastic life?). It is in the more open times that follow the Middle Ages, in the centuries of geographic and scientific discovery, that confinement becomes, according to Foucault's description and analysis, necessary.

Once this is understood, we can proceed to a reading of the very interesting and powerful concept of sequestration presented by Foucault. First of all, it is important to understand that the aim of sequestration is inclusion and normalization; whereas confinement excludes marginal individuals and reinforces marginality (Foucault 2000: 79). Even here we see that, however, Foucault's distinction cannot really hold. Think about our own society and how inclusion and exclusion go hand in hand and reinforce each other; think of the *favelas* in Rio de Janeiro, the city where Foucault gave his lectures. What is important in the institutions of sequestration, but also holds for those of confinement, is that they take "all or nearly all of individuals' time. They are institutions that, in a certain way, take charge of the whole temporal dimension of individuals' lives" (p. 80).

As we shall see, institutional sequestration is twofold: it is a sequestration of both time and bodies. Through it, time becomes labor time and the body becomes labor power. Again, the concept is very powerful and sound in its generality, yet it is difficult to see how it would apply exclusively to the specificity of capital. In fact, it applies to slavery and serfdom as well, or to those forms that share in both slavery and serfdom, such as the corvée system.

Foucault presents four functions or characteristics of institutional sequestration: control of time, control and molding of the body, the micropower which is equal to judicial power (polymorphous and polyvalent), and finally epistemological power, "a power to extract a knowledge from individuals and to extract a knowledge *about* those individuals who are subjected to observation and already controlled by those different powers" (p. 83).

Let us look at the first function of sequestration, which has to do with time. Here Foucault speaks of a distinction between modern and feudal societies. The distinction is the classical and correct one that sees the serf as tied to the land and the industrial worker as "free" to move wherever a demand for labor is present. We have already shown that the modern worker enjoys a forced freedom and that he is freely forced to a form of attachment. So, sequestration we have in both societies, but of a different kind. We could add a third, yet different, form of sequestration, that of the slave who is neither absolutely attached to any place like the serf, nor is he "free" to move from place to place, from the countryside to the city, from one industrial town to the other, like the modern worker, but is staying or leaving according to his master's will. Yet the slave is also not confined but attached—although within the modality of attachment, he also might be confined.

The four functions of institutional sequestration are responsible for the "transformation of time-power and labor-power and their integration in production" (p. 84). In other words, these institutions of sequestration ensure the set of mechanisms responsible for the transformation of "men's time and their bodies, their lives,... into something that is productive force" (p. 85).

Before we look again at Foucault's conclusions it would be good to say that, yes, it is true that these institutions of sequestration accomplish the passage from living labor to productive labor: they do so, under capitalism, according to the capitalist mode of production; under feudalism, according to a feudal mode of production, and so on. This means that institutional sequestration per se is not responsible for the specificity of the capitalist mode of production, as it is not responsible for the feudal mode of production. Rather, the opposite is the case: each mode of production chooses those techniques of sequestration capable of ensuring its efficiency and continuation. Yet, Foucault's direction of thought and analysis still indicate the way to the solution of our original question, that is, the question as to the difference between living and productive labor. I mean to say that it is still true that productive labor is living labor institutionalized, but it is institutionalized along capitalist lines. In fact, living labor also can be institutionalized along feudal lines, but then it does not become productive in the sense in which Marx uses that word—a sense given to it by the most central of the modern social sciences, political economy. It is also probably true that these institutional forms are not merely superstructural constructions erected on the economic base but are, as Foucault says in his conclusions, part of the structure. To say that they are part of the structure does not mean that they are responsible for the essential difference of any mode of production; rather, it means to say that a mode of production is not limited to the economic sphere, nor simply and ephemerally to the superstructural sphere, but is, rather, as we must repeat, "a general illumination" (Marx 1973: 107). This, again, does not mean that the new institutions bring about a different mode of production; rather, they themselves are made possible and become necessary because a new order of society, not limited to either the economic or cultural sphere but stretching through both, is called into being. This new order is called into being by the dissolution of the old order, and this dissolution is, in turn, occurring because there is a crisis that invests both the relations of production and the institutions of society. What is important in Foucault's analysis is that it shows the intimate link between relations of production and institutions of sequestration, but it does not really show that this link is a characteristic of capital alone. Still, what is important is that this analysis, up to the conclusions at least, emphasizes the fact that living labor and productive labor are two different things, and that productive labor is nothing but living labor institutionalized, the sequestration of the individuals' time and bodies under capital.

Let us go back to the conclusions. Here, as we have seen, Foucault criticizes the Marxist understanding of the concept of labor and, in a sense, he undoes what he has accomplished so far. I say this because, at this point, we lose sight of the distinction between living labor and productive labor. Labor as such becomes again the culprit of society's problems and, consequently, it again appears as pertaining exclusively to the specificity of capital. Foucault says, "I don't think we can simply accept the traditional Marxist analysis, which assumes that, labor being man's concrete essence, the capitalist system is what transforms that labor into profit, into hyperprofit [*sur-profit*] or surplus value" (p. 86). It is not the capitalist manipulation of labor but the very fact that there is labor that now accounts for exploitation and control. Foucault continues: "The fact is, capitalism penetrates much more deeply into our existence" (ibid.). This is absolutely true, but I do not think it is true in the sense in which Foucault understands it. We have already seen how capitalism is not merely a mode of production, or rather how the expression "mode of production" is something that goes much beyond the economic sphere and defines the whole spectrum of the social. The fact that capitalism, as Foucault says, "was obliged to elaborate a set of political techniques, techniques of power, by which man was tied to something like labor" (p. 86) does not make labor responsible for it, nor is it a proof that labor is not man's concrete essence. By way of analogy, the fact that feudalism tied man to the land (and to a different kind of labor) does not make the land responsible for the feudal social relations of production. In other words, it is the way in which labor (or the land) is constructed and used, not what it is in itself, that creates the modalities that translate into a mode of production. It is the relation, not the thing, which should be emphasized. Certainly, in the nineteenth century, man could be tied to something like labor (in the industrial sense) because there was something like labor to be tied to; yet, this tie was defined by the set of political techniques, not by labor. Indeed, labor as a concept also was redefined by them; or, rather, labor was being reconstructed by and through a specificity that made those techniques effective and meaningful. It is in those techniques and in a transformed concept of labor that the essential difference of capital must be sought, not in the sudden appearing of something like labor as the ground of attachment. It is interesting that Foucault, who makes it possible to discern and grasp concretely the working and meaning of those techniques of power as specific institutions, should then make the mistake of losing sight of this important intuition and shift the discourse back to the vague vogue of a critique of labor as labor.

To be sure, Foucault does not lose sight of the importance of the relations of power. The problem with his exposition does not lie in this but in the implicit rejection of the positive, and thus revolutionary, dimension of labor. By and through the capitalist institutional sequestration people's bodies and their time do not simply and generically become labor power and labor time: they become so in the specificity of the capitalist mode of production. Labor is not simply what they are tied to, but, fundamentally and essentially, what they are. No longer attached to the land or to the owner, workers are attached to themselves as "mere" possessors of labor power; but because this labor power only counts insofar as it is able to become a commodity, they are ultimately attached to themselves as to nothing. In this new attachment we see again the meaning of the word "proletarian" as used by Marx in the *Manuscripts*: modern industrial workers are attached as proletarians. They are attached to their own freedom—a double freedom, which, as we have seen, has the form of a double negation. The techniques of power elaborated by capital do not create labor as a human necessity, a human reality and competence; rather, they use this necessity, this reality and competence, in order to extract surplus-value (hyperprofit). And surplus-value is not merely the result of the process of this extraction (or production); it is its *projected* ground.

Foucault says that what he meant to do was "analyze this infrapower as a condition of possibility of hyperprofit" (p. 87). That the infrapower exists, no one denies. Yet this infrapower (the set of techniques of control) is devised because hyperprofit is the conscious end of production; or else hyperprofit would merely be its epiphenomenal consequence. True, "[t]here is no hyperprofit without an infrapower" (p. 86), yet not all forms of infrapower are geared toward hyperprofit. Foucault is correct when he says that this infrapower makes men into "agents of production, into workers" (ibid.). Yet, how would this be possible if labor were not essential in man? In fact, it seems to me that the real question is not whether labor is or is not the essence of man. I think that to this question one could easily answer that labor is *one of* the essential moments of human life, but of course there is labor and labor. Instead the question is whether the reduction of man's full being to his laboring capacity (and only to it) does not turn the potentially joyful and meaningful moment of labor into his crucifixion. Under capital, this crucifixion has the specific form of productivity; other forms obtain under different modes of production, and this is why Marx can say that a class struggle has underlain all history. Yet, this would not be possible if labor were not an essential moment of human life, coterminous with freedom.

KNOWLEDGE, BIOPOLITICS, AND THE FACTORY

In *The Order of Things* (1966), Foucault had already analyzed the question of production by describing the passage from a regime of exchange (typical of the Classical Age) to a regime of production proper, that is, capitalist production, when labor, as we are trying to show becomes *productive* labor. For Foucault this is a passage from one order of knowledge (typical of the eighteenth century) to another (typical of the nineteenth century). He says that, in the Classical period, "there is no political economy, because, in the order of knowledge, production does not exist" (Foucault 1970: 166). This is different from Baudrillard's extreme view that there is no production, and no labor, before the emergence of capitalist production. And Foucault makes this very clear when he places the birth of labor and production in general (that is, not in a capitalist or specifically capitalist sense) at the time of the first agricultural revolution, which begins the Neolithic age (ibid., 256–257). Although labor and property begin, in the most classical interpretations, before agriculture, with the "first gathering" (Locke 1980: 19). Thus, when Foucault says that "production does not exist" in the Classical period, he evidently means production in a capitalist or specifically capitalist sense.

However, the use of the concepts of exchange and production as shortcuts for two different regimes—epistemic, as well as socioeconomic and existential regimes—may still create other ambiguities, for, of course, there is production during the regime of exchange and there is exchange during the regime of production; not only that, capitalist production begins with a fundamental act of exchange, the sale and purchase of labor power. What is important is that during the regime of exchange, "the ground and object of 'economy'... is that of *wealth*" and not of production (p. 166). The *analysis of wealth* precedes political economy in the same way in which *general grammar* and *natural history* precede philology and biology, respectively. However, this does not mean that the new orders of knowledge take the place of the old ones: "Philology, biology, and political economy were established, not in the places formerly occupied by *general grammar*, *natural history*, and the *analysis of wealth*, but in an area where those forms of knowledge did not exist, in the space they left blank, in the deep gaps that separated their broad theoretical segments and that were filled with the murmur of the ontological continuum. The object of knowledge in the nineteenth century is formed in the very place where the Classical plenitude of being has fallen silent" (p. 207). This only means that the systems of knowledge and discourse, which are the same as the essential or individuating differences of history, are grounded upon an ontology (the *ontological continuum*) which may remain silent or find a measure of expression. The conditions for the implementation of a "choice" of this kind (that is, silence or expression) must be extra-epistemic, sustained, yes, by a fundamental ontology, but of a thorough historical character. For our discourse, this means that what comes into being as *productive* labor, that is, labor productive of capital, is sustained by the ontological potentiality of labor as such, but it does not exhaust it.

For Foucault, the passage from a regime of exchange to one of production constitutes one of the domains of a general epistemic passage from a taxonomic and horizontal model based on resemblances, analogies, and relations, to a vertical model which points toward human finitude, the finitude of time and history, and the depths of this finitude. Needless to say, it seems that in these depths, and going beyond analogy, one is more likely to find a different plenitude, of a tumultuous nature perhaps, which sustains and shapes all history. I mean to refer to a univocal ground. The danger, however, here lies in the possibility of hypostatizing any of the concepts that characterize a given historical age, as Marx clearly shows in his critique of political economy, with the concept of capital in particular; or as Foucault himself shows when he says that by introducing historicity into economics, Ricardo, paradoxically, "makes it possible to conceive of [the] immobilization of History" (p. 259). This only means that, in dealing with the modern age, and particularly if one follows

Foucault's thesis of an epistemic shift, it is important to keep in mind the continuous interplay (one would say, against Foucault, of a dialectical nature) between ever-new historical forms and their ontological ground inhabited, not by metaphysical entities as finished and real objects always somehow present at the historical surface, conditioning and determining it, but by potentialities. Only with this in mind can one make sense of the changes, displacements, and replacements that for Foucault happen at the *archaeological* level, and that is to say, the level of ontological potentialities and of the manner in which they relate to and sustain specific historical forms. Indeed, Foucault stresses the fact that this mutation is not due to a new discovery (e.g., the economic role of capital; and one could add: the invention of labor), nor to a more adequate approximation of knowledge and science to their object. Foucault's hypothesis is that to mutate was knowledge itself in its transcendental disposition: "...if there were those who began to study the cost of production, and if the ideal and primitive barter situation was no longer employed as a means of analyzing the creation of value, it is because, *at the archaeological level*, exchange had been replaced as a fundamental figure in the space of knowledge by production, bringing into view on the one hand new knowable objects (such as capital) and prescribing, on the other, new concepts and new methods (such as the analysis of forms of production)" (p. 252; emphasis added). What is lacking in this analysis is an explanation of how exchange was replaced by production "in the space of knowledge." If production brings into view capital as a new knowable object and, at the same time, prescribes new concepts and methods of analysis, it seems that production functions as the middle term of an ontological (and epistemological) syllogism constitutive of the phenomenal world. What comes to mind is Kant's doctrine of the *transcendental schema*, that is, the need for "some third thing" capable of mediating between an object and a concept, the category and the appearance (Kant 1929: 180-187). Production may very well be this "third thing," *intellectual* and *sensible* at the same time, but, moving away from Kant's level of representation, and even from Foucault's level of knowledge, the sensible or *practical* nature of production must still be explained in actual historical terms. Thus, if production replaces exchange, it is at the level of the unknowable or not-yet-known object that this actually takes place. That is the level of labor, which may translate into a system of simple exchange or bring about a new object such as capital. What takes place "in the space of knowledge"—a knowledge, for Foucault, always "invested in complex institutional systems" (Foucault 1997: 5)—is its institutionalization.

In recognizing the importance of labor, as he describes the labor theory of value in Ricardo, Foucault again reduces labor to productive labor, and it is here that the inadequacy of the concepts of exchange and production as pertaining to two different regimes becomes evident. Foucault says, "Whereas in Classical thought trade and exchange serve as an indispensable basis for the analysis of wealth (and this is still true of Smith's analysis, in which the division of labour is governed by the criteria of barter), *after Ricardo, the*

possibility of exchange is based upon labour; and henceforth the theory of production must always precede that of circulation" (Foucault 1970: 254; emphasis added). This is, evidently, an inadequate description of the difference
between the two ages. The possibility of exchange is always based upon labor,
unless one exchanges something one has found by mere accident, or merely
gathered (although, Locke held, there is labor there too). What Foucault is
saying is that we are now in a regime of productive labor as productive of capital. But in this sense, too, there needs to be more precision, for in the Classical period we are already governed by capital—albeit, traditionally, in a non-
specific sense. Again, Foucault is far from believing that before Ricardo there
was no labor. And, in fact, he soon says that the displacement taking place
with respect to labor is one from representation to "a region where representation has no power" (p. 255). Yet, Foucault's lack of precision and uncertainty
with respect to the use of the concept of labor (as well as that of production)
is only a further proof of our urgency to attempt a rethinking of it. Certainly,
Foucault's main interest here is not discussing the concept of labor but in
describing the shift from a modality of simultaneous relations in knowledge
to the constitution of an historical paradigm capable of understanding the
temporal succession of events—"a new arrangement of knowledge" (p. 262).
This is what for Foucault is taking place, and not the reduction of all living
labor to productive labor as productive of capital. Thus, he misses the real
nature of Marx's theory of revolution when he reduces it to one alternative
among others in the broader, and more significant, interplay of forces constituting the modern world—at the basis of which, to be sure, he places the
notions of scarcity and labor. But his critique of Marxism becomes even
harder at the end of this section of *The Order of Things*, for he sees it as
absolutely well adjusted to the modern order: "Marxism exists in nineteenth
century thought like a fish in water..." (p. 262). It "introduced no real discon-
tinuity; it found its place without difficulty" (p. 261). Ultimately, the real subject of history is for Foucault, at least at the time of *The Order of Things*, that
eventful mutation of paradigms of knowledge capable of prescribing ways of
seeing and acting; the real subject of history is "an event that any archaeology can situate with precision" (p. 262). Yet, in our reading we have at times
longed for more precision.

It is already in *The Order of Things* that the concept of *biopolitics*, developed by Foucault in the 1970s, is adumbrated. With this concept, the motives
and manners of the institutionalization of labor become more evident and
clear. Biopolitics is the way in which life is regulated within a horizon of an
always possible and imminent death. Indeed, it is by and through the specter
of death that life acquires political value. When the human being is discov-
ered in its finitude, then the modality of negation is no longer the promise of
the infinite, but, rather, the institutional ability of manipulating and using the
residual or marginal elements of that finitude, the moments when it seems to
come to an end: birth, death, sickness, and so on; the moments of crisis. It is
when the plenitude of the finite softens or tears up that an artificial negation

(not the structural negation that sustains it) takes hold of it. So is it with living labor, which finds the character of finitude in the need of reproducing itself. Yet, this character alone would not be a sufficient condition of its reduction or negation, if it had not been divorced from its instrument and object. Foucault says, "And thus economics refers us to that order of somewhat ambiguous considerations which may be termed anthropological: it is related, in fact, to the biological properties of a human species, which, as Malthus showed in the same period as Ricardo, tends always to increase unless prevented by some remedy or constraint; it is related also to the situation of those living beings that run the risk of not finding in their natural environment enough to ensure their existence; finally, it designates in labour, and in the very hardship of that labour, the only means of overcoming the fundamental insufficiency of nature and of triumphing for an instant over death" (p. 257). It is on the basis of these fundamental needs that a biopower is able to arise.

According to Paolo Virno (2002), one can understand the concept of biopolitics only if one starts from the concept of labor power, which is instead often neglected. Labor power, say Virno, means *capacity to produce*; it is this *potency* (*dynamis*), a *pure* potency, and not the act of production itself (Virno 2002: 80–81). In this, Virno is simply and faithfully rendering Marx and his Aristotelian mind-set. However, Virno continues, always following Marx, this potency has the characteristic of a commodity and, as such, the ability of being bought and sold. What is unusual and paradoxical is that potency is, by definition, something that is "not present, not real" (p. 81). All the same, this is what the capitalist wants. For Virno, it is precisely in the paradoxical nature of labor power that one finds the premises of biopolitics: "The living body of the worker is the substratum of that labor power which, in itself, does not have an independent existence. 'Life,' the pure and simple *bios*, acquires a specific importance only as a tabernacle of *dynamis*, of mere potency" (p. 82). Capital is interested in the living body of the worker only as this substratum: "Life is placed at the center of politics when at stake is the immaterial (and in itself not present) labor power. For this, and only for this, is one allowed to speak of 'biopolitics'" (ibid.). Thus, Virno correctly unveils the real, "nonmythological" origin of biopolitics (p. 83). And he concludes: "One should then not believe that biopolitics includes, as its particular articulation, the handling of labor power. To the contrary: biopolitics is only an effect, a reflection, or precisely an articulation, of that primal fact—which is historical and philosophical at the same time—consisting in the exchange of potency as potency" (p. 84).

Let us take a look back at this chapter so far. We have started from the idea that the distinction between living labor and productive labor (which is a form of living labor, yet not the only one) might be found in living labor's institutionalization and the way in which it is institutionalized. We have seen that aspects of the work of Foucault might help in that respect, although we have encountered some problems pointing toward the same direction of the criticism that Virno moves against Foucault. And we are back to the funda-mental, "harsh and paradoxical" (Virno 2002: 80), notion of labor power. Virno is certainly correct in his analysis of the concept of labor power as potency. However, he does not recognize that, insofar as labor power becomes a category of political economy, it presents the same ambiguity as productive labor. Labor power, more than paradoxical, is equivocal; so is the potency it describes. This means that we have to understand what kind of potency we are dealing with. As we have seen, the term "productive" also can be under-stood, philosophically (that is, ontologically) as *poietic*. Yet, when it becomes a specific category of capital, without losing its fundamental poietic nature, it tears itself away from all living labor, which, because of capital, must be understood as *not productive*, or neither-productive-nor-unproductive. How-ever, it is this latter form of labor, which remains at the level of ontology without entering the realm of political economy, that can be identified as true potency. Certainly, living labor as such *is* productive (i.e., creative) in a non-capitalist sense, but it is not "productive labor" in the sense of capital. The same holds in the case of labor power. This potency that becomes a commod-ity, once it has become a commodity, ceases to be what it *could* be, or could have been, and enters the *ought to* and *must* of capital. For "labor power," aside from what it means literally, has a specific meaning in the logic of cap-ital. Thus, if it describes the generic capacity to work and the concept of potency, it cannot be *pure* potency. Instead, this pure potency, which resem-bles the neither/nor of labor, is the *subjective power of labor*, of which "labor power" is only its reified form, its commodity form—its *transfiguration*, as Guy Debord says, into *labor-as-commodity* (Debord 1995: 28). This means that "labor power" is no longer a subjective, but already an objective force. It is in this sense that that which is not an object can be bought and sold as if it were already one. The women and children who work in the sweatshops around the world are not employed on the basis of their pure potency, of what they *could* do and *could* be, of their subjective power; they are employed on the basis of very specific functions and tasks for which an objectified potency (labor power) will suffice. With the designation of labor power, the subjective power of labor becomes the productive power of capital, or part of it, embodied in it without return to itself. Instead, the subjective power of labor maintains the freedom of its potency; it is this power that may defect and withdraw, whereas labor power is already a commodity; it must be conceived and constructed as one. To be sure, labor power is not different, at the level of its ontological sub-stance, from the subjective power of labor. The difference lies in its institu-tional construction and use. Finding a market for one's labor power means entering the domain of productive labor; failing to find a market for it means falling into the category of unproductive labor. Yet, the subjective power of labor has no regard for the categories of political economy; rather, it relates immediately to the neither/nor of labor, to that labor that is *not productive* with respect to capital, but that grounds productive and unproductive labor alike. What precedes does not intend to be a criticism of Virno's important clarification of the real origin of biopolitics and of his ability to see, beyond the economic horizon of labor power, the ontology of pure potency. It is only an attempt at a further clarification in the light of a critique of productive labor, and a suggestion. An example may prove useful. The pirates or the maroons who, in Rediker's description (Rediker 1987), exited the "virtual incarceration" of what could be called the *institutional* ship, can hardly be said to have made use of their labor power in constructing an alternative way of life. Rather, they destroyed the very concept of it, but undoubtedly retained their subjective power of labor with its ontological promise of a full potency.

True, Marx himself defines labor power in the same way as Virno, who quotes Marx's definition. Marx says, "We mean by labour-power, or labour-capacity, the aggregate of those mental and physical capabilities existing in the physical form, the living personality, of a human being, capabilities which he sets in motion whenever he *produces a use-value of any kind*" (Marx 1977: 270; emphasis added). The words I set in italics disprove the possibility of following the hypothesis I suggested above on the basis of Marx's own definition of labor power. However, the problem is that, if Marx has the merit of having distinguished between labor and labor power, this does not mean that the category of labor power itself is free from ambiguities. I have already said that these are the same kind of ambiguities inherent in the concept of productive labor. Marx himself gives content to them when he qualifies, from an historical point of view, the initial, general definition of the concept of labor power. Without a doubt, the sale of labor power constitutes the basis of the capitalist system: "The whole system of capitalist production is based on the worker's sale of his labour-power as a commodity" (p. 557). But he continues: "The division of labour develops this labour-power *in a one-sided way*, by reducing it to the highly particularized skill of handling a special tool. When it becomes the job of the machine to handle this tool, the use-value of the worker's labour-power vanishes, and with it its exchange-value" (ibid.; emphasis added). When this happens, what follows is, in Marx's account, a great tragedy for the working class, that is, misery and starvation, but also the development of the basic and structural opposition of labor to capital "into a complete and total antagonism" (p. 558). Evidently, the subjective power of labor as pure potency does not cease; it will lose its economic status, but economy is not what constitutes its innermost nature, which is instead ontological and political. This power is labor which precedes even the possibility of capital; labor as life activity before (an ontological 'before') it is channeled in the productive modality of capital. But insofar as labor power still retains its useful and valuable features, what the capitalist wants from the worker is not simply his capacity to work, but also his *willingness* to work in a certain way, in accordance with rules and regulations set by capital, to accept and follow a certain discipline, to be obedient, docile. In this sense, Foucault's work on the nature of the institution comes back in all its importance. The capacity to work may also, as far as capital is concerned, be wasted; in fact, part of it must be wasted—a truth that belongs to the very core of the logic of capital, as we have seen. What is required is that the worker, or rather the proletarian who needs (and thus 'freely' chooses and tries) to be a worker, get rid of his subjectivity and take on the institutional role provided to him by capital. It is only at this point that the capacity to produce "a use-value of any kind" can be channeled toward the production of value and surplus-value. What I am saying is that in Marx's definition there are two different levels. The first level has to do with what Virno calls *pure potency*, the capacity to produce any use-value—a general and generic capacity;[12] yet, at this level we do not yet encounter the category of socially necessary labor that limits and qualifies that potency in accordance with the requirements of a given mode of production. In other words, if my capacity to work does not meet those requirements, it cannot be constructed as labor power. This is, incidentally, very important with respect to the question of uneven development, as well as with respect to the question of the relation between *abilities* and *disabilities*. Even at the level of its *reproduction*, this pure potency, or subjective power, differs from labor power as a power (potentially) of capital. In fact, if the reproduction of labor power as a special commodity requires that the worker remains, for the most part if not for all of his everyday life, within the economic and cultural values of capital—or, as Ernst Bloch says, "the commodity of working power does not shake off its commodity character even during recuperation" (Bloch 1995: 907)—the reproduction of the pure potency does not. We already see what the second level of Marx's definition of labor power has to do with: no longer production of use-value in general and in any possible way (a production that may be creative and genuinely inventive), but, rather, production of value and surplus value in accordance with a labor process that is external to the nature and interests of the worker, to which the worker remains attached as *a living appendage*.

Let us see what happens to this potency constructed as labor power in the factory. Marx says, "Factory work exhausts the nervous system to the uttermost; at the same time it does away with the many-sided play of the muscles, and confiscates every atom of freedom, both in bodily and in intellectual activity. Even the lightening of the labour becomes an instrument of torture, since the machine does not free the worker from the work, but rather deprives the work itself of all content. Every kind of capitalist production, in so far as it is not only a labour process but also capital's process of valorization, has this in common, but it is not the worker who employs the conditions of his work, but, rather, the reverse, the conditions of work employ the worker" (Marx 1977: 548).

The passage above is from the section entitled "The Factory" in Chapter 15 of the first volume of *Capital*, "Machinery and Large-Scale Industry." The whole section is on the passage from a regime of manufacture to the machinery regime, and that means, again, from formal to real subsumption. The description just quoted above pertains particularly to the machinery regime; or rather it is in that regime that the *inversion* described above "acquires a technical and palpable reality" (ibid.). The inversion is this, that the worker no longer handles the conditions of his work, but the conditions of work handle the worker. This section relates to the "Fragment on Machines" in the *Grundrisse*, which we have seen in the Remarks section at the end of Chapter 1. In the *Grundrisse*, the positive aspects of machinery, once freed from the capitalist relations of production, are perhaps accentuated. However, the difference between the *Grundrisse* and *Capital* is, again, not extreme. In *Capital*, too, in which perhaps Marx presents a more thorough and one-sided critique of the machinery mode, care is taken to distinguish between machinery and the use (or *misuse*; Marx's word) that capital makes of it. This is already evident in Marx's commenting, at the outset of this section, on Ure's two descriptions of machinery. The first description, in which "the combined collective worker appears as the dominant subject, and the mechanical automaton as the object" is "applicable to every possible employment of machinery on a large scale" (pp. 544–545); the second, where "the automaton itself is the subject, and the workers are merely conscious organs..." is "characteristic of its use by capital, and therefore of the modern factory system" (ibid.). This is a very important point because, among other things, Marx distinguishes between the machinery mode and the factory system. It is not the machinery itself that deprives the worker of her subjectivity (for machinery could simply liberate time, free the worker from her work), but the modern factory system, that is, the most specific institution of capital. Machinery could then be used outside of the factory system, that is, outside of the logic of capital, and this use would be of a completely different nature. This different use entails a radically different way of conceiving the construction of that potency that, under capital, becomes a mere, though special, commodity, labor power. To make this point even clearer, Marx also says, "Here, as everywhere else, we must distinguish between the increased productivity which is due to the development of the social process of production [which in the *Grundrisse* takes on the name of *General Intellect*], and that which is due to the exploitation by the capitalists of that development" (p. 547; brackets added).

But the most important thing for our discourse has to do with the construction of labor power, or rather of the *living body* of the worker (i.e., his physical and intellectual functions, his *culture*, his whole being), without which labor power itself could not subsist. This construction presupposes a thorough education, a detailed discipline, such that a living body can become a *working* body, a worker's body. Marx says, "All work at a machine requires the worker to be taught from childhood upwards, in order that he may learn to adapt his own movements to the uniform and unceasing motion of an automaton" (p. 546). This *learning to labor*, to use the title of a book by Paul Willis, may also take the form of the future worker's conscious and deliberate rejection of other forms of learning, other ways of seeing and living life (Willis 1977). Willis calls it a form of "self-damnation," which is, however, "experienced, paradoxically, as true learning, affirmation, appropriation, and as a form of resistance" (p. 3). However, this is true only insofar as one remains within the domain of a given mode of production, that of capital. There, the potency of social being, which is the same as pure potency, appears only as labor power. Willis says, "The processes through which labour power comes to be *subjectively understood* and *objectively applied* and their interrelationships is of profound significance for the type of society which is produced and the particular nature and formation of its classes" (p. 2; emphasis added). This is close to the critique of labor power I am presenting here. Indeed, the way in which labor power is *subjectively understood* and *objectively applied* is equal to its possible instantiation within a given mode of production. What I mean to say is that if it is not *thus* understood and applied, it does not count as labor power. And if it does not count as labor power, it is something else. Thus labor power does not precede its being understood and applied in a certain way; rather, the processes of "subjectively understanding" and "objectively applying" are the very processes through which labor power is constructed and comes into being. What precedes all this is pure potency, the subjective power of labor, which may be employed by capital or not. If it is employed by capital, it becomes labor power, either as *actually* employed or as constituting the reserve army of labor, and, again, either as productive or unproductive labor. If it is not employed by capital, that is, if it finds no place in capital's categories, it remains in its original state of freedom. This subjective power of labor is still present at the moment of production, at its interstices, its dead times, in the void which must accompany the necessary presence of the worker during the labor process, a void which may be the presence of an absence. The subjective power of labor, the pure potency, is that which resists subsumption, which refuses to be constructed as labor power, to subjectively understand and objectively apply an externality. Instead, it always retains a regard for the *could*, the plurality of potentialities inherent in its own nature, for what superficially appears as mere utopia.

The concept of labor power is related to the concept of class, and particularly of the working class. We do not speak, as a general rule, of the labor power of capitalists, executives, or high-rank professionals. When we speak of labor power we know, and tacitly assume, we are opening up a space of discussion oriented toward the condition of relative or absolute *powerlessness* of the workers, their double freedom. With the concept of *class struggle* and *antagonism* this powerlessness can change to a powerful force. But antagonism and class struggle are not given with the concept of labor power as such. That is, what enters in an antagonistic relationship with capital is not the labor power constructed as a commodity, but the living body of the worker, her whole being, as it stands, at one and the same time, inside and outside the capitalist relations of production, for what stands there is not labor power alone, but always with its possessor. It is the subjective power that remains heterogeneous with respect to the capitalist labor process that may be able, in the dialectic between inside and outside, to move *against* the labor process itself, against production as valorization of capital. There is here the same relation that Stanley Aronowitz, in his recent book on class, sees between class and *social formation*. For Aronowitz, class is, fundamentally, always *class-in-formation*, where the political and cultural domains are as important as the economic. He says, "Thus I propose a shift in the concept of class from a cleavage based exclusively on relations of ownership of capital, that is, of productive property, and the correlative idea that the core classes were arrayed on the basis of productive labor—that which produces surplus value—to relations of power in all of its domains, including the power to construct historical memory" (Aronowitz 2003: 58–59). With respect to the question of labor power and of the potency that sustains it, it is evident that, "relations of power in all of its domain"—a power that exceeds the logic of productivity—do not ground only the constitution of a commodity (however special it might be) and perhaps of the consciousness of being such a commodity, but, rather, they constitute the totality of a human being, a whole way of being, which, yes, includes the economic function, but it is not reducible to it. In other words, this totality, a whole culture, cannot be reduced to, or explained by, one's capacity to labor in such and such a way. Rather, this capacity is acquired by means of an external discipline, as well as, paradoxically, as we have seen in Willis, as a form of "self-damnation."

In the passage from manufacture to large-scale industry, it is not the technical but the political aspect that counts most from the point of view of a critique of capital. As Gramsci says, they together form that technopolitical nexus that is proper to capital and that changes the subjective power of labor to the productive power of capital in an ever more sophisticated and powerful way. For Marx, "although, from a technical point of view, the old system of division of labour is thrown overboard by machinery, it hangs on in the factory as a tradition handed down from manufacture, and is then systematically reproduced and fixed in a more hideous form by capital as a means of exploiting labour-power" (Marx 1977: 547). The difference is that the tool is now replaced by the machine, yet what follows—which would be inherent in the concept of the machine—is not liberation from work, but greater enslavement of the worker: "The lifelong speciality of handling the same tool now becomes the lifelong speciality of serving the same machine" (ibid.). It is here that Marx speaks of the *misuse* of the machine and reiterates the concept of learning to labor we have seen earlier, the concept of the construction of a discipline and of the constitution of labor power itself: "Machinery is misused in order to transform the worker, from his very childhood, into a part of a specialized machine" (ibid.). The institutionalization of labor, that is the becoming *productive* of living labor, is not a function of the machinery regime, for the machine could instead free the worker from work (where 'freeing the worker from work' is to be taken, not as the end of labor, but as the end of the *workerness* of the worker)[13]—rather, that institutionalization precedes the machine and welcomes the latter within the same paradigm of oppression and exploitation. In fact, that paradigm even worsens now, for the relative independence offered by the tool is completely taken away. Marx says, "In handicrafts and manufacture, the worker makes use of a tool; in the factory, the machine makes use of him. There the movements of the instrument of labour proceed from him, here it is the movements of the machine that he must follow. In manufacture the workers are the parts of a living mechanism. In the factory we have a lifeless mechanism which is independent of the workers, who are incorporated into it as its living appendages" (p. 548). In the factory, and thus in society as a factory, this institutionalization becomes complete; it gives rise to a "barrack-like discipline" (p. 549). But this means precisely that all aspects of the worker's everyday life are shaped by it, dominated by it. As Marx says, this is the victory of dead labor over living labor power (p. 548)—dead labor, that is, capital, the "master" (p. 549), the "general intellect." Marx concludes this section by reiterating, with strong and passionate language, the main point: that is, the notion that there is a difference between acknowledging the potentialities of machinery, of accumulated social knowledge and skills, and the use made of them under the capitalist mode of production—a difference between machinery and the factory. He says, "The economical use of the social means of production, matured and forced as in a hothouse by the factory system, is turned in the hands of capital into systematic robbery of what is necessary for the life of the worker while he is at work..." (pp. 552–553). And he concludes by mentioning Fourier: "Was Fourier wrong when he called factories 'mitigated jails'?" (p. 553). In our days, these mitigated jails have transcended the domain of the factory proper and become widespread throughout society. The "economical use of the social means of production" is precisely what a critique of productive labor intends to highlight and isolate. This main point, however, becomes extremely clear in the next section of the same chapter of *Capital*, where Marx, after a reference to the Luddite movement, says, "It took both time and experience before the workers learnt to distinguish between machinery and its employment by capital, and therefore to transfer their attacks from the material instruments of production to the form of society which utilizes those instruments" (pp. 554–555). What presents itself as an absolute necessity, in Marx's times as in our own, is that the capitalist relations of production be subverted and destroyed; only thus will the inner potentialities of the machinery mode find a way to their actualization.

CONCEPTS AND CONTRADICTIONS: THE MEANING OF UTOPIA

Foucault says that "there are two sorts of utopias: proletarian socialist utopias, which have the property of never being realized, and capitalist utopias, which often have the unfortunate tendency to be realized" (Foucault 2000: 75). By "capitalist utopia," Foucault means the factory or any of the other institutions he describes. The factory, the industrial city, are examples of the capitalist utopia, notwithstanding the fact that they also are present in societies that claim (or have claimed) to be against capitalism. Then, the point is to understand the meaning of the word "utopia." Insofar as an institution entails and produces that loss of reality of which Marx speaks, it becomes, *eo ipso*, a utopia—a utopia of a peculiar kind, certainly, to which the name of *dystopia* is more appropriate. Its utopian or dystopian quality is reflected in the alienation experienced by the subject in it. The original place of being is taken away and replaced by a form of nonbeing (alienated being). The place is transformed to the point that it really becomes a nonplace.

The proletarian socialist (or communist) utopia, by contrast, which for Foucault has the "property of never being realized," is in reality what lies in the realm of potentiality and the *could*. This utopia is always already in that realm, at least conceptually. It is what for Marcuse lacks actuality only because impeded by the opposing forces of constituted power. Obviously, its potential reality is always ready to become actual, and this readiness must posit itself at the level of the concept. Yet, let us be very careful and avoid the mistake of considering the level of the concept as the level of the unreal. The concept is, rather, the most real, and it is in this sense that the modern capitalist dystopia can also be called utopian: an unreal reality, an empty paradox which lingers and, desperately, though up to now efficiently, wants to remain in control; yet, a reality which has lost the logical and ontological (as well as ethical) support of the concept. When one looks at the conceptual structure of capital, one realizes that it is empty, for there is no rationality in it, and this lack of rationality is, with Hegel, also a lack of *real* reality. But if the word "rationality" is too strong and overdetermined, we can also say that capital lacks any reasonableness. Today, capital justifies itself rhetorically through all the ideologies that seek to portray it as the defender of freedom. Yet, it is easy to see that by freedom what is meant is only free trade, and free trade (with its euphemistic "open doors") is what legitimizes and deepens the system of exploitation and oppression at the global level, augments and worsens the tragic conditions of the *global South* (i.e., with the new international division of labor, the proletariat of the entire world).[14] When this rhetoric fails, capital resorts to military action, or rather it always manages to maintain ready a mélange of its rhetorical and military instruments. The result is utter hypocrisy, but it works, it has worked very well so far. Yet, deception and military might are not (and cannot be) substitutes for the concept. Capital lacks the support of the concept because the concept only welcomes what aspires to universality and totality, but this is not the case with capital, a mere partiality. Capital rests, in fact, on the particularistic interest of a partial will. In Marx's classic argument capital has proved instrumental in creating the conditions for the possibility of a different world, but this different world cannot be willed by capital for, as one of Dante's devils would have it, "la contradizion che nol consente" "the law of contradiction won't allow it."[15] This is why all talks about eliminating the world's poverty, whether they are held at some U.N. summit or at a fortified New York's Walford Astoria, are pathetic and ridiculous. Capital cannot seriously and sincerely will the elimination of poverty, for that would be its self-annihilation. Instead, capital replaces the original univocity of labor with the univocity of poverty; global poverty, or, as Debord called it, "the unity of poverty" (Debord 1995: 41). The world for which capital has laid the foundation is capital's direct and absolute negation. It then comes as no surprise that capital should employ all its might to check and at all costs impede social and political transformation. Yet, the passage from one world to the other, from one essential difference to the other, cannot be a matter of necessary and mechanical transition. It must be willed. It needs an agent with a rational will, a subject able to call forth from the future the ontological substance that fills the conceptual structure of this difference. This agent, or subject, can be no other than living labor itself. As against the decaying utopias of capital, which rest on an empty concept, or rather on no concept at all, living labor has an immediate and intimate relation to the plenitude of the concept—a concept full of being. But this is a living labor that rests outside the categories of capital and capitalist production, either because it has been rejected by them or because it has subtracted itself from them.

Yet the problem is that living labor is apparently totally subsumed under capital. We have seen that one of the effects of this subsumption is to divide labor into a productive and an unproductive modality, and we have seen that both modalities are categories of capital and its productivist logic. Yet, living labor as a concept and as a reality surpasses capital and actually grounds it. To the objection that under real and total subsumption there actually is no living labor outside of capital, we reply that there *could* be. This is why it is extremely dangerous to say that labor is a creation of capital. To say that means to lose sight of the ontological dimension of labor and thus miss the possibility of transcending the limits that upon labor are imposed by capital. Again, it means to accept the logic of capital as a metaphysical reality. Instead, when living labor is considered in its concept, free from the manipulations it undergoes under capital, then it appears in its neutral and pure form, as being *neither-productive-nor-unproductive*, but simply creative. It then appears as the ontological foundation and motor of social reality as a whole, and, as we have seen, this is the only reason why capital wants it.

When we reach into the ontological roots of the concept of labor, we find labor's fundamental and grounding freedom. As Jean-Luc Nancy says, "Freedom can only be *taken*: this is what the *revolutionary* tradition represents. Yet taking freedom means that freedom *takes* itself, that it has already received itself, from itself. No one begins *to be* free, but freedom *is* the beginning and endlessly remains the beginning" (Nancy 1993: 77). We may think that manorial labor, slave labor, and finally productive labor are forms of necessary, rather than contingent, constraints put on labor as labor. In so doing, we overlook the fact that such constraints can be applied at all only insofar as *there is* something such as labor to which they can be applied, and that before being constrained in such and such a way, labor must logically and ontologically be free and unconstrained. Or we may be led to think that labor is eventually granted a freedom which is external to its constitution, a freedom that works by degrees and through ameliorations and reforms, in the same way in which slaves "were granted" their freedom. We then capitulate before the very logic we wished to combat (that of capital in our age) by conceding the most fundamental point: that a relative degree of freedom may be given to labor, but that originally and absolutely labor is not free.[16] Instead, we should bear in mind that, logically and ontologically, the freedom of labor does not succeed, but rather precedes, labor's enslavement and subsumption. To recuperate the conceptual freedom of labor is not to philosophize in vain. Rather, it is to show that the thisness of production, the essential difference, or the historical age under consideration, is not a given of nature but an historical contingency which, as it came to be, can also pass away. To prepare the new essential difference, we have to reach back into the purity and neutrality of the concept of labor. Yet, this reaching back is in reality also a reaching forward. It is there that, beyond *what merely is*, we can get a glimpse of *what could be*.

THE REALITY OF UTOPIA

In a polemic essay against Marxist orthodoxy written in 1969,[17] Murray Bookchin repeatedly emphasizes the distinction between what-is and what-could-be. He correctly describes this distinction as a tension, which he also calls the tension between the actual and the possible. By doing so, he is able to overcome the limits imposed on society and on revolutionary theory and practice by political economy and by an often misguided critique of political economy and move the discourse toward two equally necessary directions: toward a deeper theoretical understanding of the potentiality of labor (though this remains in this essay by Bookchin only a suggestion which is not fully developed philosophically) and toward a more meaningful, and truly revolutionary, revolutionary praxis.

Bookchin starts with the quest for creating "a movement that looks to the future instead of the past" (Bookchin 1971: 174). In support of this, he quotes from *The Eighteenth Brumaire of Louis Bonaparte* where Marx says, "The social revolution of the nineteenth century cannot draw its poetry from the past, but only from the future" (ibid.).[18] The same, Bookchin holds, can be said of the social revolution of our own times. In the polemic vein of the essay, Bookchin says that "Marxism has ceased to be applicable to our time not because it is too visionary or revolutionary, but because it is not visionary or revolutionary enough" (p. 177). However, he says that "the problem is not to 'abandon' Marxism or to 'annul' it, but to transcend it dialectically" (ibid.). Bookchin does not criticize Marx's work and philosophy, but the Marxist tradition and orthodoxy. In particular, he criticizes the thoughtless and mechanical way in which would-be revolutionaries apply Marxism to the problems of society. He criticizes the everyday dimension of Marxism, so to speak; the fact that adherents to this philosophy have forgotten that in order to revolutionize society they also have to revolutionize themselves. It is here that the question of labor and production becomes central, for the revolutionary quality of ideas stands or falls according to whether one refuses or accepts to enter into, and uplift, the logic of capitalist production.

cf. Bettelheim – Calcul économique ...

In this sense, Bookchin says, "The worker becomes a *revolutionary* not by becoming more of a worker but by undoing his 'workerness'" (p. 188). We have already seen how Marx draws a distinction between the proletarian and the worker.[19] Now this distinction can be more adequately understood as a distinction between living labor and productive labor. Bookchin's *workerness* is nothing but productivity. This productivity was earlier described as the result of the institutionalization of living labor. When we spoke about Foucault and, then, Marx, we saw how one of the most conspicuous examples of this process of institutionalization occurs, precisely, through the institution of the factory, at the point of production. Bookchin is saying something very similar, or rather what he is saying can be understood in terms of the same concept of the institution. In polemic with Marxist orthodoxy, which privileges the point of production as the strongest link in the process of proletarian unity and organization, Bookchin says, "The factory serves not only to 'discipline,' 'unite,' and 'organize' the workers, but also to do so in a thoroughly bourgeois fashion. In the factory, capitalistic production not only renews the social relations of capitalism with each working day, as Marx observed, it also renews the psyche, values and ideology of capitalism" (pp. 183–184).

Bookchin is here dealing with the difficult question of the transition from a class society to a classless society. He says that it is "vitally important to emphasize that [Marx's] explanation [of this transition] was reasoned out almost entirely by analogy with the transition of feudalism to capitalism— that is, *from one class society to another class society*" (pp. 181–182; Bookchin's emphasis; brackets added). But, Bookchin notes, going from one class society to another class society is not the same as going from a class society to a classless one. This may be true, although everything here becomes somewhat foggy and slippery; that is, the problem may be more apparent than real, or rather it may have to be sought somewhere else, perhaps in the concept of transition itself. Yet, Bookchin's point remains important because it makes us think of what may take place during the so-called transition. Obviously, the new bourgeois class did not arise in modernity because it was "attached" to feudal institutions. Rather, the opposite is the case. It is precisely because it was detached from those institutions and left to itself that it was able to take initiatives and exploit opportunities that lay at the margins of the feudal world but became gradually more important and central as that world began to crumble. The bourgeoisie was a class of merchants and entrepreneurs. Neither the serfs nor the feudal petty officials, both attached to feudal institutions, became bourgeois with the crumbling of the feudal system. Reasoning this time deliberately by analogy, one could say that the workers *as* workers, attached to production, would not cease to be what they are in the case of a hypothetical "transition" to socialism insofar as *work*, in the productive sense of the factory and thus of capital, is not completely dismantled. This also requires that one rethink, as some authors have done, the adequacy of the concept of the transition.[20]

It is in this sense that we can read Bookchin's idea of an *un-class,* which prepares itself before the coming of a fatidic transition. I will quote a long passage for its strength and clarity: "The worker begins to become a revolutionary when he undoes his 'workerness,' when he comes to detest his class status here and now, when he begins to shed exactly those features which the Marxist most prize in him—his work ethic, his character-structure derived from industrial discipline, his respect for hierarchy, his obedience to leaders, his consumerism, his vestiges of puritanism. In this sense, the worker becomes a revolutionary to the degree that he sheds his class status and achieves an *un-*class consciousness. He degenerates—and he degenerates magnificently. What he is shedding are precisely those *class* shackles that bind him to *all* systems of domination. He abandons those *class* interests that enslave him to consumerism, suburbia, and a bookkeeping conception of life" (p. 189). In other words, the worker stops believing in productivity, performing productive labor, supporting capitalist production. This is not very un-Marxian when one considers Marx's distinction between the worker and the proletarian in the *Manuscripts,* or the description of this *un-*class in the *Introduction to the Critique of Hegel's Philosophy of Right* (Marx 1975b). Here Marx describes the *proletariat,* this "class with *radical chains,*" as a "class of civil society which is not a class of civil society" and "a class which is the dissolution of all classes" (p. 256). The concept of *un-*class is evidently present in this description. Here the task of the proletariat is not that of strengthening its position by adjusting to an ideal of 'workerness' and productivity before dissolving all classes. The proletariat is already that dissolution, that "*total loss* of humanity" which, as such, that is, in this negativity, can posit the "*total redemption of humanity*" (ibid.). Marx also emphasizes the fact that the modern proletariat is not naturally poor, but *artificially* poor. In this artificiality, there are the reasons of its loss of humanity. By stopping being a worker, the proletariat exits that artificiality, described by both Foucault and Bookchin as institutionalization at all levels of life. He becomes a human being again, perhaps now naturally poor, yet expressing a living labor that refuses to be subsumed, a total being with time and with a body at its disposal. This does not mean that he becomes inactive and idle. Bookchin's "degeneration" is to be understood in terms of an involution away from institutional constraints and superimposed norms, almost a purification and a *return to the principles.* This *un-*class consciousness describes what we have otherwise called the *condition of neither/nor,* a condition that immediately, that is, naturally, reaches back into the neutrality of living labor, its concept, and does not remain idle but lays the foundations for a radical essential difference. For Bookchin, such is the situation of the revolutionary who "begins to challenge not only the economic and political premises of hierarchical society, but hierarchy as such. He not only raises the need for social revolution but also tries to *live* in a revolutionary manner to the degree that this is possible in the existing society" (1971 190). Bookchin gives the example of self-management as the most important expression of this new consciousness. And he continues: "He [i.e., the revolutionary] not only attacks the forms created by the legacy of domination, but also improvises new forms of liberation which take their poetry from the future" (pp. 190–191).

I will not go through the historical part of Bookchin's essay. What I have noted is sufficient to understand the tension between the actual and the possible, the what-is and the what-could-be, the reality of utopia. This tension is, first of all, presented by Bookchin as an explanation of social revolutions. Bookchin admits that social revolutions occur "because the 'masses' find the existing society intolerable (as Trotsky argued)" (p. 192). Yet, for Bookchin, this is only part of the explanation. In fact, social revolutions also occur because of the tension between what-is and what-could-be. In Bookchin's explanation, the terrain is covered from economy to culture, from the structure to the superstructure: the explanation is both socioeconomic and philosophical. *The tension between what-is and what-could-be is the tension of the concept.*

In a discussion that followed the publication of "Listen, Marxist!" Bookchin, speaking of the question of the class struggle, reiterates this point: "The class struggle... does not begin and end at the point of production. It may emerge from the poverty of the unemployed and unemployables, many of whom have never done a day's work in industry; it may emerge from a new sense of possibility that slowly pervades society—the tension between 'what is' and 'what could be'..." (p. 227). As he explains later (p. 231), it is when what-is appears in all its irrationality that the new modality of what-could-be becomes more adequate. I would suggest that, at this point, such modality of the future takes on the character of a *rational will* as against the irrationality of the merely given. In fact, an irrational real seems to be a contradiction in terms, and it certainly is if one follows Hegel; it is a place that becomes a non-place, a utopia that, as we have seen, is really a dystopia. The rational and real utopia lies forward, in a future already included, as possibility, in the structure of *this* time, that is, already somehow determined; it lies in the realm of the concept and of the *could*—the opposite of a mere ideality.

In the introduction to the book that also contains the essay we have been discussing, Bookchin goes even further in clarifying the meaning of the tension of utopia and in emphasizing its importance. He says, "The foremost contradiction of capitalism today is the tension between what-is and what-could-be—between the actuality of domination and the potentiality of freedom" (1971 12). This contradiction is particularly felt, not at the point of production, but when and where workers are not working, in everyday life (not that production isn't part of it, but it is not all of it either, as any economicism would make it appear), or even more urgently by those who simply do not work: Bookchin emphasizes the privileged position of young people in this respect. To say that this is the foremost contradiction of capitalism is no exaggeration, and after thirty years from Bookchin's essay this statement still holds true. To say that the contradiction is felt less at the point of production means to acknowledge that, at that point, the what-is becomes absolutely triumphant and all-pervading. At the point of production, only a disruption of production can allow one to get a glimpse of what-could-be, or else one is left with the alternative of daydreaming and with the numbing of the creative sense. When the actuality of domination becomes absolute, the potentiality of freedom is reduced to nothing. Yet, it is important to understand that this is so only in appearance. In reality, freedom can never be completely destroyed, and, in particular, its potentiality always remains—although hidden somewhere, as it were, or withdrawn into its original and irreducible dignity. It is precisely because of this irreducibility, because of this ultimate and ineradicable stronghold, this cave in the forest of the earth, this unalterable and undiminished plenitude of freedom, that the contradiction faced by capital becomes absolute—as absolute as its actuality of domination and exploitation. Under the regime of real subsumption, when all labor is subsumed under capital, capital appears as a totality. Yet capital has totalized itself only in view of productivity and profit, but it has had no regard for the true totality and complexity of social life, and thus it is not a totality but a partiality. All subsumed labor is in reality only the labor that becomes productive or unproductive. Yet, *that-there-is-labor* is not a category subsumable under capital, though capital tries to make it appear so. *That-there-is-labor*, that is, the neutrality or neither/nor of labor, points to labor's self-discipline, adequate application, as well as to enjoyment and play, and it constitutes the standing there of what-could-be. And what-could-be precisely stands where what-is reaches the limits of its partial being. Beyond what-is there stands its negation. This negation, however, is not nothing but, rather, what-could-be.

To say that capital is a partiality rather than a totality, or, rather, that it is a totality only in appearance, does not mean to deny its reality and power. Moreover, appearance should be taken in the Hegelian sense and not be confused with illusion. Certainly, totality and omnipresence of capital are not illusory. But they are reflected realities. It should not be forgotten that the essence of capital is labor. It is labor, not capital, which has immediate totality and simple commonality, which is, in other words, univocal. Once this is understood, it is easy to see that even the what-is of labor under capital (i.e., productive labor) cannot exhaust labor's potential being. Subsumed under capital, labor leaves its immediacy to enter the sphere of reflection and produce the appearance of capital. Once it subtracts itself from this task and returns to its immediacy, it counts nothing for capital because it has left the sphere of appearance, that is, it has disappeared; yet, it counts a lot for itself. Thus, this disappearing is not annihilation; rather, it is the beginning of a subterranean process that brings the contradiction between actuality and potentiality, appearance and essence, domination and freedom, to the utmost degree. It is the beginning of the guerrilla of living labor.

For Bookchin, this subterranean process has the name of anarchism, or anarco-communism: "a subterranean movement in history which conflicts with all systems of authority" (p. 211). Here, I do not wish to enter into the complex and really dated question of the relationship between anarchism and communism (or Marxism). Nor am I sure that Bookchin sees this subterranean movement in the labor terms I have described it. Indeed, I think that

I make use of a wider and more complex concept of labor than Bookchin does, for it seems to me that he tends to describe an attitude, or perhaps a disposition in everyday life, but not necessarily an *ontological* disposition. Yet, Bookchin, differently from others, always maintains the centrality of labor (through the concept of self-management, for instance), nor does he make the mistake of distinguishing between a liberated (creative) labor and leisure time. Thus, he says, "A point has now been reached where the 'masses' can begin, almost overnight, to expand drastically the 'realm of freedom' in the Marxian sense—to acquire the leisure time needed to achieve the highest degree of self-management" (p. 216). This point is very important, for the tension must not be between leisure and labor time, labor and play, but, rather, between what-is and what-could-be, the actuality of domination and the potentiality of freedom. When the potentiality of freedom is not curtailed, labor and leisure can be one and the same thing, or, as it seems to have been the case among the Arawak of the Caribbean islands, to be equal and integral components of the organicity of the same time.   ↳ Paradise Lost of...

NOT YET: THE TABLE OF LABOR, BEYOND LABOR[21]

> For the human soul embraces everything, including the other side which is not yet.
> —Ernst Bloch

The category of Not-yet is the same as the category of the *could*. It describes the structure of real utopia, and it aspires to a real, and Bloch says, *critical*, totality. We have seen that capital is a partiality, which presents itself as a totality, thus a totality only in appearance. For Ernst Bloch, the *critical totality* recuperates the elements of the genuinely noncontemporaneous dimension, that past that is not yet past, but is part of a broader Now. This Bloch says in an essay entitled "Noncontemporaneity and Obligation to its Dialectic" of 1932 (Bloch 1991). The essay begins with a definition of the concept of noncontemporaneity, which reads: "Not all people exist in the same Now." And it continues: "They do so only externally, through the fact that they can be seen today. But they are thereby not yet living at the same time with the others" (Bloch 1991: 97). Toward the end of the essay, the main noncontemporaneous groups are identified as the youth, the peasantry, and the poor urban class, all of which, discontented in their accumulated rage and unfinished past, became a target of the populist rhetoric of National Socialism (p. 142).

Bloch presents a multilayered dialectic descriptive of the complexity of the "turbulent Now" (p. 113). The dialectic distinguishes between contradictions that are contemporaneous and noncontemporaneous and, within each contradiction, between a subjective and an objective dimension. Perhaps the passage where this is most clearly explained is the following, which is in italics in the text: "*The subjectively noncontemporaneous contradiction is accumulated rage, the objectively noncontemporaneous one unfinished past; the*

subjectively contemporaneous one is the free revolutionary action of the proletariat, the objectively contemporaneous one the prevented future contained
in the Now, the prevented technological blessing, the prevented new society
with which the old one is pregnant in its forces of production" (ibid.). The first
thing we have to notice is that, according to Bloch, the subjectively noncontemporaneous contradiction (i.e., accumulated rage) and the objectively noncontemporaneous contradiction (i.e., unfinished past) would not be so sharp
and visible if an objectively contemporaneous contradiction did not exist to
utilize them in a specific political way (p. 109). To this latter contradiction he
also gives the name of *modern capitalism* (ibid.). Capitalism is able to use the
noncontemporaneous contradiction for its own purposes, to its own advantage by ideologically relying on the past and preempting the future of its revolutionary content. Indeed, "the non contemporaneous contradiction, even
if it is released by growing impoverishment, disintegration, dehumanization
in the womb of late capital, by the intolerable nature of its objectively contemporaneous contradiction, does not become dangerous to capital for the
time being" (ibid.). And Bloch continues: "On the contrary, capital... uses the
antagonism of a still living past as a means of separation and combat against
the future dialectically giving birth to itself in the capitalist antagonism"
(ibid.). The objectively contemporaneous contradiction is the merely given, the
what-is that impedes the vision and coming of what-could-be; it easily manip-
ulates those who live in a past which is not yet past and prevent the future
that, as Bloch says, is *also* contained in the Now. Another important point to
be noticed in the formulation of the multilayered dialectic has to do with the
question of technology (also dealt with in *The Spirit of Utopia*, as we shall
see). For Bloch, the objectively contemporaneous contradiction *is* "the prevented technological blessing." We go back to the idea we saw above when we
spoke of the distinction between machinery and the factory, an idea also present in the work of Marcuse in the notion of the rationality of technology as
liberation.[22] Thus, the objectively contemporaneous contradiction is a contradiction precisely because it presents itself as the age of technology, but, at the
same time, it politically withholds the benefits of technology from the social
sphere. For Bloch, the exit from this situation of impasse lies in the possible
alliance between the genuinely noncontemporaneous contradiction and the genuinely contemporaneous one; it is then that the concept of *critical totality* comes
into view. Totality must be *critical* precisely in order to avoid falling into a "false
similarity with the idealistic 'totality' which is a mere one of the system" (p. 115).
The "critical" aspect of this totality, which points to its rationality, to a "con-
crete-materialist reason" (p. 135), does not impede, but it actually makes possible, the true concept of utopia. For Bloch, Marxism is such a critical totality[23] and utopia: "The rescue of the good core of *utopia* is... overdue...; the
concrete-dialectical utopia of Marxism, that grasped and alive in real tendency,
is such a rescue" (p. 136).

In *The Spirit of Utopia*, first published in 1918, the question of technology
and its use made by capital is also dealt with in a fundamental, structural way.

The book begins with a comment on capital, technology, and labor: "For progress and capitalism have till now constructed technology, at least in its industrial application, solely for the purposes of fast turnover and high profits, and certainly not, as is so often claimed, in order to alleviate our labor" (Bloch 2000: 11). This is a relatively common view among writers who share a certain political vision, but no less important only for this fact. Bloch envisions a "humanistic technology" capable of correcting the dysfunctional use of technology in capitalism: a "consciously functional technology" (p. 12) in which *art* is also able to overcome the limits imposed on it by a traditional and narrow concept of fine art—one based on taste and stylization. The machine is "just a link in a chain," and not at all the motor of a "monstrous transformation" (ibid.). Bloch is unambiguous in this respect: the machine can abolish poverty, perform the work that, from the point of view of the spirit, is "inessential," and therefore liberate time and make *great expression* possible: a democratization of art (p. 15). In other words, there is here the possibility of an overcoming of the craft/art distinction, once toil is delegated to the machine, in the sense that all craft would be art, as it already ultimately is (pp. 15–17). The concept of art is presented as *comprehended life*, and thus it has the form of a *totality*. This does not mean that art is reduced to craft, for if in the latter technical mastery may be sufficient, it is not sufficient in the former. Rather, the forms of expression which constitute the essential moment of art become the rule rather than the exception; the *extraordinary* goes back to its ontological principle, which is the principle of individuation, its metaphysical foundation, where each difference, identical with itself, is, *eo ipso*, extraordinary. Here, artistic production replaces mere production, which is more and more delegated to the machine. In this sense, we begin dealing with an esthetics that is already ontology, a political and social ontology, but a fundamental one, that is, related to the "what," the substance of the real. Bloch says, "The issue for such art, is absolutely not any of the objective or normative formal problems of aesthetic 'pleasure,' *which are the least important things in the world*, insofar as the concept of *aisthesis* already means not an emotionalized sensation, but absolutely the same as perception, phenomenology, adequate realization. The issue, *every time*, is the content-'what' of what is upper-case Human, and of the pure ground, held open but still mysterious" (p. 116; "aisthesis" is in italics in the text; other emphasis added). The distinction between "fine" art and art as ontological practice and ethical disposition is here made very clear. The problems of fine art, stylization, esthetic pleasure, and so on, are inessential: *the least important things in the world*. To the contrary, artistic expression and production as ontological practice is *every time*—namely, according to the principle of individuation which in naming a difference also names its absolute self-identity, or conversely, in naming an identity also names its absolute difference from everything else—a question of the "what" and of the pure ground. Here the interplay between the open and the closed (or mysterious), which we shall see again in the next chapter speaking of Heidegger, is present. In Bloch, it points to the necessity, in constituting a new human reality, of going beyond the what-is, the merely given, into the indeterminate terrain of the *could*, the mystery of "inwardness," as well as, in general, *of the other side which is not yet* (276).

This is the terrain of the real utopia, announced, by Bloch's own admission, in the "revolutionary Romanticism" of *The Spirit of Utopia* according to a *Sturm und Drang* mood and later developed and defined in other works, including *The Principle of Hope* (cf. the afterword to *The Spirit of Utopia* of 1963; Bloch 2000: 279). The real or critical utopia, differently from an ideal one, is characterized by the possibility of an actual *crossing over* to the other side. Speaking of the philosophy of music, to which he devotes the longest chapter of *The Spirit of Utopia*, this utopia has the character of "a *not yet conscious knowledge* of what will occur over there one day, in an 'over there' that has not yet happened." But this *crossing over* is also a *recollection* and a *finding-a-way-back-home*: "but precisely to a home where one has never been, which is nevertheless home" (p. 145). Music, just like in Schopenhauer, represents the highest moment of this process of crossing over—a crossing into the mystery whose articulation is precisely the task of music and philosophy together; a mystery in which, however, the *word* of redemption is heard, the word expressing what remains "otherwise unsayable" (p. 163). It is, Bloch also says, a "release toward an ethics and a metaphysics of inwardness" (p. 161), that is, the place where what is inessential is seen as such, but the union with the *not yet* is already established: "Now still a fervent stammering, music, with an increasingly determinacy, will one day possess its own language: it aims at the word which alone can save us, which in every lived moment trembles obscurely as the *omnia ubique*: music and philosophy in their final instance intend purely toward the articulation of this fundamental mystery, of this first and last question in everything" (p. 158).

Beyond the inessential, and thus beyond the narrowness of both the non-contemporaneous contradictions and the objectively contemporaneous one, the mystery remains as the most essential, the *comprehensible-incomprehensible* (p. 162), which constitutes the "proper object of humanity" (ibid.), but an object which is "*objectively* veiled from itself" (p. 163). The word "objectively" must be understood in the sense of the objectively contemporaneous contradiction that prevents the future society from realizing itself. That is, it prevents the real or critical utopia, the "renewed reality" (p. 171) from coming about. For Bloch, the important thing is being able to posit the essential questions for humanity, which, as we have seen in speaking of contemporaneous and noncontemporaneous contradictions earlier, is not necessarily an easy task. The questions are those of the *Self* and the *We* beyond the merely given, the empirical, the what-is, the "unfruitful power of the merely existent" (p. 163), and they constitute the structural moments of real utopia. Bloch says, "This intending toward a star, a joy, a truth to set against the empirical, beyond its satanic night and especially beyond its night of *incognito*, is the only way to find truth; the question about us is the only problem, the resultant of every world-problem, *and to formulate this Self- and We-Problem in everything, the*

opening, reverberating through the world, of the gates of homecoming, is the ulti-
mate principle of utopian philosophy" (p. 206). This home, which has always
been one, yet not found, not yet; perhaps, in the traditional language of philosophy, the good life. Bloch speaks of a *joy* that is, at the same time, a *truth*,
for which alone philosophy, poetry, music, have been given, but perhaps mis-
construed in the sense of a direction away from home. This false sense of a
direction brings about the loneliness that Bloch, speaking of Kant, points out:
"We are lonesome, and stand in the dark of an infinite, merely asymptotic
convergence toward the goal" (p. 177). Yet, for Kant, practical knowledge
opens up a space of hope, a future that is not necessarily unattainable. It is in
this turn toward subjectivity and inwardness, where philosophy is "a solitary
light meant to burn up the night of this world" (p. 185), that Kant proves perhaps superior to Hegel, who brings "all inwardness outside" (p. 179) but in so
doing also transforms the dialectic between the closed and the open into a
"panlogical objectivity" (p. 181), an "explicitly concluded system" (p. 179).

We have repeatedly made reference to the concept of inwardness. Yet, this
inwardness, seen from the point of view of the concrete utopia, does not leave
this world; it is, rather, of this world, but it constitutes the passage from what-
is to what-could-be; in other words, it is of this world when the reality of this
world also includes possibility as its essential moment. Then, this inwardness
also meets the *state of society*, this solitude meets the *dream of the external*
world. In this sense, inwardness and solitude in the world of the merely given
incarnate the subjectively contemporaneous contradiction, that is the spirit of
conscious rebellion and revolution, the active proletarian disposition. For,
Bloch says, "how could there be an inwardness, and how could it notice that
it was one, whether as sorrow or as truly paradoxical joy, if it stopped being
rebellious against everything given" (p. 238). It is from the section on Marx
that we are reading, and we shall go back to this in our conclusion with a reference to the last chapter of *The Principle of Hope*, which reiterates similar
themes as we find now in *The Spirit of Utopia*.

In this section, the structure of the concrete utopia, which for Bloch Marxism is, becomes evident. The structure is given by the relationship between
the We and the What For, which describes the most fundamental problem of
humanity. And communism is the solution to such problem. For Bloch, communism is this way of relating economy to culture, and in this sense Bloch's
discourse is very close to our own. The question is then that of a different
conception of labor, and this different conception points toward creative
labor, that is, a labor which is not subsumed or subsumable under the imperatives of the economy but that uses those imperatives, as basic needs, for a
total, comprehensive, understanding of the What For defining humanity.
However, the What For is inscribed in the modality of the *could*, not of the
ought to, for if the latter were the case, we would be dealing with a teleology
capable of placating any free and conscious revolutionary position into a pure
waiting and a mere hope, that is, not the hope which, as Bloch stresses, is contained in the passage to a critical totality. In Marx's utopia, and according

to the principle of creative labor, "pleasure in one's ability will replace the profit motive as a sufficient motivation, at least for practical occupations" (p. 245). The structure of utopia does not get rid of the economic dimension, without which life would not be possible, but it certainly eliminates its present equation with profitability. It is not labor that must be abolished, but its productive use. Bloch says, "Hence utopia's distant totality offers the image of a structure in no way still economically profitable: everyone producing according to his abilities, everybody consuming according to his needs, everyone openly 'comprehended' according to the degree of his assistance, his moral-spiritual lay ministry and humanity's homeward journey through the world's darkness" (pp. 245–246). Bloch's messianic language, its spiritual and ethical tone, should not make us believe that the structure of utopia he is describing is less concrete than he maintains. The difficulty here lies with the nature of the concept he is dealing with, which entails a movement of transcendence within immanence. This can be easily seen in Bloch's description of the original Christian utopia in the second volume of *The Principle of Hope*. There we read that "the coming of Jesus himself was by no means as inward and other-worldly as a reinterpretation since St Paul, which always suited the ruling class, would have us believe" (Bloch 1995: 499). And again: "Jesus never said 'My kingdom is not of this world'; this passage is interpolated by St John (John 18, 36), and it was designed to be of use to Christians in a Roman court" (p. 500). What is important for us here is Bloch's clarification of the expressions "this world" and "the other world," which stand in the same relation to each other as the expressions "what-is" and "what-could-be." Bloch says, "'This world' is synonymous with that which now exists, with the present 'aeon,' whereas 'the other world' is synonymous with the future 'aeon'" (ibid.). And he continues, "What is thereby intended by these contrasting terms is not a geographical division between this world and the other world, but a *chronologically successive one in the same arena, situated down here*." And again, "'The other world' is the utopian earth, with a utopian heaven above it.... The aspiration is not another world after death, where the angels are singing, but the equally terrestrial and supra-terrestrial kingdom of love" (ibid.). Such is Bloch's description of the "communism of love"; so much more real and terrestrial must the concrete utopia of genuine communism be. Indeed, it must be terrestrial and supraterrestrial in the sense that the true spiritual dimension of life is, not eliminated, but, rather, recuperated over and beyond the need for religion in the critical totality that finds, in the passage beyond labor, the table of labor. The transcendence of the "what-is," of the merely given, of "this world," is a transcendence of the logic of productivism toward the essence of creativeness, in which earth and heaven, the utopian earth and the utopian heaven, open up their plane of immanence closed up to now because resistant to the logic of subsumption, withdrawn into its solitude, hidden in the earth's forest. "The other world" of which Bloch speaks is then the world of a labor that has finally come back to itself, and that means, away from profitability, yet in accordance with the equally important moments of pleasure and need.

To go back to *The Spirit of Utopia*, we find that the subject of this transcendence within immanence is labor itself; labor, that is, "We," our deeds, history, as the univocal ground of the social. This is that *orientation toward humanity* that is captured in the expression the Son of Man (Bloch 2000: 262ff), that is, the being that comes after man—an expression that also gives substance and meaning to Nietzsche's concept of the Overman. For Bloch, this is "what the resurrection of all the dead in the simple dogma of immortality indicates" (p. 266), that is, the meeting, in the sense of that orientation, of the problems of the We and the What For; or, as he says, the fact that "the house of humanity must remain" (ibid., italics removed), which of course implies the necessity of its construction—a construction that we are far from having begun, for its beginning necessitates the exit from the logic of productivity that enslaves even the spirit, the emancipation "from all questions of economics" (p. 267). There is here a reference again to a technology capable of liberating labor from the regime of alienation and exploitation to which it has been tied so far. Then time outside of work will become a reality, rather than being the "real unreality" still governed by the dominant mode of production in the form of the spectacle (Debord 1995: 13); each occurrence of human activity will be inscribed in the realm of the extraordinary; but this will happen only by way of a political reversal of the use of technology, and that means, by way of the proper use of the concrete will.

In the last section of *The Spirit of Utopia* on the Will, Bloch emphasizes the potentialities of what he has otherwise called the subjectively contemporaneous contradiction, that is, the revolutionary action of the proletariat—in which "proletariat" must be understood in the sense we have discussed in Chapter 1; and that means not necessarily as the human being invested by the category of "workerness," whether this human being is currently employed or not. It is in this contradiction, or even more simply "condition," that the will is exalted as the modality capable of either directing or countering all other contradictions defining the Now: the unfinished past, accumulated rage, and the technopolitical web of institutions characterizing the objectively contemporaneous contradiction. The Will, which opens up to the immanence of the *could*, to "the other world," to the Not Yet, constitutes the path to the structure of utopia in the sense that it remains open to the principle of hope—a real hope. Thus, Bloch says, "And yet what is left for us here, we who suffer and are dark, is to hope far ahead" (p. 276). For "hope will not let us go to ruin" (ibid.). It is here that the sentence I chose as an epigraph to this section occurs: "For the human soul embraces everything, including the other side which is not yet" (ibid.). This sentence, besides its poetic strength, as is often the case with Bloch, philosophically means that reality includes possibility. The structure of hope is that whereby this truth first comes to be understood, against the antagonistic will of the objectively contemporaneous contradiction and its efforts to preclude the vision and falsify the truth. However, the possibility included in reality is not a mere possibility but, rather, a real one. Bloch stresses this point by actually moving from the "formally possible" to the "*simply necessary*" (p. 276)—a move that we will not follow because that would redirect the openness of the *could* toward the *ought to* once again. What remains important at this point is Bloch's description of the "*essential* reality" of utopia. He says that "because of this final antifactual, antimundane, world-sharing homogeneity between idea and *not*-being, *not-yet-being*, it is now only the empirically factual and its logic [i.e., the objectively contemporaneous contradiction], and no longer the utopically factual, the imaginatively constitutive, which appears inaccessible or transcendent to the *creative concept*, indeed appears as the 'metaphysics' forbidden by Kant" (ibid.; brackets added). It is the description of a totality, perhaps not as critical as it will more evidently become in Bloch's later works, but one in which the essential relation between what-is and what-could-be is certainly brought to the fore—a relation that, if denied, only generates imbalance and grave forms of social pathology, in Bloch's time, but even more so in our own. This totality, in which Marxism and religion are united—and that means, the conscious, critical revolutionary action together with what, not yet being, belongs to the world of the spirit—is for Bloch the "*a priori* of all politics and culture" (p. 278). Here labor, as the inner substance of human praxis, takes on the role which essentially belongs to it: that is, of being the univocal concept between creation and need, the economy and culture, the totality of what is visible and invisible in the human experience and adventure. But what is invisible, which the regime of technology and machinery also exalts, must be willed, and not accepted as a form of ineluctable imposition. Instead, it must be willed with a view to a promised liberation, really a return, from a false metaphysics of separation and powerlessness.

4   The Solitude of Labor

*On the Relationship between Creative Labor and
Artistic Production*

Art's declaration of independence is... the beginning of the end of art.
—Guy Debord

Every nature must produce its next, for each thing must unfold,
seedlike, from indivisible principle into a visible effect.
—Plotinus

THE ESTHETIC DIMENSION OF LABOR

When the concept of labor is considered ontologically, it takes, within social
ontology, the place that the concept of being has in pure ontology. This means
that labor is still *being,* but it is not being as such, "pure" being; rather, it is
practical, "impure" being: it is what enters into the constitution of the whole
spectrum of social life. As such, labor is not a category of political economy,
yet that does not mean that it has no economic function at all. The economy
itself, economic life, is now understood in a completely different way; to be
sure, it remains an essential part of social life, but it does not stand in a relationship of opposition (of determination as opposition) to culture. Nor is
culture the superstructural product, the epiphenomenal appearance, of the
economy. Labor occupies an intermediate position *between* economy and culture, it functions as the middle term of a syllogism, which means that a synthesis now obtains such that the categories of economy and culture appear as
merely analytical names for what is in fact a totality: the totality of social
being. In this totality, all events have equal value and necessity. These events
can go from the production of useful objects to artistic production, from
exchange to language, from language in its everyday use to poetry, from the
system of laws to the knowledge and management of one's habitat as well as
of the universe as a whole. Labor performs the function of the universal concept present in the constitution of all these events—of the most common concept. These are events or expressions of nature, yet they go beyond nature.
Labor, which is in itself a natural and objective force, reshapes nature, and it
is the modality or direction of this reshaping that becomes problematic.

Labor is being as sensuous human activity. The concept of being of traditional metaphysics can only be understood, within a project of social ontology, in terms of the concept of the sensuous, and this, in turn, is nothing but
labor itself. It is not, of course, labor as a curse, nor labor as wage labor, but,
rather, labor as the transforming and self-transforming activity of human

beings; it addresses both questions of scarcity and the question of desire. The discourse of metaphysics and ontology now enters a *poietic* and practical dimension.

The emphasis on the concept of the sensuous brings us into the domain of esthetics. For political economy, the regulation of the totality of life can only happen through a fragmentation of that same totality. In that sense, esthetics would be a separate domain, one that is reached on a second thought and, as it were, after having satisfied more fundamental and pressing questions. However, from the point of view of poetic ontology, the esthetic dimension of labor is labor's fundamental and univocal disposition. The sensuous, as labor, invests all expressions of life: it is not limited to the sphere of "mere" production, nor is artistic production a superstructural moment of limited and special interest. The esthetic disposition becomes a metaphysical disposition.

Here one should consider Nietzsche's thought. Nietzsche is in fact the thinker who said this in the clearest and most forcible manner. For Nietzsche, the destruction of traditional metaphysics is followed by a regime of sensuous and artistic activity. Yet, this artistic activity must be metaphysical in character. In *The Will to Power*, Nietzsche says, "An anti-metaphysical view of the world—yes, but an artistic one" (1968: #1048). Here, art replaces metaphysics. Yet, to say that art replaces metaphysics means to give art a much wider meaning than it usually has. If art replaces metaphysics, then art is no longer an ephemeral expression of human activity, it is not a special modality of life reserved to special circumstances and people. Rather, it becomes a common concept, a subversive and radically new regime, and its movement is equal to that of the emancipation of the senses described by Marx (see Chapter 1). It is a metaphysics of immanence, metaphysics of this world, *the world we are.* In the world we are, art *becomes* metaphysics—a poetic metaphysics, to be sure. Thus, Nietzsche also says, "... art as the real task of life, art as life's *metaphysical* activity" (ibid.: #853, IV).[1]

The fact that art becomes a common concept does not entail a lowering of esthetic values. The word "common" here must be understood ontologically: "common" in the sense in which being is said to be a common concept, and that means "univocal." It has the meaning that Debord gives to it when he says that "a new *common* language has yet to be found" (Debord 1995: 133; emphasis added). For Debord, this new common language will have the form of "a praxis embodying both an unmediated activity and a language commensurate with it" (ibid.). As for the question of values, there are new and higher values, the values after their transvaluation. They become possible only after the last man follows God's destiny, and the new man, the Overman, replaces him. *The Overman is nothing but the artist as a metaphysician.* After the death of God and the destruction of metaphysics, a secular and earthly plenitude can finally become actual. Here, Nietzsche's "most difficult thought" that occurs "at the peak of meditation," that is, the eternal recurrence of the same, as well as the will to power as the closest approximation of being and becoming, shows its most fruitful result. In his work on Nietzsche, Heidegger shows this very well. He says, for instance, that "[t]o be an artist is to be able to bring something forth. But to bring something forth means to establish in Being something that does not exist" (Heidegger 1979: 69). The problem with Heidegger's interpretation is that he reduces Nietzsche's thought to a traditional metaphysics. Accordingly, Nietzsche does not overcome metaphysics but only brings it to completion. Yet Heidegger says this only on the basis of his misunderstanding of Nietzsche. For instance, Heidegger overlooks Nietzsche's emphasis on the sensuous and on *this world,* and he reintroduces in Nietzsche's thought the supersensuous and thus the metaphysical split that Nietzsche explicitly rejects. In *The Twilight of the Idols,* he says, "The 'real' world—an idea no longer of any use, not even a duty any longer—an idea grown useless, superfluous, *consequently* a refuted idea: let us abolish it!" And he continues: "We have abolished the real world. What world is left? the apparent world perhaps?... But no! *with the real world we have also abolished the apparent world!"* (Nietzsche 1990: 50–51).

After the abolition of the supersensuous (i.e., of the imaginary world of traditional metaphysics), the sensuous is no longer constructed as the nonsupersensuous. Rather, the sensuous is "the world we are." It is then not at all the empirically given, the datum of the senses, the *positum.* The sensuous includes the visible and the invisible, and in this sense it also includes the spiritual. But, as Lucretius shows, this invisible and spiritual sphere of reality does not have to be immaterial (Lucretius 2001). With Nietzsche, too, the sensuous is not a lifeless world of matter, but one endowed with life. What remains invisible to the *positum,* to what-is, is neither supramaterial nor immaterial. The will to power, is always at work in the invisible movement, the constant becoming, which takes the sensuous away from the narrowness of what-is. This is similar to what happens to the atoms in Lucretius (on account of Epicurus's concept of free will) when they swerve slightly in their movement because of the "power of will wrested from destiny" (Lucretius 2001: 41). The sensuous is sensuous precisely because it is crossed through by this power. Thus, with Nietzsche, in order to have life, creation, poetic metaphysics, art, power, and even the "spirit," we do not need to turn to the nonsensuous—as if the sensuous were deprived of precisely these essential moments, deprived of movement and becoming, of life; as if the sensuous only constituted one part of a totality. In fact, the sensuous is this totality: the open totality of being: 'totality' and yet 'open' because of the asymptotic movement whereby becoming nears being. Without ever becoming the same, the character of being is impressed upon becoming. "To impose upon becoming the character of being—that is the supreme will to power" (Nietzsche 1968: #617).

Thus, Nietzsche's new metaphysics of art does away not simply with the supersensuous, but with the split between the sensuous and the supersensuous. This is the meaning of the destruction of metaphysics: it is not simply the true world of ideas that becomes useless, but also this world as a world of appearances. What remains is *this world, the world we are,* in its plenitude and unsurpassable finitude. Even the spirit is not rejected and destroyed as such; it rather

φύσις ?
βούλησις

becomes secular and earthly. The will to power is everything; thus even the
transforming and self-transforming sensuous human activity is will to power.
Will to power is what the Greeks called *phusis,* but human activity, labor, is
also this *phusis.* Here *phusis* takes on the character of art not because it is
humanized, but rather because it is *over-humanized.* It is not because man naturally and deterministically expresses the *phusis,* which also constitutes him;
in other words, it is not because man is this generic and compulsory will to
power that he also becomes an artist. Rather, man becomes an artist (and in
this sense a true metaphysician) when *phusis,* or with Nietzsche will to power,
is raised above the level of the merely given, and one of the most eminent ways
in which this happens is, as we shall see, through and because of language.
One cannot speak of consciousness with Nietzsche, but one can do so with
Marx. In any case, what one finds in both Nietzsche and Marx is the discovery and upholding of the sensuous, the discovery of life as practical and poetic
activity, as what remains once the abstractions of traditional metaphysics and
political economy are shown in their falsity. The world that remains after the
true world of ideas and the false world of appearances collapse is neither true
nor false, neither ideal nor apparent. It is the living approximation of being
and becoming. In the same way, the destruction of productive and unproductive labor leaves us with a labor that is neither productive nor unproductive,
a living labor, a "form-giving fire" that also brings about the closest and
asymptotic approximation of being and becoming, of time and human temporality. What is important is that becoming does not turn into being, whether
this is the true world of ideas or the world of dead labor. This also means that
being does not turn into an empty abstraction, which would be the same as
nothing. Yet, the plenitude that follows from this position is not fixed and
immutable. The fact that being and becoming approximate each other without ever becoming one and the same force is a function of the expansive and
ever-changing nature of this plenitude.

When labor is understood as the sensuous (*aistetikos*) human activity, it
becomes a concept of both esthetics and ontology. Or, rather, esthetics *is*
ontology when the latter is understood not in its pure sense, but, rather, as a
practical and poetic disposition or power. In this sense, the distinction
between mere production and artistic production becomes problematic
because it is now evident that it is not a necessary distinction. The fact that
it is constantly made only says that it has become a commonplace, but it does
not say that this commonplace has any philosophical validity. It seems easy
to show that at the basis of this distinction there are at least two prejudices:
one is the division of labor and the other, which follows from the first, is the
view that mere production cannot share in the freedom and creativeness of
artistic production. By problematizing this distinction, I do not mean to suggest that all production should be exactly of the same type. Even in artistic
production as usually understood there is difference between one work and
the other, as there is greatness and mediocrity. Rather, what I am saying is
that the disposition with which one approaches *any* type of production should

and could be re-directed toward the discovery and the experience of one's creativity. In other words, to say that all production could become artistic does
not mean that we are all expected to create great works of art. Rather, it
means to give the concept of production, through creativeness and freedom,
its due dignity. No activity is too low or uninteresting unless it is made so by
deliberately devised social categories. One thing is certain: the coming of an
esthetic regime cannot amount to making great works of art available to an
ever larger majority of people, or to everybody. This is easily done today by
way of technology, but that is also the way of devaluing the content of art.
Instead, an esthetic regime requires that everybody be socially and existentially
able to explore and actualize his or her creative potential. And in order to do
this, one has to have time for it.

I will try to show here how the difference between production and artistic
production can be overcome if the concept and the practice of creative labor
become the universal and common subject of the social. What is important
to realize is that we are now dealing with a philosophy that posits praxis, that
is, human sensuous activity, at the center, and it does so in the most conscious
and explicit way. This praxis we have already identified with poiesis. This
identification runs counter to the traditional Aristotelian distinction of the
two terms. For Aristotle, action (praxis) has its end in itself, whereas production (poiesis) does not. But in Aristotle, this distinction serves the purpose of
emphasizing the meaning of ethics as a practical science and, indeed, as part
of political science. With modernity and the emergence of capital, a new split
occurs, this time within poiesis itself, within the theory of production. However, this was not the case throughout antiquity, the Middle Ages, and the
Early Renaissance, when the distinction between crafts and arts was not what
it later became with modernity. With modernity and capital, the distinction
between crafts and arts becomes vitally important because of the formulation
of a new concept of *the end:* the end of production is now no longer only external to action; it is even external to production itself, for the end is no longer
the product, but merely surplus-value and profit. With modernity, we can
then distinguish between mere production and artistic production. Certainly,
in the Late Middle Ages and the Early Renaissance, capital was already emerg-
ing, but it was far from having attained its specificity—a specificity centered
on the concept of productive labor and its counterpart: unproductive labor,
which was however only needed as the horizon of productive labor, only
needed to justify the necessary social category of exclusion. However, the
important question here is the question of *the end:* If the labor which counts
is productive labor (i.e., that which has its end outside itself), it is then also
important to ask what this end is. We have already seen the answer: the end
is no longer usefulness, but profit. In fact, when the end of production is usefulness, creativeness can still be a part of it—as it was in the case of the crafts-
man/artist. But when the end of production is profit, creativeness must be
pushed away from the realm of production proper (mere production), it must
become artistic production, now seen as a luxurious appendage to everyday

life, a wholly individual endeavor, an "esthetic compensation," as Mumford would say.

How can then a philosophy of praxis recuperate the lost sense of the original concept of production? For it is no longer enough to say, with Aristotle, that action and production are different because "production has its end in something other than itself, but action does not, since its end is acting well itself" (Aristotle 1999: 1140b). And actually one has to go against Aristotle who explicitly says, "Nor is one included in the other; for action is not production, and production is not action" (p. 1140a). In reality, the difference does not lie in the fact that action has its end in itself and production has its end in something other. Rather, the difference lies in the fact that one and the same concept, that of action, can be interpreted in two ways: as having its end in itself or as having its end in something other. Once this is done, it is easy to see that production is nothing but action that has its end in something other than itself; a special kind of action, but not a different genus. Yet, this end, its otherness notwithstanding, must still relate to the specific kind of action performed and to the material used. To make a concrete example (one of Aristotle's examples), the end (and the good) of house-building is certainly something other than house-building itself, but this something other has to be something that relates to both the activity of house-building and the material employed. Thus, the end of house-building is a house. It cannot be something altogether other than the action itself. Yet this heterogeneous result is precisely what obtains under capital where the *true* end (and the good) of house-building is no longer a house, but it is profit.

Thus poetic ontology, which posits the unity of poiesis and praxis, cannot accept the new split within production itself operated by capital, nor can it recuperate the original Aristotelian distinction, for we now see that production is indeed a kind of action. Instead, poetic ontology (a philosophy of praxis) will seek to bridge the gap between the two terms (action and production) in the direction of their actual identification. The concept of creative labor, which the philosophy of praxis puts at the basis of the constitution of a new totality of the social, is in fact a synthetic expression in this sense: labor is, fundamentally, action; but its creative dimension relates to the original sense of production as *poiesis,* the transformation of the acting self and of what is acted upon *into another:* a production of difference. It certainly has nothing to do with production as understood by capital and political economy; there is here no productivity and profit, no productive and unproductive labor but, rather, an active, synthetic, and subjective withdrawal from these categories.

CREATION AND MERE MAKING

The question of production (the question of *poiesis*) must be seen in its relation to the question of action (the question of *praxis*). Once it is established that poiesis and praxis cannot be considered in separation from one another,

[handwritten margin note: the difference between the po-litics-in-command view of revolutionary society and . . .]

the question of production moves from being a question of political economy to being a question of ontology.

When considered critically, a fruitful way to look at this is offered by Heidegger's interpretation of production as *poiesis,* although Heidegger attempts a passage, not of course from political economy to ontology, but from traditional metaphysics to poetic metaphysics (or poetic ontology). For Heidegger, production as poiesis is, fundamentally, *bringing forth.* Yet, this bringing forth can be creation (*Schaffen*) or mere making, the making of equipment (*Verfertigen*). On the basis of this distinction, between creation and mere making, Heidegger explains the difference between art and reality. It is this difference (ultimately a function of the division of labor) that constitutes the object of my critique.

Traditionally, production is seen as radically different from action. In the *Nicomachean Ethics,* as we have seen, Aristotle says that action and production are two different things. According to Agamben, whom we have already cited in this respect, the history of Western metaphysics after the Greeks is the history of the blurring of this fundamental distinction (Agamben 1999a: 71). We have seen that for Aristotle what distinguishes production from action is really the concept, or the function of the concept, of *the end:* production has its end outside itself, action has its end in itself. But we have questioned the adequacy, within modernity, of the Aristotelian distinction. It is in fact true that this distinction loses meaning in the history of western thought. With Vico, production and action can no longer be seen in separation, and with Marx they truly become the constituent parts of the same process. But this is seen by Balibar as the *removal of a taboo* and as a *revolutionary thesis* (Balibar 1995: 40). Agamben takes a transhistorical approach not dissimilar from Heidegger's, but Balibar bases his understanding of the Aristotelian distinction in terms of the division of labor and of class. He explains the distinction as follows: "Since the Greeks (who made it the privilege of "citizens," i.e., of the masters), *praxis* had been that "free" action in which man realizes and transforms only himself, seeking to attain his own perfection. As for *poiesis...,* which the Greeks considered fundamentally servile, this was "necessary" action, subject to all the constraints of the relationship with nature, with material conditions. The perfection it sought was not that of man, but of things, of products for use" (pp. 40–41). Balibar's argument is very important. In his *Politics,* in a way that anticipates Hegel's dialectic of master and slave, Aristotle sees action, insofar as it pertains to the slave, as *instrumental* action, rather than action as such, or pure action. Here we find the link between action and production. Of course, the action of the slave is simply a mediation, to use Hegelian terminology, and indeed a vanishing one—a mediation between the desire of the master and the object of his desire; the slave is a minister of action, an instrument of action, a possession also endowed with another possession from which he can be separated: his capacity to work and produce, what becomes under capital the laborer's labor power. But life is action, contrary to production (*Politics*

1941: I, 1253b–1254a). Thus, because the action of the slave is geared toward production, the instrument of action is really an instrument of production. This also anticipates Marx's dialectic between living labor and dead labor, between labor and capital, between labor power as a special component of the means of production and production itself. It is then correct to say that poiesis and praxis collapse into the same concept and that the Greek distinction is blurred. For Balibar, however, the identification of poiesis and praxis is dynamic and dialectical; in other words, he does not say that we only have one concept instead of two; rather, he says that this identification constitutes "the revolutionary thesis that *praxis* constantly passes over into *poiesis* and vice versa" (p. 41).

Thus, the question of production (i.e., of a specific making) is necessarily related to that of a wider sense of human activity: doing. Poiesis is making; praxis is doing. For Heidegger, however, the traditional distinction between poiesis and praxis becomes the distinction, within the concept of poiesis, between creating and making: creating has its end in itself; making has an end other than itself. However, peculiar to Heidegger's interpretation is that both concepts have the thinking and knowing of *techne* as their transcendental structure. Creation is not, therefore, the exact equivalent of human praxis. But what is important is that the concept of production, understood as "bringing forth" in general, is, for Heidegger, of different kinds. In *The Origin of the Work of Art* (1935—1936), Heidegger distinguishes between creating and mere making. He says, "We think of creation as a bringing forth. But the making of equipment, too, is a bringing forth. Handicraft... does not, to be sure, create works, not even when we contrast, as we must, the handmade with the factory product" (Heidegger 1971b: 58). Then he asks a very important question: "But what is it that distinguishes bringing forth as creation from bringing forth in the mode of making?" (ibid.). What distinguishes them is poetry: "The nature [*Wesen*] of art is poetry. The nature [*Wesen*] of poetry is the founding of truth" (p. 75).

In *The Origin of the Work of Art*—and particularly in the final section, "Truth and Art"—the issue is posed in a special way. The second section ends with the following question: "What is truth, that it can happen as, or even must happen as, art? How is it that art exists at all?" (p. 57). These are questions that Heidegger also asks in the first series of his lectures on Nietzsche, then published in the first volume of his *Nietzsche* as *The Will to Power as Art*. The time of the two series of lectures, on Nietzsche and on the origin of the work of art, is about the same, the late 1930s.

In *The Will to Power as Art,* Heidegger distinguishes between the guiding (or penultimate) and the grounding (or ultimate) questions of philosophy. The former asks: What is the being? The latter asks: What is being? The grounding question, Heidegger says, "remains as foreign to Nietzsche as it does to the history of thought prior to him" (Heidegger 1979: 67). This means that Western metaphysics up to Nietzsche (i.e., according to Heidegger, up to the time of its completion) only asks the question as to what the being is, that is, the question about the being of beings, not the question about being as such. The guiding question, however, is as essential to philosophy as the grounding question. Moreover, it is not a question that metaphysics also could not ask. It is part of the history of the truth of being; part of this history's destiny. In fact, both questions ask "what beings and Being *in truth* are" (p. 68). The phrase "in truth" is not to be understood in the rhetorical sense of "truly," "really"; rather, "in truth" has a spatial and temporal meaning—an ontological meaning. It designates the open region of being and its essence: "Beings are to be brought into the open region of Being itself, and Being is to be conducted into the open region of its essence" (ibid.).

But the "where" of this open region is not fixed once and for all. It itself is a happening and a framing. It is in this sense that the "where" of the occurrence of truth is spatial *and* temporal. More than just a place, "in truth" designates a *placing* (*Stellen*) and an *occurrence*, an *event* (*Ereignis;* also rendered in English as "enowning"). Thus, it is "in truth," that is, within this placing and this occurrence, that truth as *alētheia* (unconcealment) comes to the fore. But "in truth," truth is, at the same time, concealed in the *space* (*Raum*) in which it stands together with being. This space is the "realm of the grounding question" (ibid.)—not a ground, but a grounding; there, truth and being are not simply inhabiting the same space; rather, they are "united in essence and yet foreign to one another" (ibid.).

The passage from the guiding to the grounding question of philosophy is a passage to the question of being *as* truth, where the latter, in its concealedness, is untruth, and the former, also in its concealedness, is nonbeing. When Heidegger speaks of art—both in his interpretation of Nietzsche and in *The Origin of the Work of Art*—he speaks metaphysically. He says, for instance: "The work... is not the reproduction of some particular entity [*Seienden*] that happens to be present at any given time; it is, on the contrary, the reproduction of the thing's general essence [*des allgemeinen Wesens der Dinge*]" (Heidegger 1971b: 37). Heidegger opposes the view that art belongs to esthetics and truth to logic. Instead, he affirms the metaphysical nature of both concepts, provided that they are essentially related to each other in and through poetry. There would be no esthetics and no logic without the essential relation of art and poetry and without the simultaneous founding of truth. That the essence (or nature) of art is poetry and the essence of poetry is the founding of truth should not be understood in a hierarchical order. The word "essence" [*Wesen*] is not to be taken here as that which lies behind or beyond. Rather, the word "essence" relates all beings to itself as to their unavoidable destiny. It is to be understood as the Parmenidean *moira* (fate). Thus, Heidegger says, "What is, is never of our making or even merely the product of our minds" (p. 53). Man is not the measure of all things; for Heidegger, a fateful measure grounds all things, as well as man, as historical beings.

However, the relation of art, poetry, and truth uses man as its essential measure. Man finds himself in the center of the place that opens up in the midst of beings and *because of* man. "Because of man" does not imply that this is in fact what man autonomously wills, as if he could also choose not to will it; rather, it means that what opens up pertains to man's being there.[2] But what is there? Heidegger says, *Eine Lichtung ist,* "There is a clearing" (p. 53), a lighting center that "encircles all that is, like the Nothing which we scarcely know" (ibid.). There is no essential relation and no human measure without the open and lighting center within which all beings must stand. "Only this clearing grants and guarantees to us humans a passage to those beings that we ourselves are not, and access to the being that we ourselves are" (ibid.). Heidegger makes no mention here of either Parmenides or Protagoras. However, it is evident that *the passage,* not man, is the measure of things that are and of those that are not, of those which *we* are not and of *that-we-are.* The passage, which for Heidegger the artist experiences in a special way (and more than the artist, the poet), is the space where what is concealed and what comes to the fore as unconcealed (yet always concealed in its *not,* in the "un-" of unconcealedness) fight their ambivalent battle by both following and refusing to follow their fatefulness. Thus, truth as happening is founded in its historicality. This history, which is not one of dates and factual events, is the founding of truth as truth-in-the-world. Yet, the world is there only because of its *not,* namely, because of the earth. The latter, however, is not a solid, external, and ultimately abstract ground on which the world can merely stand. As Heidegger says, "What this word [i.e., "earth"] says is not to be associated with the idea of a mass of matter deposited somewhere, or with the merely astronomical idea of a planet." Rather, "Earth is that whence the arising brings back and shelters everything that arises without violation." The arising is *phusis* ("nature"; really, that which manifests itself of its own accord), and it relates earth and world. This means that the relation of earth and world is not an external one: "In the things that arise, earth is present as the sheltering agent" (p. 42).

In the open, where everything finds its place, there is a relationship between earth and world. Once again, this relationship expresses the concept of *alētheia,* the play of concealment and unconcealedness. The earth is a self-secluding essence out of which a self-opening and worlding world emerges, though it remains sheltered and concealed by the earth. "World and earth are essentially different from one another and yet are never separated. The world grounds itself on the earth, and earth juts through world" (1971b: 48–49). As Heidegger explains, "the world is not simply the Open that corresponds to clearing, and the earth is not simply the Closed that corresponds to concealment" (p. 55). In Heidegger's reading of the history of philosophy, this relation corresponds to the relation between the guiding and the grounding question. Indeed, "the world is the clearing of the paths of the essential guiding directions with which all decision complies. Every decision, however, bases itself on something not mastered, something concealed, confusing" (ibid.). But what is confusing also has some clarity, for it still happens within the clearing. The question as to what the being is, is a worldly question of this kind. Even Nietzsche—who, according to Heidegger, brings the series of guiding questions to completion—is only able to point confusedly (and yet clearly) to something different, something unthought. By contrast, the earth is "that which rises up as self-closing" (ibid.). The question as to what being is, is an earthly question of this kind.

The guiding and grounding questions, the world and the earth, are in the same open region, that is, in the region of *alētheia*. They are not external to one another, but, at the same time, they are not the same thing. A political ontology would be able, on the basis of what Heidegger himself says, to individuate the earth and the world, respectively, in the ethical and political realms. This political ontology would draw stronger consequences than Heidegger does from the fact that the worlding of the world is immediately an earthing of the earth. In fact, this entails the consummation of the world and the appearing of the earth. It is true that a world must open up for the earth to rise (p. 63), but the earth is also what makes a world collapse and disappear. It is the ontological power of creation capable of creating as well as of destroying a world.[3] Insofar as human praxis is also an expression of that same power (the general *phusis*), this praxis is responsible for the kind of world created; it then bears responsibilities for the potentialities of its destruction as well.

Fundamentally, when Heidegger asks the question as to the difference between the two modalities of bringing forth, he works on the basis of the unspoken, tacitly accepted concept of the division of labor. He makes it clear that his main interest is not that of formulating a discourse on art or esthetics. He admittedly starts from the ontological plane of being. When bringing forth has the character of creation, there is something in it, according to Heidegger, that goes beyond what is simply human. To be sure, the ontological power of creation is always historical for Heidegger, but of a history that grounds human history: the history of the truth of being. Thus, he does not distinguish between the power of *phusis* and the power of that specific and only human form of *phusis* which is *praxis*. The consequence is a transhistorical concept of history. Yet, it is only within the realm of praxis and human history that the distinction Heidegger draws between creation and mere making, the work of art and the making of equipment, can be understood. Only there can it also be criticized and perhaps overcome or rejected.

Heidegger says that the question as to what distinguishes the different modalities of bringing forth is a difficult one, for even the Greeks are supposed to have understood these two modalities by means of the same concept, that of *techne*. Heidegger explains that "*techne* signifies neither craft nor art"; it "denotes rather a mode of knowing" (p. 59). The neutrality of *techne* (its neither/nor) has a metaphysical configuration. This means that *techne* comes before the division into creating and making. It is bringing forth in general, or the possibility of bringing forth, and as such, it constitutes the univocal ground upon which analogies are to be established. This univocal ground is what Heidegger calls, even in *Being and Time*, the *as*-structure. Through the "as," something comes to the fore *as* something, and it is also understood and interpreted *as* something. But the *as* itself does not pertain to one particular something in an exclusive manner; instead, it pertains equally to any and all.

The *as* is the structure by and through which the power of bringing forth expands into everything that can be and is. In fact, any being is only insofar as it rests upon this structure. In their transcendentality, both the *as*-structure and the concept of *techne* cannot be responsible for the difference between creation and making, nor for the subsequent growth of relations of analogy. They constitute the potentialities through which any given *this* presents itself in the world. But these potentialities rest on a univocal and neutral ground.[4]

In sections 31 and 32 of *Being and Time,* Heidegger shows the nature of understanding and interpretation and the development of the former into the latter. Understanding develops into interpretation. In interpretation something is explicitly understood (i.e., named) *as* something. However, this is not what merely occurs at the ontic level of the statement: when I say, for instance, of a table that it is a table. Rather, in interpretation, to be explicitly understood and named is the *as* itself, and this is what the poetic experience is all about. Heidegger says that "what is named is understood *as* the *as* which what is in question is to be taken" (Heidegger 1996: 139). To understand what is named *as* the *as* of something means to avoid falling into the jungle of analogy and likeness and to move toward univocity and *thisness*.[5] To say of something, not merely that it is something, but that it is something *as* something, means to see it in its difference from any other thing and thus in its absolute self-identity. Yet, the *as,* which is discerned in it, does not belong to it in an exclusive fashion; it is, rather, a common concept. The sameness of difference and identity is what the concept of *thisness* stands for. In real interpretation, as different from mere opinion, what is understood and named is grasped as *this* on the basis of its *as*. Heidegger says, "The 'as' constitutes the structure of the explicitness of what is understood, it constitutes the interpretation" (p. 140). But this structure is not an original feature of the statement, for it precedes the statement. Indeed, "[t]he articulation of what is understood in the interpreting approach to beings guided by the 'something as something' lies *before* a thematic statement about it. The 'as' does not first show up in the statement, but is only first stated, *which is only possible because it is there as something to be stated*" (p. 140; second emphasis added). Such is the ontological reality of the *as*.

In section 33 of *Being and Time,* Heidegger draws a distinction between the existential-hermeneutical *as* (namely, the primordial "as" of circumspect interpretation that understands) and the apophantical *as* of the statement (p. 148). This distinction is, in reality, one between ontology and predication. The existential-hermeneutical *as* pertains to what something really is. In other words, naming something is not simply adding to its being; it is rather understanding something *as* something, that is, understanding something in its very being, as it really is or comes to be. Of course, the existential-hermeneutical *as* is a feature of language. But what does Heidegger mean by language? The best way to answer this question at this point is to say that Heidegger has two different concepts of language. One is a language built on the hermeneutical *as,* a language to which the *as* is constitutive; a solid language, one could say, which has the same structure as *Dasein* (being there). This is the language that is rooted in the *there*. The other is a language of the statement, which is built on the apophantical *as* and which is used in many ways; for instance, as an instrument of communication. The language of the poet, of poiesis, of production as poiesis, is of the first type, for it expresses the univocal ground of the *as*-structure. This can be seen from the special place that poetry occupies in the relation between art and truth. In fact, even though all art is essentially poetry, Heidegger gives priority to the linguistic work. In *The Origin of the Work of Art* he says, "Nevertheless, the linguistic work, the poem in the narrower sense, has a privileged position in the domain of the arts" (Heidegger 1971b: 73). But this requires that we have "the right concept of language" (ibid.), which is, precisely, that which pertains to the existential-hermeneutical *as*. Indeed, "language is not only and not primarily an audible and written expression of what is to be communicated" (ibid.). Rather, "language alone brings what is, as something that is [i.e., something as something], into the Open for the first time" (ibid.; brackets added). Language names beings for the first time, but this naming is not an external feature of the being of a being. Rather, it is constitutive of its nature and structure. To name is the same as to say, and saying is the essential activity of the poet: "Such saying is a projecting of the clearing, in which announcement is made of what it is that beings come into the Open *as*" (ibid.). I cannot call enough attention to the importance of this sentence. What it means is that, to paraphrase Heidegger, beings come into the Open *as* the beings they are *and yet* "are" not. The saying that is a projecting of the clearing is poetry itself. But what is poetry if not labor? It is perhaps the most supreme form of labor, to which of course belongs the all-consuming effort of remaining in touch with the language of the existential-hermeneutical *as*. Here, being and the "not" of being are both contained; the tension between what-is and what-could-be is more urgently felt, and the structure of utopia—we now read beyond Heidegger—is quite conspicuous, for the "nothing" appears as that which is *not yet,* and yet it is not nothing. But why should the possibility not be posited that all labor may acquire this same substantial form? Heidegger says, "Poetry is the saying of the unconcealedness of what is" (p. 74). But in its concealedness, namely, without and before the "un-" of manifestation, what is "is" not, or rather it is "not yet." Thus, in the truth of what is, there remains the "un-" of un-truth, namely, the concealed in the unconcealed: "In unconcealedness as truth (*alētheia*) there occurs also the other "un-" of a double restraint or refusal" (p. 60). This "not" actually occurs in the world: "Projective saying is saying which, in preparing the sayable, simultaneously brings the unsayable as such into a world" (p. 74).

I will argue that, for this ground (namely, the *as*-structure) to be rediscovered and for its potentialities to be actualized and practiced in everyday life, *poiesis* must become *praxis,* that is, production must become one moment of action, of human activity. This would be a modality not dissimilar from the solitude of labor that, by abandoning or destroying the categories of capital, is able to return to itself. We would then be able to move toward the concept of poetic (or creative) labor.

When I say that Heidegger does not distinguish enough between the power of *phusis* and the power of *praxis,* I mean to say that there is not, in Heidegger, an adequate conception of human agency and freedom. Furthermore, I would like to argue that this lack of clarity and adequacy comes from an acritical acceptance of assumptions that, as far as the question of production is concerned, derive from the realm of political economy, although Heidegger in no manner concerns himself with it. Heidegger says, "The artist is a *technites* not because he is also a craftsman, but because both the setting forth of works and the setting forth of equipment occur in a bringing forth and presenting that causes beings in the first place to come forward and be present in assuming an appearance. Yet all this happens in the midst of the being that grows out of its own accord, *phusis*" (Heidegger 1971b: 59). The artist is *also* a craftsman, and the craftsman often *also* an artist. The structure of the *also* constitutes the possibility of analogy resting upon something univocal. This does not mean that Van Gogh (whose painting of the peasant shoes Heidegger discusses in *The Origin of the Work of Art*) was also a shoemaker. Rather, it means that shoemaking and painting, as well as any other art and craft, are related by an *also* to a third something, which is included in both. This third something is nothing other than the transcendental structure discussed earlier, the *as*-structure. Thus, I find it difficult to understand why the doing of the artist "is determined and pervaded by the nature of creation, and indeed remains contained within that creating" (p. 60), whereas that of the craftsman is not and does not. Ultimately, the creative power is, for Heidegger, not the doing of the artist, but nature, *phusis,* a general and transcendent doing or bringing forth, notwithstanding the fact that a specific modality of bringing forth must be there.

I would then like to suggest that the difference between creating and making is untenable from the point of view of radical political ontology. This difference can be made only on the basis of three fundamental principles, whether they are made explicit or not. The first is a metaphysical principle (of the traditional kind of metaphysics, i.e., ontotheology) according to which a power, equal to the One, remains hidden behind world and social phenomena; the second is a political principle that regulates and legitimizes class distinction on the basis of the division of labor; and the third is the economic principle of the division of labor itself. By contrast, the abolition of the difference between creating and making does not entail the end of creating, or of what Heidegger calls *the extraordinary;* rather, it moves toward a different understanding of creating and of the extraordinary itself. More in the manner of Nietzsche: everything that is, is *eo ipso* extraordinary; more in the manner of Marx, living labor itself is a creative power, once it abandons and destroys the categories of capital (and its creative dimension would not be, of course, confined to the economic sphere). Both positions are also present, as we have seen, in Bloch's concept of concrete utopia.

In Heidegger instead, the difference between creation and making presents many problems. In his work on Nietzsche, for example, he says, "Art induces reality, which is in itself a shining, to shine most profoundly and supremely in scintillating transfiguration" (Heidegger 1979: 216). It then seems to be a question of degrees. Heidegger explains this order by speaking of the concept of truth. In *The Origin of the Work of Art,* he says that art really is the founding of truth, and truth particularly needs what is not ordinary. But this is highly problematic, and we shall see why.

When in *The Origin of the Work of Art* Heidegger speaks about truth, one may very well start suspecting that his discourse on art is a mask for something else. We have seen what the relationship between art and poetry is. Poetry constitutes the essence of art, but it is also what founds truth. Poetry then distinguishes "bringing forth" from "mere making" on account of its intimate relation with truth. The distinction then lies in the fact that in creation createdness is contained and preserved and, furthermore, truth is founded. Yet, this is not all. Heidegger also says, "Founding, however, is actual only in preserving" (ibid.). This preserving is history itself. The preserving that follows the happening of truth and its establishment in the open is what lets truth, not only originate and happen, but also persist in its being. Yet, what are the examples of this historical happening? Certainly, we have poetry as versification, and we also have the work of art in general. But Heidegger also says, "Another way in which truth occurs is the act that founds a political state" (p. 62). For Heidegger, again, this is not a question that belongs to the history of men and women in the world, but to the history of the truth of being, to the struggle between world and earth. The concept of founding is in itself "essentially historical" (p. 77). And founding, together with preserving, is also the true nature of art. With art as founding, "history either begins or starts over again" (ibid.). But what is history? Heidegger's answer is almost unintelligible: "History is the transporting of a people into its appointed task as entrance into that people's endowment" (ibid.). The subject of such "transporting" remains ineffable, and this people's "appointed task" is lost in the order of fatefulness. At the same time, the relation between art and history is a very intimate one: "Art is history in the essential sense that it grounds history" (ibid.). The act that founds a state is then an historical act as well as a work of art. But this founding, as well as the subsequent preserving, has nothing of the radicality of the truly historical praxis (of the history of men and women in the world), which may also tend toward the destruction of the state (in its actual and transcendental forms); nothing of the secular radicality which justifies the concept of the state as a work of art in the age of the Renaissance. Instead, both art and history are removed from the human plane and become demiurgical forces. For Heidegger, founding is an extraordinary act, but the extraordinary never becomes an earthly and worldly practice. He says, "Truth is never gathered from objects that are present and ordinary" (p. 71). Yet, the ordinary, the what-is, the empirically given is fashioned as such by deliberate political measures. Heidegger breaks the tension between what-is and what-could-be, the ordinary and the extraordinary by excluding the former almost as a nuisance from the realm of authenticity. Yet, an essentially different and truly radical way of thinking would look for the extraordinary in the ordinary, or, rather, it would challenge the distinction between the ordinary and the extraordinary—a metaphysical distinction at the direct service of a political ideology.

In his work on Nietzsche, Heidegger says, "Art is affirmation of the sensuous" (Heidegger 1979: 162). Furthermore, because of Nietzsche's alleged reversal of Platonism, "truth is the same as what art affirms, i.e., the sensuous" (p. 162). By looking at Nietzsche's philosophy as an inversion, rather than the abolition, of Platonism, Heidegger can reintroduce the nonsensuous alongside the sensuous in Nietzsche's thought and justify the distinction between art and mere reality. To be sure, the fundamental distinction is not between art and reality, but between art and truth. In fact, "[a]rt and truth are equally necessary for reality," but "[w]hile [they] are proper to the essence of reality with equal originality, they must diverge from one another and go counter to one another" (p. 217).

In *The Origin of the Work of Art*, Nietzsche's abolition of the distinction between appearance and truth is neutralized by "the appearance that artistic creation is also an activity of handicraft" (Heidegger 1971b: 64). Indeed, "the making of equipment is never directly the effecting of the happening of truth" (ibid.). Handicraft uses up the material that it employs. Art, by contrast, brings createdness into the work. Heidegger makes it clear that createdness has nothing to do with the name of a great artist. Yet, if this it not the case, then createdness can also express itself as handicraft. Without trying to solve the problem present in Heidegger's position, I would like to point it out for consideration. The point is this: even though one can accept that createdness expresses itself in the "simple 'factum est,'" and that this means, fundamentally, "that unconcealedness of what is has happened here," one cannot accept that "as this happening it happens here for the first time" (p. 65). In fact, each time is a first time. Even an infinite series of repetitions would simply be repetition of first times. Instead, what Heidegger does is ask again the fundamental metaphysical question, namely, the question as to whether "such a work *is* at all rather than is not" (p. 65). The existential "*that* it is" that answers the question cannot be—and Heidegger is aware of this—a prerogative of the work of art. However, what distinguishes the "*that* it is rather than is not" of the work of art from that of the equipment is that whereas the latter's "disappears in usefulness" (p. 65), the *that* of the former finds a unique place in its solitude. Thus, createdness "stands as the silent thrust into the Open of the 'that'" (p. 66).

The word "silent" in the above quotation is important, for silent is what remains concealed in *alētheia*. Silent is also the origin of language and poetry, and silent is the passage of man from thrownness to projection. Creation is the passing over of *Dasein*. Createdness is its having passed over and its remaining preserved in history. To be sure, all this is unusual and extraordinary. However, the point is not separating the usual from the unusual and the ordinary from the extraordinary; rather, the point is establishing the unusual and extraordinary nature of any moment. The most usual—what, for example, comes out of mere habit—is the most unusual. Heidegger knows that. Let us consider the peasant shoes, not as they are presented by Van Gogh's painting in their workly character, but, rather, in their equipmental character, that is, in their usefulness and, above all, their reliability. This time, Heidegger brings us from the work to the equipment by crossing the unstable bridge, often present in his work, hanging over an abyss. The name of this bridge is: *Und dennoch, and yet.* In the "undefined space" (*unbestimmter Raum*) we see "A pair of peasant shoes and nothing more. And yet—" (33). Heidegger ends the paragraph with the words "And yet" closed by a dash. The "and yet" modality, which opens up onto the undefined and neutral space, is another way of naming the configuration of neither/nor. "And yet" does not mean both/and; it does not, in other words, describe the positive but superficial changeability of positions, as if everything were really possible. Rather, "and yet" indicates that what-is is not necessarily all there is, that the "nothing more" that precedes it is *actually* a world of *hidden potentialities.* "Nothing more/and yet-": one assertion denies the other. It is, in fact, a way of calling into question the principle of noncontradiction and the entire foundation of positive science. "And yet" is an end that is also a beginning. Through it, the "nothing more" is posited as the "undefined space" in which language dwells and from which it speaks. In fact, Heidegger says, "This painting spoke" (p. 35). It is only through the artwork that we know "what shoes in truth are" (ibid.). However, what here comes to the fore is a world of labor and everyday life that grounds the painting. The "and yet" modality points to the double negation of refusal and dissembling, to an alternative but/also, to the what-could-be that is barely visible from one's stance in the what-is. In and through the "and yet," the work (in its workly character) and the equipment (in its equipmental character) relate to the same common and neutral structure. It is here that what is most fundamental in both comes to the fore. Thus, Heidegger says, "From the dark opening of the worn insides of the shoes the toilsome tread of the worker stares forth" (pp. 33–34). The "where" of truth is here too; and this is a "where" of labor. In fact, truth cannot be saved for special occasions, as it were. Truth is rather a question of everyday life. But Heidegger says, "Truth is never gathered from objects that are present and ordinary. Rather, the opening up of the Open, and the clearing of what is, happens only as the openness is projected, sketched out, that makes its advent in thrownness" (p. 71). The presentness and ordinariness of truth is a concept also introduced by Hölderlin, but, though sadly and nostalgically, to a different end. In one of the fragments, Hölderlin says, "but you have all forgotten that the first fruits belong/not to mortals, but to the gods./more common, more daily a thing/must the fruit become, before/it pertain to mortals" (Hölderlin 1984: 227). Here, the direction toward immanence is more clearly shown. After all, for Hölderlin, even the poets, though spiritual, must be worldly: "Poets, too, men of the spirit,/Must keep to the world" (p. 87). Certainly, there is in Hölderlin a strong dimension of the transcendent, and the idea of fate weakens an interpretation whereby the ordinary could be the same as the extraordinary. In "Patmos," he says, "For man does not govern, the power lies/with Fate, and the work of the immortals moves/Of its own pace, hasting towards completion" (p. 99)—a view very similar to that of Leopardi with respect to nature (see note 3). Yet, a few lines below he also says that nothing is too common: "For nothing is too lowly" (ibid.). Then, the view that Heidegger's critique of everydayness points toward the overcoming of its inauthentic and empty status cannot easily be accepted. What is important in his critique is the implied critique of positivism, which informs science as well as everyday life.[6] With respect to Hölderlin, we should also notice his view on the similarity between the work of gods and ours. In "Patmos," he says, "For the work of gods resembles ours" (p. 97). This resemblance, however, does not name the structure of analogy, but that of univocity: one and the same labor pertains to the gods and to humans. The relationship between the concepts of being and labor, of "pure" and social ontology is here evident. The resemblance mentioned by Hölderlin is due to time itself, for his next line reads: "The Almighty does not wish all things at once."

Thrownness and projection bring us to the center of poetic metaphysics, an immanent metaphysics, and that is, to poetry itself. To be sure, the important concept here is projection, that is, the time when the fruits of production will be proper to mortals, and not thrownness, that is, the fact of realizing that the first fruits are, in their essence, denied to them. Thrownness (a problematic concept) simply reinscribes poetic metaphysics within the general framework of ontotheology. Thrownness implies transcendence of some sort, whereas projection is an immanent standing out. Of course, poetry is projection, and thrownness should rather be understood as a finding oneself there, without any allusion to "a having been thrown." For, in reality, one does not come *from somewhere else.* Rather, the "where" of coming and being-there is equal to its "when," and this is the meaning of the *event.*

Heidegger's next step is to link art to poetry: "*All art,* as the letting happen of the advent of the truth of what is, is, as such, *essentially poetry.*" He rightly explains that "[i]t is due to art's poetic nature that, in the midst of what is, art breaks open an open place, in whose openness everything is other than usual" (p. 72). This is the place described by the "and yet" modality: what-is-not, or not-yet, what-could-be, in the midst of what-is. Thus, Heidegger is not wrong in saying that the poetic nature of art brings about the unusual, the "other than usual." But he does not explain why this should be limited to exceptional forms of human existence rather than become itself usual and proper to the human being—a real exception, as Benjamin would say. In fact, the "midst of what is" must be our everyday life, though that is a manifestation of a *phusis* to which we ourselves belong—but one in which we also determine things. Is this everyday life really usual? What indeed is usual, especially today that, to use Heidegger's own language, the worlding of the world shows nothing but the absence of the gods? What is usual if the irreducible, poetic power of men and women in the world is all subsumed under capital? That is, if the passage that *Dasein* itself is, is not a passage into an "illuminating projection" (Heidegger 1971b: 72), but one, without return, into a spiral of madness? Poetry, then,—and by poetry I mean production as poiesis inextricably linked to free praxis—is more than a mere letting truth happen. As Antonio Negri wrote in his work on Leopardi, "poetry breaks the surface of being, to build new and more universal being" (Negri 1987: 304). However, the constitution of this other being is not the creation within which alone createdness remains as opposed to everyday making and doing; nor is it a founding. Poetry does not found anything, but rather it unleashes ever-new forms of power—"power" as the potency painstakingly contained by the power of what-is, which, for its part, invents and founds the usual and the ordinary. Poetry represents a completely heterogeneous modality to that of the present, to everyday making and doing, production and action.

For Heidegger, "Truth happens only by establishing itself in the conflict and sphere opened up by truth itself" (p. 61). Truth, then, "unconcealment," comes to the fore by affirming itself in its own destiny out of (yet bound to) a double negation in which it is, "in truth," what is and "is" not. But indeed, what if, as we have suggested, the essence of poetry is not the founding of a truth that keeps concealed the double negation from which it arose? What if the power of poetry lies instead in the exploding of concealment itself, if the double negation is a battle to be fought in the open—a political battle, a struggle between enemies—and the "founding of truth" an enduring process which opens a new ground at each founding? What if, in other words, the forgetting of those fruits that do not belong to humans, of the ineffable being, is not a problem at all, but, rather, the path to the immanence of a human and earthly plane?

POETIC DOING - See p. 154

> It shows what is there and yet "is" not.
> —Heidegger

"... [O]ut/of exploited depths:/no word, no thing/and both with a single name" (Celan 1996: 66). These lines by Paul Celan capture the essential meaning of Heidegger's thinking the doing of language. It is that *single name,* that is, language, being—really, the name of univocity—which comes to the fore at the point where words break off. This single name is the saying that is a projecting of the clearing. It is the saying of the poet in which the unsayable also comes to the fore. It is the single and unspoken poem of every great poet. But it is also the *new common language* sought by Debord.

I will introduce the discussion of Heidegger's essay on the essence of language (*The Nature of Language*) with some preparatory remarks on other works by Heidegger, particularly *Hölderlin and the Essence of Poetry* and *What Are Poets For?*

We have seen that Heidegger's work revolves on one main question: the question of being. At the outset of *Being and Time,* published in 1927, Heidegger says that today the question of being has been forgotten. Obviously, "today" does not mean 1927. Rather, "today" names the time of forgetfulness. The time of the forgetfulness of being, the time of its concealment, is the time of the history of western metaphysics—a history that goes from Plato to Nietzsche. For Heidegger, Nietzsche brings metaphysics to completion. However, this does not mean that, after Nietzsche, there will no longer be any metaphysics. In other words, even after Nietzsche, the grounding question of philosophy, the question about being as such, the question about the region where being and truth stand together, is, according to Heidegger still not asked. As we shall see later, this question is very much related to the question of the essence of language. Heidegger calls into question the "where" of the standing together of being and truth, as well as the "how" of their being united in essence and yet foreign to one another; a "where" and a "how" to which the essay on the essence of language answers with the metaphor of a neighborhood in which, this time, language and thinking dwell.

It is important to note that the grounding question does not reach the ground. It does not because the grounding itself is groundless. The grounding, which the projecting of the clearing is, grounds itself as an ungrounded ground. In *The Origin of the Work of Art* we read: "the ground is first grounded as the bearing ground" (1971b: 76). This groundless ground is equal to the abyss. This is the nothing that remains beyond the *what* of all metaphysical questioning. And this is why, for Heidegger, even positivism, the science of the *positum*—which for its founder, August Comte, is the absolute and positive overcoming of metaphysics—remains intrinsically metaphysical. The question that must now be asked is then one that leaves nothing besides, "not even nothingness" (Heidegger 1979: 68).

Yet, how can one overcome metaphysics and thus ask again the question of being? For Heidegger this is accomplished through a descent into the *nearness of the nearest*—a figure with Taoist overtones, which constitutes the open region where truth as *alētheia* and being, thinking and language are neighbors. It constitutes the *ēthos,* namely, according to Heidegger's reading of Heraclitus fragment (Fragment 119): *ēthos anthrōpōi daimōn:* "Man dwells, as far as he is man, in the nearness of god," the originary place in which man himself dwells (Heidegger 1977: 233). This means that man dwells in the same neighborhood, but he dwells there in such a way that his dwelling is characterized by *brokenness.* Man is, indeed, the being who is broken. The human condition is one in which something, perhaps being itself, breaks off, and yet, at the same time, it breaks onto the open region of its own manifestation. Man is for Heidegger *Da-sein,* being-there, a temporal, historical being defined and sustained by language. Language is "the house of the truth of Being" (p. 199), but its essence is denied to any question which does not move toward a grounding of itself but remains, metaphysically, on this side of nothing. Asking the grounding question would not seem to be a very difficult task, for, as Heidegger says,

"Being is the nearest." However, he adds, "the near remains farthest from man" (p. 210), and this means that man is condemned to blindness and forgetfulness. This until the descent into the nearness of being can be accomplished.

In a 1968 lecture called "Time and Being," Heidegger says that "our task is to cease all overcoming, and leave metaphysics to itself" (1972: 24). And in "The End of Philosophy and the Task of Thinking" of 1966, he calls for a thinking which is less than philosophy (Heidegger 1972). This thinking is poetic thinking. There is here a move (or an attempt to a move) from vulgar metaphysics to poetic metaphysics.

The task of thinking as poetry, or poetry as thinking, is already clearly present in *Hölderlin and the Essence of Poetry* of 1936. In this essay, Heidegger discusses five pointers, that is, five quotes from Hölderlin, whom he calls "the poet of the poet."

1. Writing poetry: "That most innocent of all occupations."
2. "Therefore has language, most dangerous of possessions, been given to man... so that he may affirm what he is..."
3. "Much has man learnt.
   Many of the heavenly ones has he named,
   Since we have been a conversation
   And have been able to hear from one another."
4. "But that which remains, is established by the poets."
5. "Full of merits, and yet poetically, dwells
   Man on this earth."

The first pointer, says Heidegger, defines poetry as *play:* "This play thus avoids the seriousness of decisions, which always in one way or another create guilt" (Heidegger 1968: 273). However, the play that avoids the seriousness of decisions does not endanger deciding as separating, as cutting oneself off, as being broken and breaking at the same time. For this is what language does. To decide is to be resolute, and this is man's disposition when, through language, he affirms himself. Indeed, as Heidegger says, "The affirmation of human existence and hence its essential consummation occurs through the freedom of decision" (p. 274).

There cannot be freedom of decision without language. The essence of language is to be seen in the fact that language is not a tool, but the condition for "the possibility of standing in the openness of the existent" (p. 276). It is through language that the descent into the nearness of the nearest is made possible. Language makes the world. This is what it means for Heidegger to speak of poetic metaphysics. He says, "Only where there is language, is there world..." (ibid.). This statement prepares the ground for an understanding of the line by Stefan George Heidegger discusses in *The Nature of Language:* "Where word breaks off no thing may be."

Language becomes actual in conversation. This happens because in conversation the being of man (*Da-sein*) becomes actual. But Da-sein is grounded in language. Conversation, however, is not to be understood as the idle talk of the "they," which Heidegger analyzes in *Being and Time*. In fact, conversation is no idle talk at all. It is not the talk in which there is no essential hearing. Rather, conversation is the ability to speak *and* hear (p. 278). But hearing presupposes silence. Conversation is the time and place of silence in which language becomes essential and thus the possibility of undergoing an experience with language (explored by Heidegger in *The Nature of Language*) becomes possible.

Then Heidegger asks the question, "Since when have we been a conversation?" (p. 278). And the answer is: since time arose; namely, since man placed himself into the open region in which permanence and change both belong (p. 279); which for Heidegger means since Parmenides and Heraclitus. This is the time in which the gods acquire a name and, at the same time, claim us. Hence, it is the time in which a decision must be made "as to whether we are to yield ourselves to the gods or withhold ourselves from them" (p. 280).

It is through this decision (pointer 4) that the establishing of that which remains occurs. This establishing is poetic creation: making as *poiesis*. This is where Heidegger and Hölderlin are very close to Vico, who also says that the poets are the true founders of social being.

The poetic dwelling (pointer 5), which characterizes the human condition through and by the "and yet" modality which makes man's merits tremble, is nothing but the presence of man in the nearness of the nearest, in the proximity of being itself. It is then the poet who, by means of an innocent and yet most dangerous occupation, lays down the foundations that sustain history and the world. The poet occupies for Heidegger the intermediate position *between* men and the gods. And poetry itself occurs according to the innocent and most dangerous modality of neither/nor. Indeed, poetry determines a new time: "the time of the gods that have fled *and* of the god that is coming" (p. 289). But this is a destitute time, "because it lies under a double lack and a double NOT: the No-more of the gods that have fled and the Not-yet of the god that is coming" (ibid.). The poet, this messenger of the gods, is exposed to one of the greatest conceivable dangers, for, as Heidegger says in *What Are Poets For?*, the poet has to reach—beyond metaphysics—into the abyss, find out what the danger is, and show it to the mortals. The poet, Heidegger says, is exposed to divine lightning (p. 284).

What Are Poets For? was published in 1950, but it was delivered as a lecture in 1946. The title comes from a poem by Hölderlin: "... and what are poets for in a destitute time?" (*Bread and Wine*). This essay, which deals particularly with the poetry of Rilke, can be seen as a continuation of *Hölderlin and the Essence of Poetry*. In *What Are Poets For?* Heidegger says that the time—again, the time of the concealment of the truth of being, namely, the history of metaphysics—is destitute because of "the god's failure to arrive" (1971b: 91). This failure implies the withholding of the ground that grounds and sustains the world. Because of this, the world and the age hang over the abyss. Now, for Heidegger, the only hope to salvation is that the world "turns away from the abyss" (p. 92), but it must do so in a fundamental and radical way.[7]

However, this turn requires that the abyss of the world, the nothing metaphysics hypostatizes, "be experienced and endured" (ibid.). And for this, "it is necessary that there be those who reach into the abyss" (ibid.). These are the poets, whom Heidegger, with Hölderlin, sees as the most mortal among mortals, for they are those who are closer to the abyss and more exposed to the danger. But because the poets can reach *sooner* into the abyss, it is their responsibility not to decline the task.

Fundamentally, the poets are the most mortal because they are *the most daring*. And they are the most daring because they dare language (p. 132), which is for Heidegger the house of the truth of being and the grounding power of the world. The act of daring language plunges the poet into the abyss in which the danger is. We now fully understand how this innocent occupation is also the most dangerous of possessions. Indeed, the saying or singing of the poet, his esthetic-ontological occupation or disposition is immediately ethical, for the poet is there to appropriate time as language and as being and consequently turn the world away from the abyss. The world is in need of salvation because there is a danger. This danger is, not simply technology, but the essence of technology, namely, "the threat that assaults man's nature in his relation to Being itself, and not in accidental perils" (p. 117). Technology, in fact, in its essence, dissolves the relation of man to being by creating the illusion that the world is under control, that being itself is under control, and that everything—as God is dead—is actually possible.

The salvation cannot come from technology, but "from where the danger is," namely, "from where there is a turn with mortals in their nature" (p. 118). This turn in the nature of mortals occurs precisely at the site of the double NOT, namely, "where all ground breaks off" (p. 119). This is also the site in which thinking as thinking becomes possible. And here Heidegger uses Hölderlin's lines: "But where there is danger, there grows/also what saves" (p. 118). This is strikingly similar to Marx's view according to which, in the age of machinery and real subsumption, a radical change cannot come from technology, from a change in the technical aspect of production, but from politics. This is, however, a politics that implies a radically new way of thinking and acting, of theory and practice. It is a politics that operates at the ontological level of the double not, the neither/nor, in which the neutrality of the act, that is, its potentiality, can redirect the act itself toward a new task and a new definition of what it means to be human—and thus toward the dissolution of itself as politics. This is so with Marx, too, and that is the meaning of his *critique* of political economy, the ground breaks off showing the abyss on which the whole logic of capital rests. It is the abyss of labor—the groundless grounding of the social world.

For Heidegger, the ground that breaks off is language, for language is the grounding power of the world. Yet the link between language and labor is self-evident, for language must not be here understood merely as predication, but as the *as* constitutive of the world: "Only where there is language, is there world…" (Heidegger 1968: 276). I can then proceed to a discussion of Heidegger's first lecture of *The Nature of Language,* which is mainly built on the following lines by Stefan George: "So I renounced and sadly see: / Where word breaks off no thing may be."

The Nature of Language consists of three lectures given by Heidegger between 1957 and 1958 and published in essay form in 1959. My discussion is limited to the first lecture. The essay as a whole represents an exploration in the "possibility of undergoing an experience with language" (1971a: 57). Heidegger calls attention to the word "possibility," for this exploration or attempt remains for him at a preparatory stage (p. 70).

Heidegger starts the essay by highlighting the ambiguity of our relationship with language. As in our relationship with being, we are at the same time close to and far from it. Our experience with language, as well as our relation to being, is not—Heidegger says—"of our own making" (p. 57). We do not choose language; the opposite is the case. However, the experience with language will not occur if we choose the channels of "analytic" philosophy, that is, the channels of technology, metaphysics, and positivism. As Heidegger says, this scientific enterprise has its own validity, but it will not bring us face to face with language. Indeed, "[i]n experiences which we undergo *with* language, language itself brings itself to language" (p. 59). Language speaks itself as language not when, for instance, the solution to a problem is enunciated in a proposition, but, rather, when the word looked for does not come to us; in other words, language speaks itself as language when there is a crisis. In keeping with the etymology of the Greek *krisis,* a crisis occurs, when something breaks off, when there is a division, a separation, at the time of a struggle; but this is also the time when a decision must be made, the time for a resolution which requires that something be questioned, explored and interpreted. This is when critical thinking begins. In this case, language "distantly and fleetingly" touches us "with its essential being" (ibid.).

Looking or waiting for the word capable of speaking that which "has never yet been spoken" (ibid.) defines the situation of the poet. With the poet, language is immediately poetry, that is, language that speaks itself essentially. Here we recognize the language of the existential-hermeneutical *as* which counters the language of the apophantical *as* of the statement, of which Heidegger spoke in *Being and Time.* Language comes to the poet who is waiting and singing. Thus Heidegger chooses a poem that he calls "almost songlike" (p. 60): Stefan George's "The Word." In this poem, the poet is given a gift by the goddess of fate, the norn. It is this gift that prepares the ground for the poet's sad (and yet joyful) renunciation, which is the condition for entering into the openness of language itself, the condition for reaching the neither/nor of its univocal being.

Heidegger asks whether in a poem there is thinking too. And he answers: yes, "and indeed thinking without science, without philosophy" (p. 61). This new or different thinking requires that we listen to language, which is the "there" where both being and truth belong, or the "there" where being *in truth* belongs. This *in truth* has the structure of concealment where something is but at the same time "is" not, can be but can also not be. In George's poem, the listening occurs through renunciation, and that means, through a withdrawal. The colon that comes before the last line is interpreted by Heidegger as the limit beyond which there is *not* nothing, as metaphysics would have it, but the "relation of word to thing" (p. 66). This relation is not a mere connection between the thing and the word but the word itself. In *Being and Time,* Heidegger already explained that word, *logos,* is also *relation* (1996: 30). But this is only, as it were, its final meaning. In fact, originally, this relation that the word itself is, is nothing but the *as*-structure.

But how does the renunciation occur? It occurs when and because something has transformed the poet's relation to the word, and thus to the world (Heidegger 1971a: 67, 73). The poet has undergone an experience with language. "To experience is to go along a way. The way leads through a landscape. The poet's land belongs to that landscape, as does the dwelling of the twilit norn, ancient goddess of fate. She dwells on the strand, the edge of the poetic land which is itself a boundary, a march" (p. 67). This march, or border region, is the neighborhood in which thinking and poetry belong. It is the "poetic site" (*der Ort des Gedichtes*) of which Heidegger speaks in *Language in the Poem* (Heidegger 1959: 38).

But in what sense can thinking and poetry be said to dwell in the same region or neighborhood? In order to answer this question we need a different understanding of thinking—different from the one that usually prevails: thinking as representation, abstraction, calculation, and even conceptualization.[8] Indeed, Heidegger says, "[t]hinking is not a means to gain knowledge" (1971a: 70). And he continues with a powerful metaphor: "Thinking cuts furrows into the soil of Being" (ibid.). The meaning of this metaphor is that thinking *does* something. The fact that this doing is the doing of labor is not coincidental or inessential. That the metaphor employed by Heidegger relates to work in the fields only stresses the relationship between thinking (and language) with a labor which is not productive in the capitalist sense, but, rather, productive of use-values, constitutive of a world where everyday life becomes possible. Thinking does not create the conditions for acting and action, as it would be in a traditional way of understanding theory and practice as belonging in two separate domains. Heidegger is very clear on this point, and his *Letter on Humanism* he says, "Thinking does not become action only because some effect issues from it or because it is applied. *Thinking acts insofar as it thinks*" (1977: 193; emphasis added). However, this does not imply, for Heidegger, the notion of German Idealism according to which thinking as knowing is mind thinking itself. Rather, Heidegger's metaphor is such that thinking is immediately labor, and the very concrete image he uses—plowing the fields—should be given some consideration. The word used by Heidegger in German is *ziehen,* which is not "cut" in a general sense but "cut" in the sense of digging a ditch.[9] Acting directly on the soil of being, thinking changes it. The furrows do not belong to that soil, as it were, *a priori.* They are the product of the labor of thinking. However, one should not see being as permanent and immutable.

Rather, being constantly changes, and the changes brought about into it by thinking are traces of permanence. Soon the furrows will disappear, they will be covered up again, and the need will arise for new labor. Thus thinking works without rest, and yet it rests, for it draws its power from waiting and listening.

As Heidegger says, "... the authentic attitude of thinking is not a putting of questions—rather, it is a listening to [the grant,][10] the promise of what is to be put in question" (1971a: 71). "Promise" in English, because of its Latin origin, is to be understood as what is produced for, what is allowed to grow, but it is also related to the idea of a gift. The German *Zusage* is immediately related to language, to what is spoken before or for, to what comes to the word. In this sense, the word that constitutes the question comes by itself; it is a self-showing word.

Heidegger analyzes and criticizes the title of his own essay: not "The Nature of Language," but "The Nature?—of Language?" can serve as a guide on the way to language. Thus, the question applies to both language and its essential being—a guiding question, still about the being of a being, which says that the phrase "the nature of language" still has a metaphysical configuration and significance.

Here Heidegger goes back to the problem of the grounding question, the ultimate question of all thinking: thinking fundamentally remains "the search for the first and ultimate grounds" (p. 71). Insofar as this is true, thinking remains a questioning, although, as we have seen, the main character of such questioning is not putting questions, but listening to the question that comes by itself and speaking back to it in essential conversation. The question comes from language when language speaks itself. When this occurs, then, "the being of language becomes the language of being" (p. 72). Here the word "being" is not *Sein,* but *Wesen,* that is, essence as essential being. This may appear problematic, but the truth is that, for Heidegger, language does not emanate from being, as it would be if he spoke of the language *of* being (*Sein*). Granted that this may be somewhat confusing, it can be said that there is no distinction between language and being (*Sein*); that, in other words, what they *in truth* are—their *Wesen*—is one and the same. We have seen that they have a single name. This single name is what Heidegger means by "einem einzigen Gedicht" ("one single poetic statement") out of which every great poet poetizes (1959: 37; 1971a: 160). Heidegger himself points out that even this inversion, "the being of language/the language of being," remains problematic and that it may only serve as a guide word on the way to language. Thus the language of being only means the language that speaks itself essentially, that is, the language of the existential-hermeneutical *as,* in which something *can be* stated *as* something. But what this language says cannot be heard if the question of being (*Sein*) remains forgotten and being itself concealed. For this, there are poets. Through renunciation, the poet accepts the breaking off of the word and the descent into the nearness of being. Yet, this breaking off is also, in turn, a breaking up and a breaking through—a breaking onto a new ground. In the last part of his essay, which I have not discussed here, Heidegger says,

"To break up here means that the sounding word returns into soundlessness, back to whence it was granted: into the ringing of stillness which, as Saying, moves the regions of the world's fourfold into their nearness" (1971a: 108). This means that the apophantical *as* of predication, to which the poem also in part belongs, returns completely into the existential-hermeneutical *as* of possibility and meaning. And Heidegger closes his essay with the following sentence: "This breaking up of the word is the true step back on[to] the way of thinking" (p. 108; brackets added).

In this passage to thinking, which is the opening up of a venue of reconciliation within the sensuous (when understood according to a philosophy of immanence), the fundamental question of the relationship between art and labor can be formulated and worked out. We have here a classic position with respect to art: the Hegelian position, which posits the truth of the work of art in the "passage through the mind" (Hegel 1993: 44). For Hegel, in artistic production there is identity of the sensuous and the spiritual. Yet, this identity is soon broken by a departure from the sensuous, although the departure is never total: "Art, by means of its representations, while remaining within the sensuous sphere, delivers man at the same time from the power of sensuousness" (p. 54). Even with Hegel, and perhaps more so with him than with Heidegger's passage through language, we still ultimately remain within the sphere of immanence. The point is to understand what kind of immanence it is.

CREATIVE LABOR AS SOCIAL LABOR

The beginning of the end of art points to art's becoming a common concept. Art is no longer relegated beyond the sphere of production proper, in that space of the social in which we (or rather some of us) rest from labor, a space from which labor is in fact excluded, or, rather, included only for the purpose of preparing and dismantling the artistic scene. On the contrary, as a common concept, art, creative labor, becomes social labor. The end of the regime of productive labor as productive of capital does not erase the fundamental structure (concept and practice) of production as such. Production is now artistic production, and it is the result of creative labor. This structure encompasses the whole spectrum of the social, it subsumes society within itself, rather than being subsumed by society as one of its epiphenomenal moments. This is what Theodor Adorno means when, toward the end of his *Aesthetic Theory*, he says, "The immanence of society in the artworks is the essential social relation of art, not the immanence of art in society" (Adorno 1997: 232). Of course, under the regime of capital, the first type of immanence is only a reflection, not always visible in a triumphant society of business and noise, of deliberate ignorance and thoughtlessness, the idiotic society that sees in the esthetic mode a weakening of the aggressive determination deemed necessary for the construction of a solid world, a "real" reality.

This first type of immanence, which appears as a reflection and an epiphenomenal moment, is held in check in many ways: it is institutionalized and normalized (as is the case with museums) or banned (as is the case with graffiti). Society and art can then be understood only as the two terms of a relationship of antagonism, which is however reduced, with systematic consistency, to the second type of immanence mentioned by Adorno: that of art in society. Yet, the immanence of society in the artwork cannot stay at the level of reflection; its meaning is not that the artwork speaks about society, but that the artwork, the result of creative or artistic labor, is constitutive of society, for, as Adorno says, "artistic labor is social labor" (p. 236). What returns in the artworks, as "mere forms divested of their facticity" (ibid.) and thus as forms of abstract labor is, for Adorno, both the social forces of production and the relations of production. The direction of a society, its specific formation, will say whether this abstract labor is merely the quantitative expression of labor to be used for the process of creation and valorization, or whether it will be, at a level which is higher than mere abstraction, the neutral form of labor, its neither/nor, incessantly creating and renewing a social ontology of plenitude. Not the spiral movement that drives capital to madness, but the very substance of the good life for everybody, where scarcity is overcome. With the overcoming of scarcity, the world of the spirit, and the work of the spirit, will also run throughout the plane of immanence and finitude.

The two types of immanence discussed here are to be understood in relation to the concepts of the empirical and the transcendental and of their relationship. The immanence of art in society is the result of the reduction of reality to what-is, the empirically given, the datum, without reference to what makes it possible, to potentiality. By contrast, the immanence of society in art points to what-could-be, the transcendental and neutral, the potential. However, this does not recreate the split, typical of traditional metaphysics, between the potential and the real, or one would lose immanence itself. At the outset of his *Aesthetic Theory,* Adorno, referring to Kant, stresses the irrevocable status of art's autonomy with respect to the empirical world. However, this again does not have to be understood as positing the existence of two different spheres, irreducible to one another, for art is of this world, or rather it is this world's constitutive power. Thus Adorno says, "Art is autonomous and it is not; without what is heterogeneous to it [i.e., the empirical world], its autonomy eludes it" (p. 6; brackets added). Art is not a social phenomenon, but the grounding of all social phenomena. This is certainly not the case under the regime of capital, where the terms of the fundamental immanent relation described here are upset and overturned. Yet it is so when one looks at art, esthetics, from the point of view of social ontology, and equates it with ontology. In this sense, it is not simply the case that, as Adorno says, art is "defined by its relation to what it is not" (p. 3). The empirical world is not necessarily only that through which art *shines,* the medium whereby art is also communicated, and art does not necessarily "achieve a heightened order of existence" (p. 4) by separating itself from empirical reality. This, which is curiously similar to some of Heidegger's propositions, is a correct description of the role of art in our society, yet the question has to do with the potentials of art in a society in which the empirical world itself is not the negation of creativeness, or, rather, with art as potentiality *tout court*. For Adorno, "it is precisely as artifacts, as products of social labor, that [artworks] also communicate with the empirical that they reject and from which they draw their content" (p. 5; brackets added). And he continues: "Art negates the categorial determinations stamped on the empirical world and yet harbors what is empirically existing in its own substance" (ibid.). If this is really how things stand, our thesis that art could become a common concept and productive labor become creative labor would be mistaken. However, this would be the same as saying that the split between art and empirical reality, artistic production and mere production is not the function of a given social formation, of specific economic interests, of a deliberate political will, but that it is inscribed in the order of metaphysics, and thus cannot change. Adorno is aware of the fact that the ontology of productive labor is the same as that of creative labor, and thus of the fundamental sameness between artistic production and mere production. He says, "The aesthetic force of production is the same as that of productive labor and has the same teleology..." (ibid.). However, this truth should not simply be noted coincidentally and as a matter of analogy: it is rather what should be called into question and become the central question. It is precisely here that our distinction between productive labor as productive of capital and creative labor (or labor which is neither productive nor unproductive) works. Although Adorno nears our position when he says that art "gives the lie to production for production's sake and opts for a form of praxis beyond the spell of labor" (p. 12), he still does not recognize that, beyond labor, labor will be found once again, as we have seen when discussing Bloch.

The question of the destruction or deestheticization of art [*Entkunstung*], central to Adorno's notion of the culture industry, certainly moves toward the correct direction in the critique of modern, capitalist society (cf. Adorno 1997: 16, 368). However, what the new and better praxis constituted by art itself can offer is not a world without labor, but one in which the functions of art and labor become identical. It is in this sense that art can really take on the function and task attributed to it by Adorno, of being the "social antithesis of society" (p. 8), not simply the "plenipotentiary of a better praxis" but also the "critique of praxis" (p. 12). This requires a new sense of totality, a new social ontology capable of eliminating the dualism between what is art and what is not art. In this sense, the destruction of art, a direct consequence of art's declaration of independence according to Debord, also lays out the groundwork for the return of art to itself, and this happens in the same way in which labor also returns to itself. Here we see the conditions for art's and labor's becoming common concepts, or rather one and the same common concept, united as they are in the sameness of *poiesis* and *praxis,* or rather in their constant passing over into each other. Certainly, from the point of view of the present, art appears precisely in the terms in which Adorno describes it: "art fragments on one hand into a reified, hardened cultural possession and on the other into a source of pleasure that the customer pockets and that for the most part has little to do with the object itself" (p. 15). Yet, it is this same present age which also produces spaces of expression that challenge the notion that there is no outside from the subsumption of all labor and all art under capital, no escape from reification. Thus, the resurgence of graffiti art in New York City, as anyone can notice by riding the subway, is certainly a visible sign of what otherwise remains invisible, *outside* the forms and spaces of visibility allowed by the institutions. It is in fact writing, intelligence, beauty, the power of transformation that is under attack by the institutions. But this comes down to attacking labor, that is labor power in act, or, rather, the subjective power of labor as the potentiality of doing and not doing, before it is constructed as a commodity and thus lost to its owner. For this is what the institutions mostly fear, that some labor remains unbridled, constructed neither as productive nor as unproductive; then the immediate sameness of labor and art becomes evident, for this labor cannot be other than creative labor (or destructive labor, to be sure; but the two concepts are really identical). We made reference to graffiti art, not to any pretentious way of creating art as art, or as fine art. For instance, the reference was not to the news as of March 25, 2004, reporting the painting in red of an iceberg in Greenland by the Chilean-born Danish artist Marco Evaristti. Apparently, the artist said: "We all have a need to decorate Mother Nature because it belongs to all us. This is my iceberg, it belongs to me." This is silly, irresponsible, and it goes in the direction of that self-destruction of art, which begins with its aspiration to constitute a separate domain within the existing social order. This is an example of the second type of immanence, the immanence of art in society, criticized by Adorno. What Evaristti did and said is similar to those political theorists who want to reform capital by holding on to it, who want to create spaces for justice, democracy, and peace without wanting to eliminate the very conditions that necessarily generate injustice, social control, and war. By contrast, the practice of graffiti, often referred to as vandalism, points toward the immanence of society in art, for here the destructive/creative power takes society by surprise and threatens its order as that which always exceeds it. A graffiti artist will not say: This is my railway wall; it belongs to me. Nor is it a metaphysical truth that we all have a need to decorate "Mother Nature"; and only a person who poses as an artist, but is not an artist, can make such a vacuous statement. Nor can one tolerate today such a thoughtless use of the concept of Mother Nature, in itself a dubious concept, for, as Leopardi says, nature is a mother but also a wicked stepmother.[11] Graffiti art, with its principle of the abstract in/on the concrete (with respect to language in particular),[12] represents an undeniable, though perhaps confused, search for the universal. The universal is also what abstract art proper seeks to point out: the universal as possibility. In this sense, the art of Piot Mondrian, as well as of the whole group around De Stijl, is an essential paradigm. Against the distortion of the object practiced by artists such as Duchamp and Picasso, Mondrian (as well as Malevich) seeks the neutralization of the object through geometrical abstraction. For Donald Kuspit, Mondrian's writing "strongly resembles that of Spinoza's *Ethics* and, together with his painting, has the same ethical purpose: to free the self from human bondage" (Kuspit 1993: 45). This ethical purpose, which is universal in character and scope, centers on the possibility of *understanding,* and that means, first and foremost, understanding the emotions. This understanding, which occurs through the adoption of a geometrical method, is not merely intellectual and abstract, but ethical and ontological. The method goes from the abstract to the concrete, or from the universal to the individual. In this sense, it is similar to the method chosen by Marx in the introduction to the *Grundrisse.* Mondrian himself says, "The artist of the future will not have to follow the path of gradual liberation from natural form and colour: the way has been cleared for him; the mode of expression is ready; he has only to perfect it. *Line and colour as plastic means in themselves* (i.e. free from particular meaning), are at his command so that he can express the universal determinately... *humanity will no longer move from individual to universal, but from the universal to the individual through which it can be realized*" (in Kuspit 1993: 145). For Kuspit the "resemblances between Spinoza's and Mondrian's philosophies are... so many that one has to assume that Mondrian's geometrical painting is an attempt to demonstrate Spinoza's *Ethics,* or at least its geometrical spirit, in visual terms" (p. 47). By freeing oneself of the natural, outward object, one reaches the inward universal, which radically transforms the self and its world. By way of interpreting and elaborating on Kuspit, we can say that the plane of inwardness and universality is the ontological plane of potentiality, the occurrence of all contraction of being in *whatever this.* To simply analyze the "this" in its thingly occurrence is to miss its contingent causation at the level of potentiality, and thus to miss its true ontological structure. In fact, the actual "this" is not merely what we concretely see, but the determined universal which is contracted as such. By distorting the object, one does not go beyond the confused intuition proper to the initial, immediate experience of the concrete, but one only augments that confusion. The true and real "this" is the potential which *becomes* actual, not something different from it—a potential which could also not become. It is at the level of inwardness and universality that we can have a clearer intuition of its structure, and perhaps an adequate grasping of it. In this sense, the geometrical method becomes the method of ontology: geometry becomes ontology. Kuspit says, "Mondrian's compositions are not concerned with the properties of space and of objects in space, as geometry classically is, but with geometry in the broader sense, as a means of abstractly articulating the universal, affording instant intuition of its primordiality" (p. 48). The *metron* (measure) by which his paintings are "measured" is a philosophical, not a geometrical concept. Again, Kuspit says, "Mondrian does not apply geometry to the world of objects in space, but invents a geometrical world in which there are no objects. This abstract world represents the universal within for him" (ibid.). This is not a geometry of exact and objective measures, nor is it a distortion, but rather a creative geometry which "differentiates wholeness, or articulates a differentiated whole" (p. 49). It is then the creation of difference itself, which turns individuality into universality: the constitution of a new political ontology. Indeed, the whole project of De Stijl (which in Dutch means "The Style"), of which Mondrian was part, was "an essential ordering of structure which would function as a sign for an ethical view of society. The single element, perceived as separate, and the configuration of elements, perceived as a whole, were intended to symbolize the relationship between the individual and the collective (or universal)" (Overy 1991: 8).

To go back to Adorno, it is of course necessary to say that we are in agreement with his critique of the destruction of art, of its reification, and of the making of the culture industry. The disagreement only comes in when we stress the necessity, absent in Adorno, of bridging the gap between art and labor, art and mere empirical reality. This bridging is not the awkward attempt at fixing the relation of elements that do not in fact match but, rather, the result of revolutionary praxis itself, and that means of the destruction of the old relations and the creation of new ones. This process of destruction and creation cannot, however, happen at the level of the empirical only; it has to reach, beyond the empirical, into the transcendental level of neutrality, which makes the empirical possible. In an interesting but difficult remark, Adorno says, "If art were to free itself from the once perceived illusion of duration, were to internalize its own transience in sympathy with the ephemeral life, it would approximate an idea of truth conceived not as something abstractly enduring but in consciousness of its temporal essence" (Adorno 1997: 28–29). A Nietzschean moment—but it is not clear where Adorno stands in relation to this. The idea of truth that art would thus approximate is the truth of labor, living labor, which endures not as a state, but as a process. And this is not so simply because the product of labor disappears in usefulness, as Heidegger says, but, rather, because, as Adorno holds, the ephemeral life would concretely reveal the essence of time. The fact that labor thus endures is a truth that goes from Heraclitus and Parmenides to Marx, for labor is nothing but the conscious dimension of becoming and being. What changes from becoming to being, understood in the regime of capital as the antagonism between labor and capital, is in reality the everlasting process of awakening and upsetting what rests: all situations and states. This endures. Here labor finds its strength: in the transhistorical nature of its movement, in its permanence as the most common concept, a permanence that it finds in its solitude. It is here that art nears labor, as well as the essence of time not abstractly understood.

The question is not placing art within the terrain of utopia as if art could bring about a different world by merely being the determinate negation of what is, for, as we have seen, there is no way to get a real, concrete grasp of what-is without also holding fast to what-could-be; but what-could-be is not utopian in the usually negative meaning given to this word. It is rather the too often overlooked presence of the potential, and it is at that level that the work of restructuring society must be done. When art is also thus understood, that is, as operating at the level of potentiality, at the same level of the neutrality of labor, then art is not at all what negates empirical reality *tout court,* but rather what negates *this mode* of the empirical, *this* essential difference, to bring about a radically new vision of the empirical; for how could the empirical cease to exist? When the empirical does not block the view of the nonempirical, when it is not the mere *positum,* which is often mistaken for reality as a whole, then the empirical and the nonempirical, the transcendental, what is neutral to the this or that of occurrence, what-is and what-could-be do not constitute a dualist structure of elements which are irreducible to one another, but the unity of experience. As Adorno says, art is and is not in and of the empirical world. It is then obvious that art cannot be the negation of the empirical, but its transfiguration; the synthetic figure of a passage. If utopia is understood as the "negation of what exists" and as what remains "obedient to it" at the same time (p. 32), it does not go to the roots of things, it does not enter the realm of what-could-be, the real structure of a concrete utopia. The argument is similar to the one we find in the *Economic and Philosophical Manuscripts* regarding the distinction between crude communism and genuine communism. There, too, the former is a mere negation of what exists, but the latter entails a radical transformation of what-is as well as of what-could-be. The fact that art might end by touching on the real structure of utopia is not a great loss, for, as we have seen, this end is also the beginning of art as a common concept and the coming of a mode of production no longer at odds with the fundamental human disposition toward creativeness. If all life is estheticized, art will no longer be a supplement, a matter of compensation; the forms and spaces of everyday life, the diversity of labor, the many forms of living labor, will touch upon the same, usually hidden or forbidden, structure. It is not here a question of holding fast to the "promise of reconciliation in the midst of the unreconciled" (Adorno 1997: 33); rather, the issue is renouncing any such promise and entering the logic of a double negation in which the fundamental tension of society, its fundamental antagonism, becomes a fight to the death. From the point of view of radical esthetics, which is the same as ontology, the emphasis is on the unreconciled as such. In this sense, only the constitution of a new totality can end the hostility toward it: not a ready-made reconciliation but the shattering of the old order of things. That this also calls forth the specter of catastrophe should not make one step back, for catastrophe is the hidden principle and drive of the present order.

Art is never antisocial; it can be, as it should be, against the institutions of society, but the social institutions and society are two different things. Labor, too, is, potentially, against the institutions of society. The fact that, as Adorno critically notes, "[s]ocial reflection on esthetics habitually neglects the concept of productive force" (p. 42) has to do with a prejudice present within the realm of criticism, and at times of the artist's perception of his own experience, not with the actual absence of the social dimension within the artwork. Adorno says, "After the abolition of scarcity, the liberation of the forces of production could extend into other dimensions than exclusively that of the quantitative growth of production" (p. 46). Yet, this will not happen if we hold on to one and the same concept of productive force. Again, if we understand "productive" in the sense of capital, the abolition of scarcity will do little to change the direction of production; and indeed the abolition of scarcity would already be an actual reality if the logic of capital did not impede its full actualization. Here, the question is not merely one of production, but of distribution, thus of circulation. The liberation of the forces of production could happen any time. But which forces? Those that pertain to the valorization process, the power of labor appropriated by capital, will never lead toward the direction indicated by Adorno. It is only the pure subjective power of labor, equal to the artistic experience of creation, which may extend into other dimensions, and in a sense it always already does. The direction of *growth* in production must, in fact, cease. It is the distribution of produced wealth that needs to be addressed in relation to the abolition of scarcity. Thus, we cannot say that one and the same force of production will be able to continue this quantitative growth, which is a mere euphemism for profit, and yet at the same time reach into the world of the spirit, as it were. As in our remark on Tronti, this force cannot simply be inside and yet against the capitalist mode of production; it must, at the same time, conceive of itself as being, and in fact be, *outside* it, not merely in a spatial sense, but in an ontological sense. It is not simply a question, as in one of Adorno's definitions of art, of "rationality that criticizes rationality without withdrawing from it" (p. 55). The movement of withdrawal is instead a necessary one; but that does not imply a relapse into an irrational or prerational realm, which is what Adorno fears and thus seeks to avoid. The point is that the concept of rationality can be understood in many ways, and certainly the rationality of a force acting against capital and its institutions, corroding them from its center and threatening them from the outside, whether this force is called labor or art, is of a higher order than the merely abstract and empty rationality of capital itself. Adorno refers to Max Weber's concepts of disenchantment of the world and rationalization in this respect. Yet, the rationality that operates at the transcendental level of neutrality and potentiality is no rationalization at all. In fact, rationalization destroys reason, precisely, and thus rationality proper. The destruction of reason does not come from any "irrationalist" philosophy. As Hardt and Negri say in one of the most interesting parts of *Empire,* it is the ideology of the world market that is against reason (Hardt and Negri 2000: 150–151). In this, such ideology is joined by esthetic approaches to the understanding of life that fall under the generic category of postmodernism: the critique of the Enlightenment, of reason, of essentialism, and of modernity.[13] If all this opens up the possibility of a politics of difference, as Hardt and Negri say, it does not mean that a critique of it from the point of view of universal reason is unnecessary. To the contrary, this is the most pressing task of our times. Such critique is what a concept of art that reaches into the univocity and commonality of labor can afford. Then, what we have is not merely a "rationality criticizing rationality without withdrawing from it," but we rather encounter that which most determinately withdraws by returning to itself as to the innermost essence of reason, to the world's *logos,* criticizing the fragments of empirical reality now detached from their sustaining ground, forgetful of it. The new empirical reality that must be constituted, a concrete utopia, must return from such a return, it must be the distinct expression of such a withdrawal.

The conflict between the work of art and empirical reality (of which the work of art also partakes) is resolved by the radical transformation of the latter. Thus the conflict is not between the work of art and that which not yet exists, postulated by the work of art itself. Adorno says, "By their very existence artworks postulate the existence of what does not exist and thereby come into conflict with the latter's actual nonexistence" (p. 59). This statement touches upon the structure of real utopia, not adequately understood by Adorno, not understood by him in the sense explained by Bloch. The conflict with what does not exist does not pertain to the work of art as a work of art, but it pertains to it insofar as it also partakes of the specific mode of the empirical reality it challenges. Yet the work of art is never part of the *merely* given. Rather, it is always already in touch with the univocal ground common to what-is and what-could-be. In this sense, it is the same as labor, which can be totally subsumed under capital (or any other mode of production) and yet always capable of exceeding that totality, *inside* the constructed totality, and yet, at the same time, always *outside* it. Adorno is not completely unaware of this, as we have already noted. Thus, the alternative he envisions at this point: "Either to leave art behind or to transform its very concept" (p. 61). In truth, this is a false either/or, for the two possibilities point toward the same direction. And, in accordance with the structure we have already analyzed with respect to the concept of labor, here, too, we find that it is the neither/nor of art, which alone is capable of exiting the terrain of art as a separate domain of experience, a domain at the direct service of an ideology, of a social and political design. The neither/nor of art, which is the same as the neither/nor of labor, grounds the possibility of the social, as well as of a new conception of the political—the political not in the sense given to it by Carl Schmitt (1996), of a fundamental and irreducible antagonism, the relationship between friend and enemy (which is indeed the most rigorous definition of the political with respect to all history up to now),[14] but, rather, as the constitution of a really livable *oikos,* which we prefer to the dubious concept of *polis.* It is here that the synthetic mode through and in which life is *lived,* rather than merely apprehended in thought, becomes evident. Of course, for this to obtain, for art and labor to really *shine,* the Schmittian, but also Marxian, form of antagonism must be completely overcome and eliminated. And this cannot happen without the utter destruction, not simply of the enemy, but of the conditions that make the enemy possible at all. The thought of the reform of humankind in this sense should not be left to a question of opinion, for the issue here has nothing to do with groups of people in their physical existence, at the empirical level, but rather with modes of thought. What must be eliminated is a mode of thought that can be safely named *social idiocy* (similar to, and inclusive of, Mumford's notion of *esthetic idiocy*), that is, the mistaking of the commonality of difference, which occurs on the horizontal plane of being, for a vertical scale of values, a hierarchical order, according to which social, cultural, and existential experience is measured. The enemy of labor is also the enemy of art, and as labor and art touch on the innermost essence of reason, it is also the enemy of reason itself and of true intelligence. Having-to-be-destroyed is what most essentially pertains to the concept of the enemy. The not-yet-existing announced by art as the *more* of nature, announced by labor, cannot tolerate a renewal of forms of subsumption which would reduce both art and labor to what they are not, and cannot, in true dignity and authenticity, be. For this reason, the not-yet-existing must operate a new clearing, whereby all the old forms of domination and oppression must disappear. Thus, those theorists who think that capital could be maintained and yet reformed really believe that profit (thus exploitation) could be acceptable to the not-yet-existing. But then the Not-Yet would be a mere extension of what-is into what-could-be. True, the *could* modality names a plurality of possibilities, as we have seen. And it is in this sense that Adorno is right in pointing out a certain convergence of the possibility of utopia and the possibility of catastrophe. The point, however, is to distinguish between a disguised form of the Not-Yet, a mere extension of what-is into what-could-be, and a truly radical change, where the Not-Yet appears in its totality and purity. How could a world geared toward business and growth, police mentality and social control, listen to and appreciate the word which comes from the neither/nor of labor, the neither/nor of art? We have no issue with Adorno insofar as he also names the structure of potentiality sustaining and making possible the manifestation of art and being, in turn, manifested by it at level of the actual. He says, "By its form alone art promises what is not; it registers objectively, however refractedly, the claim that *because the nonexistent appears it must be indeed possible*" (p. 82; emphasis added). The structure of real utopia is then revealed. The correct form of immanence, the immanence of society in art, is also first shown, for what becomes visible, although perhaps in a confused manner, is the truth of society, as well as the truth of history and time. This is the *more* present, for Adorno, in the artworks, which he calls "their spirit" (p. 86). And he also stresses that "what appears" in the artworks is not "mere appearance," but, precisely, something *more:* the "more" that transfigures nature as well as any given regime of society. That which is appropriated by capital as surplus-value is now returned to its fundamental ontological task. This is what "makes artworks, things among things, something other than thing" (ibid.). But what is a mere thing? What is *a priori* excluded from the more that comes from nature (for labor is a natural power) and yet transforms nature as it transforms society? What is barred from entering the realm of the spirit? Probably nothing. The more that breaks through the thin wall of the empirical is held in check only by specially devised institutional practices and techniques. But it is otherwise *there* from the beginning. The commodity form is the clearest and most precise example of the reduction of what is always other than thing to a mere thing; this is the process of reification. Exchange value, or simply, value, is what institutionally and legally usurps the spiritual dimension that makes a thing other than thing. This otherness has to do with the principle of individuation, the identity of identity and difference, which takes mere thinghood away from *this* thing. In so doing, it does not reduce *this* thing, no longer a mere thing, to the empirical *this,* but it opens it up, beyond contingency, to the structure of potentiality and neutrality. No longer a matter of quantity, it is now quality that determines the new form and sub-stance of value. It is the same with the concept of God, usurping the spiritual dimension without which human life would be unconceivable, and thus the truths of religion in general determining all aspects of the spirit. This is the meaning of the fetishism of the commodity. The work of art also appears as a commodity. Herein lies the problem, which is a problem the work of art shares with all other products of labor: not in its also being part of empiri-cal reality but, rather, in its being part of an empirical reality so constituted that the nonempirical, the spiritual, is excluded from it. In reality, once labor is liberated from its abstract and thingly character, once labor and art speak with one voice, sharing the same ground out of which all doing is done, all forms and spaces of everyday life are thoroughly and radically reformed, or rather transformed. This is the revolutionary task of the present. Certainly, it belongs to the concept of the revolution to eliminate forms of domination and oppression, to destroy the conditions of their reappearing. How could that be otherwise? As Machiavelli shows, class antagonism is the relation between those who want to dominate and those who want *not to be dominated.* It is a matter of self-evidence that the desire of the latter has a universal aspiration that is utterly lacking from the particularistic, "private," interest of the for-mer. But here we are seeking to reveal a structure of universality, for it is at that level that art and labor first meet. True universality and objectivity are not attained simply because something is and is present allover the world, for this could be the mere result of the dominant forms of power imposing their partiality as if it were a totality, subsuming all difference under their specific difference. The spirit of the thing, which for Adorno "appears through the appearance" (p. 87), has a more intimate relationship with true universality and objectivity, not because it shows through and in the object, but, rather, because it touches upon the structure of neutrality and univocity.

Yet, even as spirit, art cannot be simply said to be the antithesis of empiri-cal reality, "the determinate negation of the existing order of the world" (p. 89). Art is more than that, or, rather, it has the potential to be more than that: the positive overcoming of a given modality of the empirical; not of the empiri-cal as such. When art and labor meet, the split between the sensuous and the supersensuous disappears, as in Nietzsche's critique. The world of empirical reality and the world of the spirit do not necessarily have to be held in irre-ducible separation. They can be brought together in a radically transformed concept and practice of everyday life. This is what it means to live artistically or esthetically. It is not a question of choosing, an either/or between the empir-ical and the spiritual. It is rather a question of living the spiritual within the empirical and the empirical within the spiritual: a question of immanence. But Adorno distinguishes once again between the sensuous and the nonsensuous, closer to Heidegger than to Nietzsche or Marx in this matter. The spirit is not *of* another world. We should be careful and avoid the common confusion according to which it seems that the spiritual belongs to the ontological sphere, whereas the empirical does not. What remains "hidden" as ontological does not reside in a different sphere. In other words, we do not have to confuse the concept of the transcendental (without which even immanence would be inconceivable) and the concept of the transcendent.[15] Instead, we have to hold fast to the tension between what-is and what-could-be. The idea that what-is, the empirical, could be eliminated is the same as the idea that labor, production could be eliminated. In reality, the question is not eliminating the empirical as such (which would be practically impossible and theoretically the result of a philosophical mistake), but *this* form of the empirical; not eliminating what-is, but *this* what-is. Art cannot be the determinate negation of empirical reality as such, but, rather, of a specific social formation within the empirical. The emergence of a new what-is out of what-could-be, a new essential difference in Marx's terms, negates this what-is as well as what-could-have-been. From the political point of view, it is of the utmost importance that the slogan "Another world is possible" has gained so much attention. However, philosophically, its truth should be immediately evident. In fact, many other worlds are possible, and worlds within worlds (as the Zapatistas say): this is the meaning of the *could* modality. And determining the specificity of the new world to come (*which* world?) should be a matter of the most serious consideration. A world in which the spirit is no longer detached from the empirical, the nonsensuous from the sensuous, a world where the senses are emancipated, as Marx says, this is the world of the unity of art and labor, of poiesis and praxis.

We have seen how the poetic-practical modality, which relates to language, art, and labor, shows, for Heidegger, what is and what "is" not. This is the thinking of language for Heidegger; the thinking of art for Adorno; it is also the thinking of labor. The paradox of esthetics presented by Adorno is in line with this way of thinking. He asks: "How can making bring into appearance what is not the result of making; how can what according to its concept is not true nevertheless be true?" (p. 107). In a sense, we already know the answer to this question: *Making itself is not mere making.* The *more* which one finds in all life expressions, the unanalyzable moment of synthesis of which Adorno is very fond, always already belongs to making itself. For Adorno, "... in artworks, appearance itself belongs to the side of essence" (p. 109). We would like to broaden this notion and find in it a universal: appearance always and in all cases belongs to the side of essence. The possibility of the end of the separation between art and nonart with respect to making is a real possibility. Only insofar as this is true can the notion that another world is possible really make sense. Exiting the abstractions that keep us from the synthesis of expression, from the real occurrence of *haecceitas,* or thisness, and its sustaining ground,

Fusing the Manifesto's successive stages of labor into one concurrent State ---

of what makes the "this" possible, requires the overcoming of that separation; it requires the togetherness of poiesis and praxis. This is the renewed concept of labor we have presented here; or, rather, labor's deep structure, its fundamental ontology. We have talked about labor, not as it appears in any given mode of production, but as that without which no mode of production is conceivable. How can this most common concept of the social retreat before the making of art? And how can art be something other than labor? When we posit this renewed concept of labor, which is labor's true dignity, the sameness between art and labor becomes self-evident. For who would rather work for the master, the landlord, a wage, or the creation of surplus-value?

Heidegger's riddle of art and Adorno's enigmaticalness of art have to do with the synthesis of expression that could relate to and inform all aspects of life, not simply a separate artistic domain. But for this to occur, it is necessary that, as Nietzsche says, art become "the real task of life," its *metaphysical activity.* Adorno is correct in giving the imagination preeminence in artistic experience, whereby understanding is raised to its "highest sense" (p. 122). Thus, the disposition toward art, or the lack thereof, becomes a matter of inner feeling, not, of course, as an *a priori* condition, but as a form of cultivation, hence of education. The reality principle that for Adorno stands in the way of understanding and experiencing art, which deestheticizes art, is a byproduct of a society geared, not simply toward consumption, but also toward the false totality of the *positum,* which sees in the latter, and indeed in its possession and mindless consumption, the form of freedom. This is the freedom to go as one wishes from one thing to the other, of choosing without choosing. One remains within the empirically given, the what-is, but with the impression of having the totality of being at one's disposal. Excluded from this totality is what-is-not, the indeterminateness, which, as Adorno also says, is an essential component of the work of art. For Adorno it is the *inwardness* in the labor process that brings about the refusal of art (p. 116). He says, "It is impossible to explain art to those who have no feeling for it; they are not able to bring an intellectual understanding of it into their living experience. For them, the reality principle is such an obsession that it places a taboo on aesthetic comportment as a whole; incited by the cultural approbation of art, alienness often changes into aggression, not the least of the causes of the contemporary deesthetization of art" (p. 120). However, the enigma of art, the "duality of being determinate and indeterminate," or even more precisely of being the "determination of the indeterminate"(p. 124)—that is, the passage from what-could-be to a new what-is—does not cancel the necessity of the synthesis of expression, which finds in univocity and individuation its constitutive elements. For Adorno, artworks are "not univocal even through synthesis," but they remain "question marks" (ibid.). Yet, precisely insofar as esthetic experience is genuine by becoming philosophy (p. 131), that is, insofar as esthetic *is* ontology proper, the questions it asks reach into the univocal ground of social being, and that is, of labor itself. The myth of the artist, which characterizes modernism, as well as post-modernism,[16] is eliminated with the convergence of art and philosophy, if philosophy is understood and practiced as a philosophy of praxis, common to everybody, in the Gramscian sense. Art becomes *this* praxis. Only in this sense can we read Adorno's statement: "The progressive self-unfolding of the artwork is none other than the truth of the philosophical concept" (p. 130). If the truth of the philosophical concept has become one of labor and of everyday life, then the genuine experience of both, art and philosophy, finds in labor and in everyday activity its most fertile ground: a labor which is liberated time and thus time for the practice of both philosophy and art. The anthropological type that resists both is eliminated by the same movement that eliminates the myth of the artist. The possibility of the nonexistent and yet possible, of the fact that "the world *could* be other than it is" (p. 138), does not need an art which is opposed to society—at least, not for long—but rather one which absorbs society within its own plane of immanence, one which erases from the concept of the social, not the empirical, but the distinction between the empirical and the nonempirical; not the real, but a concept of the real which excludes the possible. Thus, what art must repudiate is not the world, but the fact that the world is seen as fundamentally hostile to art and that art is seen as, at best, a supplement to the world. Adorno is then correct when he says, "There is nothing in art, not even in the most sublime, that does not derive from the world" (p. 138)—a position identical to the one by Hölderlin we have considered earlier. But he continues: "All aesthetic categories must be defended both in terms of their relation to the world and in terms of art's repudiation of that world" (ibid.). And it is this that must be corrected and qualified. It is the relation of art to the world, art's return as a conqueror that eliminates the nonartistic and profane, which will be able to build a secular and earthly plenitude whereby the world can actually be experienced as a world. This is also the "implicit critique of the nature-dominating *ratio*" (p. 139) initiated by art, that is, a critique of the institutions that turn the potentially genuine experience of the world into the nightmare of total absorption within the factory and prison regime, the reduction of the openness of the world to the painful fixity of that regime. But it is Adorno we are reading here, who, notwithstanding some difficulties, is capable of maintaining operative Nietzsche's lesson on the sensuous, of giving reason a broader scope than the "nature-dominating *ratio*" might ever allow, and of avoiding falling into the quasi-mystical position we have seen in Heidegger. Thus, he says, "It is not through the abstract negation of the *ratio*, not through a mysterious, immediate eidetic vision of essences, that art seeks justice for the repressed, but rather by revoking the violent act of rationality by emancipating rationality from what it holds to be its inalienable material in the empirical world" (ibid.).

The point of labor is clearly made by Adorno when he says, "It is as labor, and not as communication, that the subject in art comes into its own" (p. 166). Indeed, the subject in art is the same as the subject in labor. For Adorno, it is "spirit bound up with, preformed and mediated by the object" (ibid.). The movement of the spirit takes place within the "more," which gives meaning not only to the artwork but also to the world as a whole. When Adorno dismisses any tolerance for bad works, he also must be able to see in a transfigured concept of labor, which accomplishes the movement of the spirit, the possibility for a commonality of art that excludes bad works by virtue of its very concept, of its actual presence. It is in this sense that art, being "the most compelling argument against the epistemological division of sensuality and intellect" (p. 174), is also, as actual praxis, the unity of both elements, the emancipation of the senses according to Marx, the ability to always have "subjectivity... achieve the objective" (p. 171), and as such always "geniality." But this concept, too, would now reach into the most common and univocal. The *more* that gives the work of art its status as a work of art does not have to be extraempirical, but, rather, it has to be profoundly empirical, that is, crossing through the entire structure of meaningful experience, for it is the very essence of meaning. Adorno says, "Artworks are something made that has become *more* than something simply made" (p. 179; emphasis mine). Indeed, the simple fact that an artwork is made does not tell us that it is an artwork. And this is what Heidegger, too, explains. Yet, it is not by negating their status as things that artworks reach into the *more* of meaning—of their meaning as artworks. The requirement that this meaning be universal should not be at odds with the structure of experience, and thus with the unity of the empirical world. Indeed, the dialectical relation of the particular and the universal which, as Adorno says, "has its model in art" (p. 202), gives the world of experience, of everyday life, the social world, its steadiest ground, provided that art is not subsumed within the social, not assigned a special place within the social, which in actuality deprives it of its ontological aspiration and turns it into a mere embellishment of the empirical. For it is the confinement of art that is then understood as art's independence from the social. Thus, ultimately it is not art that wages a war against society, but society against art. Art's opposition to society is often a reaction to its confinement and exclusion. Art's original autonomy should not, by contrast, be understood as an aspiration to stay away from society; rather, autonomy, in the Kantian sense, should be seen as its transcendental movement, thus as the ontological power able to subvert society only because, more fundamentally, it can *make* it. Adorno says, "By crystallizing in itself as something unique to itself, rather than complying with existing social norms and qualifying as 'socially useful,' it *criticizes society by merely existing,* for which puritans of all stripes condemn it" (pp. 225–226; emphasis added). No doubt, art takes on such a critical role within the established order, yet its original aspiration is much broader than that, for it can create new social space and redefine the concept of the useful. I am not here in total disagreement with Adorno. It is true that by opposing a society that opposes it, art tends to become asocial and that its asociality is "the determinate negation of a determinate society" (p. 226). But it is not the negation of society as such. Adorno is correct in saying that a *determinate* society is negated by art's opposition to it, at least, ideally negated, and the word "determinate" should be stressed here. However, his thought should be corrected in the sense that such negation does not simply engenders art as a movement of resistance, but, more than that, it gives art, in its autonomy, the affirmative power to ground and sustain a radically different concept of the social. That this remains only at the level of potentiality does not diminish its importance and its true capacity. It is this character of art that is not stressed enough by Adorno, which is approximated by him, but never fully posited. For Adorno, art "keeps itself alive through its social force of resistance; unless it reifies itself, it becomes a commodity" (p. 226). This is an either/or that excludes art's fundamental ontological power, which becomes evident in the equation of art and labor. True, for Adorno, the concept of resistance already includes that of a constitutive force, but only as reproduction. Thus, in resistance, "social development is reproduced without being imitated" (ibid.). Yet, this movement, by itself, goes beyond mere resistance, into the construction of a radically new essential difference. It is not merely a question of reproduction, but rather one of original production— the production of something entirely new and radically different. In order to be able to posit that, Adorno would have to be less resistant to the structure of utopia, of concrete utopia, which alone can negate *this* mode of the empirical without negating the empirical as such, as the mode that becomes actual as a contraction of the double power of potentiality and impotentiality, that is, maintaining that power within itself, thus immediately being something other than the *merely* empirical. Again, I am talking about a concept of the empirical, of the sensuous, which does not occur in opposition to the extraempirical, the supersensuous, which does not reproduce the split of traditional metaphysics, but, rather, has, within itself, the *more* of the unity of its structure. This is, again, the concept of labor liberated from the modality of subsumption, alienation, and exploitation—a concept of labor which is instead capable of subsuming within its structure of immanence the various expressions of social life. How can this concept be different from a renovated concept of art—one which, for Adorno, grounds the social rather than being grounded by it? Yet, it is not simply art's "immanent movement against society" (p. 227), which is social in this sense, for art's immanent movement is also *for* society. The convergence of art and society in the artwork's content, the "historical gesture [which] repels empirical reality" (p. 228), has precisely the form of the constitution of a new society, grounded in the immanent movement of art and labor. It is in this sense that "art becomes the schema of social praxis" (ibid.). The schema has the form of the unity of praxis itself and poiesis. In this sense, all expressions of social praxis, from science to politics, are part and the result of the founding power of art's categories, in a manner which is identical with the operative modalities of Vico's poetic metaphysics, informing all possible instances of social experience. Adorno is then correct in saying that the categories that are valid for science are the same categories that are valid for art. And he is, once again correct, in denouncing the political, ideological, use of art: "the political positions deliberately adopted by artworks are epiphenomena and usually impinge on the elaboration of works and thus, ultimately, on their social truth content" (p. 232). For, as we have seen, art's scope with respect to the social is much greater than making statements about it: in fact, it always moves toward the fundamental function of the constitution of the social. Thus, the immanence of society in the artworks is reached. With it, the equation, at the ontological level, of artistic production and social labor also becomes evident. Adorno says, "Social forces of production, as well as relations of production, return in artworks as mere forms divested of their facticity because artistic labor is social labor; moreover, they are always the product of this labor" (p. 236). If artworks are the product of artistic/social labor, with the elimination of productive labor, which dominates society but is really anti-social, the return of labor to itself will make possible the constitution of a society where the work of art prevails as its most common element and feature. For the return of labor to itself is the return of labor to its original esthetic disposition, the measure of a radically different political and social ontology.

Bin ich so klug als vie zuvor . . .

Notes

INTRODUCTION

1. Gilson says, "Or l'intellect de l'homme, dans sa condition présent, peut concevoir l'être sans le concevoir comme fini ou comme infini, comme créé ou comme incréé, donc le concept d' 'être' est un concept distinct de ces derniers. Sans doute, lui-même est inclus dans l'un et l'autre, mais ni l'un ni l'autre ne sont inclus en lui. De lui-même, il n'est ni l'un ni l'autre... , il est 'neutre' à leur égard; bref, il leur est 'univoque'" (Gilson 1952: 100).

2. "Le concept commun d'être est formellement neutre au fini et à l'infini, mais un être reel est nécessairement l'un ou l'autre."

3. The notion of labor as a univocal and common concept is absolutely central in the present study. Indeed, it was on this initial intuition that an original graduate paper (written in 1996) was developed into an article (Gullì 1999), then into a dissertation (Gullì 2003), and finally into a book. This understanding of labor is necessary to a new political ontology, one that is based on an adequate notion of the contingent; that is, contingency at the potential level, and thus an adequate concept of history. I become even more persuaded of its importance today that I find the concept of the commonality of labor under the pen of Hardt and Negri in their recent study of the multitude (Hardt and Negri 2004).

4. For an example of how the question of productivity is fundamental in giving a political direction to an analysis of labor, see Rifkin (1995), in which the concept of productivity plays the most central role.

5. Informalization: "Informal work is usually defined as any which takes place outside the formal wage-labour market, such as clandestine work and illegal work, but also including various forms of self-employment. It is a global phenomenon and not just pertaining to the South, although its level there is considerably higher" (Munck 2002: 111–112). Flexibility amounts to "a reduction in wages ('labor costs flexibility'), a reduction in the number of workers ('numerical flexibility'), and an increase in the number of tasks the remaining workers had to perform ('functional flexibility'). Overall, across the North the 'flexibility' offensive had created by the end of the 1990s a workforce which was much more insecure and had seen many of the welfare rights gained under Fordism wiped away" (ibid., 78).

6. In their most recent work, Hardt and Negri clarify the controversial concept of immaterial labor by pointing out that immaterial is the product of a labor that remains material (Hardt and Negri 2004: 109).

7. On neoregulation, see, for instance, Emmons (2000).

8. In this sense, see also Jean-Luc Nancy (1991).

9. The reference is to Lewis Mumford, who uses the phrase "esthetic idiocy" in his critique of modernity (Mumford 2000).

10. The United Nations is curiously shy when it comes to poverty and hunger. Goal 1 of the Millennium Development Goals adopted in 2001 seeks to eradicate *extreme* poverty and hunger, not eradicate them in their totality—a thing that our proud century could easily do (see *Miniatlas of Global Development*, Washington, DC: The World Bank, 2004).

11. When I refer to this work later, I will use the subtitle rather than the title. The second and third books on physics and ethics were never written.

12. In this respect, see Milbank (1991), who calls attention to the Aristotelian difference between *poiesis* (making) and *praxis* (doing). Even though it may be true that Vico—as Milbank says—prefers the more precise *poiesis* to the "generic" *praxis*, this does not alter the fundamental practical dimension of his philosophy. Milbank uses this distinction in an argument that intends to defend Vico's anti-Platonic metaphysics against two different readings of his thought. Milbank says, "Those who stress *scientia* at the expense of *conscientia*, understand *verum-factum* as still lying within the Platonic paradigm, and assume the priority of *verum*. By contrast, the 'humanist' group reduces the specificity of 'making' to a generic 'practice' in which we are to act on the basis of (non-mathematical) probabilities. This fails to allow that in '*making*' as opposed to '*doing*,' Vico acknowledges a specially adequate 'comprehension' of the product through the synthesis of all its different elements" (1991: 95). However, to see the Aristotelian distinction as one of opposition is very problematic. In fact, any act of *poiesis* is fundamentally practical. In this sense, a poetic metaphysics also must be a practical one.

13. This is in *The New Science*.

14. Compare this with Marx's claim, in the *Grundrisse*, that the correct method is not the one that focuses on the concrete but, rather, that which starts from the abstract and has the concrete as its arrival point (Marx 1973: 100–101). I will return to this important point in Marx in Chapter 2.

15. On this point, Milbank is absolutely correct (see note 12).

16. Here again we need to think of Marx, for instance, his *Theses on Feurbach*, particularly thesis II: "In practice man must prove the truth, that is, actuality and power, this-sidedness of thinking" (1994: 99). In Vico's philosophy, "proving the truth" means making it. This is also true of Marx's philosophy of course, with the difference that in Marx the material conditions, the circumstances, play a greater role than in Vico.

17. Vico specifies that this synthetic and totalizing activity of the human mind is not without limits. In a way that could read as an anticipation of Kant's distinction between understanding and thinking, his putting of limits to reason, Vico says, "... we cannot understand the limitless and formless, though we can think about them." And he very interestingly adds, "As we say in Italian, 'Può andare raccogliendo, ma non già raccoglierle tutte' (One can keep on picking things up, but never get them all together)" (1988: 77). The convergence of *verum* and *factum* then works toward the constitution of an open totality.

18. See Heidegger's analysis of a poem by Stefan George in relation to this (Heidegger 1971a: 57–108). I will discuss Heidegger's analysis in Chapter 4.

19. In his fourth meditation, Descartes says, "Whence, then, do my errors arise? Only from the fact that the will is much more ample and far-reaching than the understanding, so that I do not restrain it within the same limits but extend it even to those things which I do not understand."

CHAPTER 1

1. Cf. Marx's *Theses on Feuerbach,* Thesis 1 in Marx (1994: 99).

2. This fact was first recognized by Marcuse (1972a) in his seminal study of the *Manuscripts* in 1932. However, although Marcuse says that the *Manuscripts* represent "a philosophical critique of political economy," he also maintains that this critique constitutes the "critical *foundation* of political economy" (p. 5). Yet, if it is true that

To say that Marcuse did not appreciate that is puerile chutzpah. As for the rest it is pure sophistry: Catching the bull by the tail...

"a simple economic fact appears as the perversion of the human essence and the loss of human reality," it is not as true that this same economic fact can become "the real basis of a revolution which will genuinely transform the essence of man and his world" (p. 8). Thus, if Marcuse is correct in separating political economy from ontology, he remains caught within the paradigm of productivism by saying that this ontology is the critical *foundation* of political economy *and* at the same time of a theory of revolution. The end of the critique of political economy is not political economy's critical foundation, but rather its supersession and final disappearance. What this ontology grounds, once the critique is undertaken and brought to completion, is not a renewed modality of political economy, but the modalities of a total and radical alternative to the system of production conceivable by political economy. Indeed, as Marcuse's later work shows, a simple economic fact cannot be the "real basis of a revolution." (See, for instance, Marcuse 1972b.)

3. Recently, this question has received some attention. In a book on Paul's *Letter to the Romans,* Giorgio Agamben notes: "The fact that, in the course of time, the proletariat has been identified with a determinate social class—the working class, which demanded prerogatives and rights—is... the worst misunderstanding of Marxian thought. What was in Marx a strategic identification—the working class... as a contingent historical figure of the proletariat—becomes a true and substantial social identity, which necessarily loses its revolutionary vocation" (Agamben 2000: 35). Hardt and Negri, in discussing the concept of the multitude, also distinguish between working class and proletariat: "In contrast to the exclusions that characterize the concept of the working class,... the multitude is an open and expansive concept. The multitude gives the concept of the proletariat its fullest definition as all those who labor and produce under the rule of capital" (2004: 107).

4. This does not entail doing nothing at all, but only stopping producing and valorizing capital. A paradigmatic illustration of this modality of subtraction and subversion can be seen in the practice of desertion and in the mobility, particularly with respect to piracy, characteristic of the maritime world of the early eighteenth century, as described by Marcus Rediker (1987: Chapter 2).

5. I draw the concept of *organic* labor from Marx's definition of nature as "man's *inorganic body*" (1975: 328). Marx says: "Man *lives* from nature, i.e. nature is his *body,* and he must maintain a continuous dialogue with it if he is not to die" (ibid.). It is this dialogue that the word *organic* refers to. And he continues: "To say that man's physical and mental life is linked to nature simply means that nature is linked to itself, for man is a part of nature" (ibid.). Even though I cannot develop this argument here, I would like to note the importance that this passage has from an environmentalist point of view.

6. I use the word "measure" in Protagoras's sense, that is, as the reason and practice whereby nature is transfigured and culture constituted; a concept of political ontology.

7. I will go back to this theme in the final chapter of this book.

8. This is how Scotus defines univocity: "I designate that concept univocal which possesses sufficient unity in itself, so that to affirm and deny it of one and the same thing would be a contradiction. It also has sufficient unity to serve as the middle term of a syllogism, so that wherever two extremes are united by a middle term that is one in this way, we may conclude to the union of the two extremes among themselves" (Duns Scotus 1987: 20).

9. See the section on productive labor.

10. Of course, this recalls Hegel's dialectic of master and slave.

11. I will return to this when I discuss the concepts of "what-is" and "what-could-be" in the section on the reality of utopia, Chapter 3, *infra*.

12. See particularly the last two chapters of this book.

13. On this sense of "culture," within the Marxist tradition, see, for instance, Bukharin (1969: 150).

14. This is Pashukanis's argument in *Law and Marxism,* of which more will be said later.

15. I will say more about this in the next chapter.

16. The legal character of social relations is not a metaphysical given just as the economic character of labor is not. Pashukanis says: "... under certain conditions the *regulation* of social relations assumes a *legal character*" (p. 79).

17. See F. Bastiat (1964: 204).

18. See, in this respect, the *Grundrisse,* Introduction.

19. This question also will be taken up and developed by Marx in the *Grundrisse,* and it will constitute one of the main themes of recent readings of Marx's thought, which intend to stress the character of subjectivity. For a very recent discussion of this question, see Jason Read (2003), particularly Chapter 3, "The Real Subsumption of Subjectivity by Capital."

20. There is a strong visionary element in these pages of Marx, which returns, however, everywhere in his writings, even in those in which the supposedly scientific element seems stronger. I am not saying this as a critique, for a general problem with Marxism is, as Murray Bookchin has remarked, not that it is too visionary, but that it is not visionary enough (Bookchin 1971: 177). In Marx, this visionary element comes from the revolutionary passion that led him to the study of political economy and not, certainly, from political economy itself. Mario Tronti also points this out: "Marx does not start from 'the critique of political economy,' even when understood as critique of capitalism. He gets to it and goes through it, starting off from an attempt at a theory of revolution" (Tronti 1977: 186).

21. According to Burnet, even the philosophy of Democritus, subject of Marx's doctoral dissertation, depends on Parmenides's thought: "What appears later as the elements of Empedokles, the so-called 'homoeomeries' of Anaxagoras and the atoms of Leukippos and Demokritos, is just the Parmenidean 'being.'" And he continues: "Parmenides is not, as some have said, the 'father of idealism'; on the contrary, all materialism depends on his view of reality" (1957: 182).

22. This is in "A Contribution to the Critique of Hegel's Philosophy of Right. Introduction" (Marx 1975: 251).

23. Bookchin calls attention to a passage from *The Eighteenth Brumaire of Louis Bonaparte* where Marx denounces the inability of revolutionaries to actually revolutionize themselves as well as things and says how a social revolution must "draw its poetry... from the future" (cf. Bookchin 1971: 174).

24. See particularly "The Revolution against 'Capital'" in Gramsci (1990: 34–37).

25. This is also the main theme of *Il potere costituente. Saggio sulle alternative del moderno* (Negri 1992), translated into English as *Insurgencies: Constituent Power and the Modern State* (Negri 1999).

26. Murray Bookchin, among others, also has identified and explored this question in important ways. See the section on the reality of utopia.

27. If I am here speaking of Lenin's concept of the professional revolutionary, I do not mean to include Lenin himself (or other famous or less known or unknown

genuine revolutionaries) in this category. What I am saying is, rather, that the bureaucratization of the formation of the revolutionary subject goes hand in hand with the emphasis on production and productivism, with the concept that the proletarian is, first and foremost, a worker. The history of the Russian Revolution has clearly shown how it is the party, the professional revolutionaries, to lag behind, not the "objective" moment per se, but the subjective structures of desire for social change informing and defining the revolutionary subject (whether this latter is a factory worker or not)—a desire that, to be sure, is based on and is in agreement with objective structures of reality, and that is, furthermore, an integral part of that objective reality; perhaps the most important and fruitful component of it: *the possible* that enlivens the merely given. After all, with the *Theses of April 4,* "Lenin shifted the whole question to the subjective plane" (Trotsky 1959: 232). It is interesting to note that at that time, narrates Trotsky, Lenin was considered an anarchist, "a bad Marxist," by its enemies—a view accepted even by the British ambassador to Russia (p. 237).

28. It is useful to be reminded that "the term 'totalitarianism' [was] originally invented as a description or self-description of Italian Fascism" (Hobsbawm 1994: 112).

29. Obviously, the last expression refers to the Zapatista slogan "un mundo donde quepan muchos mundos."

30. See, for instance, Hobsbawm (1994).

31. Cf. Mumford (1961: 21, 25–28).

32. "The definition of man as a 'species being' has done a lot of damage in Marx-scholarship." Marcuse goes on to trace the "real origins of Marx's concept of 'species'" in the concept of universality (Marcuse 1972a: 15).

33. See the section on the reality of utopia, Chapter 3.

34. For instance, in Fichte's idea of freedom there is a moment in which the authority that the self exercises over itself supersedes the givenness of natural freedom.

35. Cf. Spengler (1991). See also Lukács's discussion of the question of time and space in *History and Class Consciousness.*

36. In the *Grundrisse,* Marx defines fixed capital as capital which "consumes itself in the production process," that is, the means of production "in the strict sense" (1973: 691). Then he describes it as "that whose physical presence or use-value is machinery" (p. 703). But then, again, as "man himself" (p. 712).

37. I also would like to suggest that "immaterial" labor might be a misnomer. Following Lucretius, it would be better to speak of "invisible" labor, for nothing is really immaterial, but also because "invisible" labor would account for other forms of labor that are certainly precisely invisible yet in no way "immaterial," not even if one accepts this denomination as reasonable for those forms of labor which only entail information and knowledge. I have already noted Hardt's and Negri's recent clarification of this problem (see note 6 in the Introduction), yet its reconceptualization (for this is what they really offer) demands a full disambiguation.

38. In this respect, cf. Chapter 4.

39. I will go back to this concept in the next chapter.

40. I will go back to this point later in Chapter 2.

41. In this sense, see Lazzarato (1996) and Read (2003).

42. I will return to this point.

43. See Aronowitz and DiFazio (1994).

44. As Augustine says, "These concepts already exist, and those who foretell are gazing upon them, present within themselves" (1942: 222).

Chapter 2

1. The distinction between living labor and productive labor is one of the main themes of this work. For an earlier formulation of the problem, see Gulli (1999 and 2003).

2. In the *Grundrisse* we read: "It has a use-value for the worker himself only in so far as it is *exchange value,* not in so far as it produces values. It has exchange value for capital only in so far as it is use-value" (1973: 307).

3. In the *Grundrisse* Marx says that productive labor is "that which produces capital" (1973: 304).

4. For Marx's own treatment of this, see his analysis of the double aspect of the commodity in the *Grundrisse.* He says: "... this double, differentiated existence must develop into a *difference,* and the difference into *antithesis* and *contradiction*" (1973: 147).

5. See, for instance, Marx (1973: 172, 708); also cf. Negri (1991a: 33).

6. In this sense, Debord is very clear. He says that certainly the proletariat "has lost the ability to assert its own independence,... lost its *illusions.* But it has not lost its being." He continues: "The proletariat has not been eliminated, and indeed it remains irreducibly present, under the intensified alienation of modern capitalism, in the shape of the vast mass of workers who have lost all power over the use of their own lives and who, *once they realize this,* must necessarily redefine themselves as the proletariat–as negation at work in the bosom of today's society" (Debord 1995: 84). In this very important thesis, Debord also makes it clear that the proletariat is not identical with the employed labor force.

7. For the incompatibility of these two concepts ("expansion" and "development"), see Samir Amin (1997: 14).

8. Cf. Kant (1929: B225, *passim*).

9. Marx returns on this important point in the chapter on Capital: "If, then the specific form of capital is abstracted away, and only the content is emphasized,... , *then of course nothing is easier than to demonstrate that capital is a necessary condition for all human production.* The proof of this proceeds precisely by abstraction from the specific aspects that make it the moment of a specifically developed *historic* stage of human production. The catch is that if all capital is objectified labour which serves as means for new production, it is not the case that all objectified labour which serves as means of production is capital" (1973: 258).

10. "Labour... as the creator of useful value, as useful labour, is a condition of human existence which is independent of all forms of society; it is an eternal natural necessity which mediates the metabolism between man and nature, and therefore human life itself" (Marx 1977: 133).

11. Capital reproduces abstract labor insofar as it "produces the worker as a wage-worker" (Marx 1977: 716).

12. In this sense, it is perhaps important to consider Debord's very interesting description of the relationship between exchange value (i.e., the specific product of abstract labor) and use-value (i.e., the specific product of useful labor): "Exchange value could only have arisen as the proxy of use-value, but the victory it eventually won with its own weapons created the preconditions for its establishment as an autonomous power. By activating all human use-value and monopolizing that value's fulfillment, exchange value eventually gained the upper hand. The process of exchange became indistinguishable from any conceivable utility, thereby placing use-value at its mercy. Starting out as the condottiere of use-value, exchange value ended up waging a war that was entirely its own" (Debord 1995: 31–32).

A Key to subsequent (Capital) articulation of "Supreme Contradiction" of CM? (philos-opher production)

13. It is also important to note that this is the indifference that will become typical and common in the age of automation.

14. In his *Metaphysics* Aristotle explains that permanence and becoming cannot exclude one another: "It is also evident that neither those who say that all things are at rest speak truly, nor those who say that all things are in motion. For if all things are at rest, whatever is true will always be true and whatever is false will always be false, yet there appear to be a change;... And if all things are in motion, nothing will be true, and so everything will be false; but this [is]... impossible" (1979: 1012b 23–28).

15. See particularly his *Dialectical and Historical Materialism.*

16. Even though I agree with Negri's characterization of the *Grundrisse* as an *open work,* I do not see why *Capital*—and this, of course, beyond the use that has been made of it—would necessarily "block" revolutionary subjective action.

17. In *Capitalism, Socialism and Democracy,* Schumpeter says: "Marx retained his early love during the whole of his lifetime. He enjoyed certain formal analogies which may be found between his and Hegel's argument. He liked to testify to his Hegelianism and to use Hegelian terminology. But this is all. *Nowhere did he betray positive science to metaphysics*" (Schumpeter 1950: 9–10; quoted in Rosdolsky 1977: xii; my emphasis).

18. Of course, "metaphysics" is here used in its vulgar sense. See Remark 2.

19. It is true that, as Negri says, "Marx's score with Hegel was settled long before [at the time of the so-called early writings]; here [in the *Grundrisse*] it is only a question of going back to him in a critical and scientific manner" (1991a: 3; brackets added). Indeed, the critique of Hegel is not at all an aspect of the *Grundrisse.* Under attack here are the bourgeois political economists and the socialists, first of all Proudhon. It is the latter who appear as Hegelians. Now, if we ask what the result of the concept of circularity is, the answer is *identity.* And it is this concept of identity that Marx wants to smash. Speaking of the problem of production and consumption–within the wider context of the concept of production as a Hegelian totality in which production, distribution, exchange and consumption are only members, "distinctions within a unity" (Marx 1973: 99)—Marx says: "Thereupon, nothing simpler for a Hegelian than to posit production and consumption as identical. And this has been done not only by socialist belletrists but by prosaic economists themselves, e.g. Say; in the form that when one looks at an entire people, its production is its consumption. Or, indeed, at humanity in the abstract" (pp. 93–94).

20. See Negri (1991a: 9, 85–104).

21. Notwithstanding Negri's denial of the dialectic in all its forms, he still retains—both in *Marx beyond Marx* and in his later writings—a dialectic of antagonism as the motor of his concept of constitutive ontology.

22. See, for instance, the lectures on *The Nature of Language* in *On the Way to Language.* For Heidegger, the time of *poiesis,* the poetic experience, "points to something thought-provoking and memorable with which thinking has been charged from the beginning, even though in a veiled manner" (Heidegger 1971: 87).

23. The translation of passages from Negri (1992) is mine, although after I first wrote these pages a translation of *Il potere costituente* has appeared in English (see Negri 1999).

24. See Duns Scotus (1987) and Deleuze (1994).

25. See Negri (1991b and 1992).

26. This latter case is explained by the law of the tendency of the profit rate to decline (cf. Negri 1991a: 100).

27. This is the question of the tendencies of capital. "It is its tendency, therefore, to create as much labour as possible; just as it is equally its tendency to reduce necessary labour to a minimum. It is therefore equally a tendency of capital to increase the labouring population, as well as constantly to posit a part of it as surplus population—population which is useless until such time as capital can utilize it" (Marx 1973: 399).

28. By contrast, Negri adds, "*the concrete... seeks in abstraction its determination*" (Negri 1991a: 48); this constitutes the process of tendency.

29. On the question of subsumption, see Marx (1977: 1019–1038).

30. "Marx's theory of crisis and its counteracting tendencies is the core of his critique of capitalist production. Contrary to the commonsense view that crisis may then sound the death-knell of capitalism, Marx held that crises were the condition of capitalist development" (Aronowitz 1981: 184).

31. The dialectic between becoming and having become is also treated by Marx, in the *Grundrisse,* in the section on the accumulation of capital (Marx 1973: 459–471). In this section, capital emerges into existence as the truth of being, namely, as the essence it has become (I am, of course, using Hegelian terminology here.) From this moment on, "it creates its own presuppositions, i.e. the possession of the real conditions of new values *without exchange,*" which appear "*not as conditions of its arising, but as results of its presence*" (p. 460; Marx's emphasis). Insofar as capital is establishing its ground, we are still within the Hegelian circle (cf. Book II of *The Science of Logic,* "The Doctrine of Essence"). Yet the spiral movement of productive capital does not cancel the dialectic between becoming and having become. Here becoming appears as living, abstract labor which changes capital from a thing to a process. "Labour is the yeast thrown into it, which starts it fermenting" (p. 298). In this process, labor is not only consumed but also objectified, that is, from *becoming* it itself changes to a *having become.* Labor, as subjectivity, acts upon an object and modifies it. In so doing, "as a modification of the object, it modifies its own form and changes *from activity to being*" (p. 300; emphasis added). In *Capital, I,* Marx says the same: "Labour has become bound up in its object: labour has been objectified, the object has been worked on. What on the side of the worker appeared in the form of unrest [*Unruhe*] now appears, on the side of the product, in the form of Being [*Sein*], as a fixed, immobile characteristic" (p. 287; see also p. 296). The product is the coincidence and the neutral result of three moments: the material, the instrument, and labor. The whole process is one of *productive consumption,* indeed it is "consumption of consumption itself" (Marx 1973: 301). The "*form-giving* activity consumes the object and consumes itself, but it consumes the given form of the object only in order to posit it in a new objective form, and it consumes itself only in its subjective form as activity" (p. 301).

32. Money is either identical with itself (M–M), or it is the form of a time of difference (M–M').

33. "The philosophical significance of money is that it represents within the practical world the most certain image and the clearest embodiment of the formula of all being, according to which things receive their meaning through each other, and have their being determined by their mutual relations" (Simmel 1990: 128–129).

34. This law is a function of the relation between constant and variable capital. Constant and variable capital are, from the point of view of the valorization process, what means of production and labor-power are from the point of view of the labor process, that is, respectively, the objective and subjective factors of capital (Marx 1977: 317). According to this law, the greater the mass of objectified labor (i.e. constant capital) set in motion by living labor, the less is the surplus-value that capital is able to

appropriate. In other words, the gradual growth of constant capital in relation to variable capital–a direct result of the valorization process—makes the appropriation of surplus-value progressively smaller, for less labor is able to produce a greater quantity of commodities. In Volume 3 of *Capital,* Marx says that this law is "just another expression for the progressive development of the social productivity of labor" (Marx 1981: 318), and he explains it as follows: "Since the mass of living labour applied continuously declines in relation to the mass of objectified labour that it sets in motion, i.e. the productively consumed means of production, the part of this living labour that is unpaid and objectified in surplus-value must also stand in an ever-decreasing ratio between the mass of surplus-value and the total capital applied. But this ratio between the mass of surplus-value and the total capital applied in fact constitutes the rate of profit, which must therefore steadily fall" (p. 319).

35. See the first section of Chapter 2.

36. Money is the *first concept* of capital and the *first form* in which it appears. Capital starts from money that *is and is not* in circulation (Marx 1973: 253). Like all other commodities, money has the ability to step outside circulation. But differently from all other commodities, which by stepping out of circulation are consumed and destroyed, money acquires thereby an independent existence as "the non-substantial general form of wealth" (p. 254).

37. This contradiction is also present in the exchange process between the capitalist and the worker. In *Capital* Marx says: "Capital cannot therefore arise from circulation, and it is equally impossible for it to arise apart from circulation. It must have its origin both in circulation and not in circulation" (Marx 1977: 268). And: "This whole course of events, the transformation of money into capital, both takes place and does not take place in the sphere of circulation. It takes place in circulation because it is conditioned by the purchase of the labour-power in the market; it does not take place in circulation because what happens there is only an introduction to the valorization process, which is entirely confined to the sphere of production" (p. 302).

38. Under capital, "living labour itself appears as *alien* vis-à-vis living labour capacity, whose labour it is, whose own life's expression it is, for it has been surrendered to capital in exchange for objectified labour, for the product of labour itself" (Marx 1973: 462).

39. For an example in philosophy, see Bernstein (1992: esp. pp. 309–314).

40. It is, in Negri's words, the power of *self-valorization* (Negri 1991a). However, Negri does not characterize it as a *neither/nor* logic.

41. "*This transformation* [of labor into capital] is *posited* only in the *production process* itself. Thus, the question whether capital is productive or not is absurd. Labour itself is *productive only* if absorbed into capital, where capital forms the basis of production, and where the capitalist is therefore in command of production." And: "Labour, such as it exists for itself in the worker in opposition to capital, that is, labour in its *immediate being,* separated from capital, is not productive" (Marx 1973: 308; cf. also Marx 2000: Book I, Chapter IV).

42. "The apogee of critical science resides in specifying the non-subsumable, " namely, the *principle of hope* or desire against need. "The counterlogic is... to define desire as that which goes beyond need and is unrecuperable by the prevailing structure" (Aronowitz 1981: 249).

43. What is meant here is, of course, capital-commanded need.

44. Cf. H. Arendt (1958).

45. Cf. Augustine, *Confessions,* Book XII, Sections III–XI (1992: 235–241).

46. For Saussure, a sign is a "twofold psychological entity" in which a concept (signified) and a sound-image (signifier) are inextricably united (Saussure 1986: 66). In Baudrillard's critique, as well as in that of many other French writers, concepts can be so "deconstructed" because the two sides of the sign are conflated into the second side only (the signifier), which becomes "floating," and it must report to an external signified: Baudrillard's "objective reality." Yet, the relationship between this objective reality and its sign, that is, the relationship between the concept and its expression, is more complex than that. Expressed is the concept, not the thing. It is the concept that is signified through and by the signifier. To say that the concept is a signifier means to have a very poor and flat vision of the world, to lose sight of its complexity. In fact, by functioning as a signified, the concept shows to be a structural moment of that objective reality to which Baudrillard refers.

47. The translation of passages from Méda (1995) is mine.

48. The *Grundrisse* was first published in the original German version in 1953. A previous limited edition in two volumes had appeared in the Soviet Union in 1939 and 1941. Rubin's *Essays on Marx's Theory of Value* was published in Moscow in 1928, two years before his arrest which was soon to lead to his final disappearance.

49. It seems to me that the difference between *Theories* and the *Grundrisse* is that in this latter Marx speaks more categorically of *productive* labor as an exclusive modality of capital, calling labor which is productive in general "not productive," namely, the neither/nor of labor. With respect to this question, very important is also the section on productive and unproductive labor in the unpublished Chapter 6 of *Capital*.

50. To use, but in a qualified sense, the controversial concept of multitude (for instance, Hardt and Negri 2000). Cf. also Hardt and Negri (2004: 102).

CHAPTER 3

1. In premodern societies, poverty had certainly a different dimension and meaning. As Hobsbawm says: "For the old traditional system, inefficient and oppressive as it had been, was also a system of considerable social certainty and, at a most miserable level, of some economic security..." (1962: 190–191). When the peasant becomes a "free" economic subject ("free" in Marx's sense of a "double freedom"), he also loses those fundamental forms of certainty and security.

2. See also Hobsbawm's classic *Bandits*, particularly the fourth edition with the new chapter "Bandits, States and Power" (Hobsbawm 2000).

3. On the importance of the Poor Law of 1834 for the institutionalization of labor, that is, for the creation of a competitive labor market, see Polanyi (1944), for whom that date marks the beginning of industrial capitalism as a social system. He says: "It is no exaggeration to say that the social history of the nineteenth century was determined by the logic of the market system proper after it was released by the Poor Law Reform Act of 1834" (p. 83). Essentially, the Poor Law of 1834, abolished the "right to live," which was guaranteed by previous laws. See also Hobsbawm (1999: 67).

4. The thesis of a rupture between a preindustrial and an industrial age in Europe is not completely invalid, but I don't think that underlying structures do not exist that, unmodified, have to do with both ages. This would become even clearer when one considered Europe not in isolation but within the global frame and order. Then, for instance, Eric Williams's thesis of the structural relation between capitalism and slavery (Williams 1994) should be considered, and one would be able to see the possibility that these continuities exist. But even Braudel's study of the Mediterranean, which

we have been looking at here, indicates that the age that immediately preceded the rise of industry was already one in which a prefiguration of future social relations existed. If the phenomenon of poverty in the classical age is different from poverty in the Middle Ages or in antiquity, it is because in the former case non-specific capitalist relations are already being delineated.

5. I would rather say that poverty is always an economic phenomenon with a moral justification. If we confine ourselves to the historical time under consideration, the difference does not lie in whether poverty is an economic or moral phenomenon, but rather in whether it represents a specific or nonspecific dimension of the nascent capitalist system.

6. Cf. Foucault (1977: 92 and 139; brackets mine).

7. Peter McLaren also calls attention to the importance of the body in his discussion of Che Guevara's revolutionary subjectivity: "For Che, the body became the revolutionary's most severe teacher. But Che's physical strength and agility were not those of the phallo-military mercenary of the ruling class, whose mindless athleticism serves the highest bidder, but rather that of the battle-tough warrior whose steely resolve pushes the body to its limits, yet never divorces it from critical, contextual analysis of the goals ahead" (McLaren 2000: 79). In other words, the body becomes the unity of theory and practice, the *organicity* of the revolutionary organic intellectual, a *great reason*, the place and measure of the senses' emancipation.

8. For a description of capoeira, see Bira Almeida (1986).

9. A nonchalant Foucault says, "Someone said that man's concrete essence is labor. Actually, this idea was put forward by several people. We find it in Hegel, in the post-Hegelians, and also in Marx, the Marx of a certain period, as Althusser would say. Since I'm interested not in authors but in the function of statements, it makes little difference who said it or exactly when it was said" (Foucault 2000: 86). In addition to the fact that "the Marx of a certain period" is more fiction than reality, a reading of the *Grundrisse*, or even of *Capital*, would show the thorough historicity of Marx's understanding of labor.

10. Of course, in premodern or precapitalist societies, labor is either absolutely free (where the only compulsion would be a sense of self-discipline and of social/communal interests) or absolutely un-free, that is, *forced* labor. It is only under capital that the contradiction obtains whereby labor becomes "forcedly free," or a *free-forced* labor.

11. Interestingly enough, attachment is what most specifically characterizes the feudal social system. I will say more about this below.

12. "Labour-power... proves its value-creating property only if it is activated and realized in the labour process: but this does not exclude it being potentially in itself already value-creating *as a capacity,* and as such it does not arise from the process but is rather presupposed by it" (Marx 1981: 505; emphasis added).

13. See "The Reality of Utopia" later in this chapter.

14. It has been said (but it is worth repeating) that the division of the world into a North and a South is not a completely accurate and adequate description of the global economic and social situation today. With the due differences (often amounting to a question of degrees), we can say that there is also a South in the North, and in perhaps less important ways, a North in the South. The former is constituted by the most exploited sections of the working class in the advanced countries, often, but not always, made of people who were compelled to leave their own original countries in the world's South, that 'exodus' incorrectly celebrated by Hardt and Negri (1994 and 2000) as a positive moment in the most recent developments of history. The latter is constituted

by the ruling classes of the South, or rather by all the sections of society that, in important ways, benefit from the mischievous machinery of free trade.

15. *Inferno*, XXVII, 120; Allen Mandelbaum's translation.

16. The absurd nature of this logic was, of course, evident to the sharp and subtle eye of Duns Scotus: "...if something is against the law of nature, it can never become just... because crimes are not ratified by their longevity, but are rather more to be condemned; now, all forms of servitude other than these two cases [of voluntary indenture and as punishment for criminal activity] are against the law of nature; therefore, no matter how long such a contrary custom has existed, it would not seem just that a master exercise such dominion over such servants" (Duns Scotus 1986: 327). And again, arguing against or correcting Aristotle, he says that no matter the degree to which a man is enslaved, he never loses his fundamental freedom. Thus, Aristotle's "damnable form of servitude, where the slave is like an animal... does not mean that in his actions he is only led and does not lead on his own, because no matter how much of a slave he might be, he is still a man and so he has free will. And on this score, it is clear what great cruelty is involved in first imposing such servitude, for it reduces a man who is his own master and free to act in a manly and virtuous fashion, to the status of a brute animal, unable to choose freely or to act virtuously" (p. 330).

17. "Listen, Marxist!" in Bookchin (1971).

18. Bookchin quotes more at length, but for our purposes this suffices.

19. See Chapter 1, *supra*.

20. For instance, when Debord notes that "*the bourgeoisie is the only revolutionary class that has ever been victorious*; the only class, also, for which the development of the economy was the cause and consequence of its capture of society" (Debord 1995: 56–57; emphasis in the original), he addresses the question of the transition, and he does that, precisely, by calling into question the "linear model" (p. 56), which makes of the transition a matter of deterministic and mechanical movement.

21. The expression is from *The Spirit of Utopia*: "Then human beings will finally be free for those concerns and questions which alone are practical, which otherwise only await them at their hour of death after their entire restless life up to then had done nothing but seal them off from everything essential. It is as the Baal Shem says: the Messiah can only come when all guests have sat down at the table; this table is first of all *the table of labor, beyond labor*, but then at the same time the table of the Lord" (Bloch 2000: 246; emphasis added).

22. For instance, in *One-Dimensional Man*, Marcuse says that "the technological redefinition and the technical mastery of final causes *is* the construction, development, and utilization of resources (material and intellectual) *freed* from all *particular* interests which impede the satisfaction of human needs and the evolution of human faculties." This, Marcuse adds, cannot happen on the basis of "technical progress per se," but it must be the result of a "political reversal" (1964: 234).

23. In this sense, Bloch's "critical totality" is close to Gramsci's "absolute historicism."

CHAPTER 4

1. Here Nietzsche is quoting himself from the "Preface to Richard Wagner," which opens *The Birth of Tragedy*. The quotation is not exact, and the original statement is even stronger: "... I am convinced that art represents the highest task and truly metaphysical activity of this life..." (1967a: 31–32).

2. In this sense, see also Agamben (2004).

3. In this sense, see Leopardi's powerful poem *La ginestra, o il fiore del deserto* (The Broom, or the Flower of the Desert). Speaking of the eruption of Mt. Vesuvius which in the year 79 A.D., destroyed Pompeii and Herculaneum, Leopardi says: "Let whoever/Likes to sing the praises of our state/Come to these slopes and see/How loving nature looks after/Our human kind. Here/He may measure exactly/Man's might, which that/Heartless nurse when least expected/Can with a little shrug, in an instant,/Almost obliterate, and with/Some barely bigger shudderings/Just as abruptly bring to nothing" (Leopardi 1997: 75).

4. The question of the distinction between analogy and univocity became a very important issue in the debate between the medieval schools of thought started by Thomas Aquinas and John Duns Scotus. It was the latter who said that the concept of being is not only analogous to God and creature but also univocal. As Éric Alliez says, "The great Scotist ontological proposition expresses the definitive *metaphysical* exit out of the sphere of the ontotheological One, within which the theory of analogy evolves (that theory is only valid through/in a metaphysics of participation that reduces ontology to a theology: every existent in its finite measure partakes in the divine nature)" (Alliez 1996: 200). If analogy is based on the modality of *likeness,* univocity, with its complementary concept of *thisness* (i.e., the principle of individuation), is based on the modality of *as-ness,* and thus it grounds absolute identity as it grounds, at the same time, absolute difference. Scotus's doctrine of univocity opened the way to a poetic metaphysics that has one of its most important representatives in Giambattista Vico who abandoned theology to itself and, on the basis of his celebrated axiom that the true is the same as what is made, laid the foundations for a secular ontology. It makes sense to see Heidegger's lifelong wrestling with metaphysics as an attempt, not to abandon metaphysics *tout court,* but to go from metaphysics as ontotheology to poetic metaphysics. I speak of an "attempt to a passage" rather than simply "a passage," because I am not sure that Heidegger succeeds in his move. In fact, even though his concept of being is certainly not the One, is still remains behind the *as* as a "there is" (*Es gibt;* "it gives") equiprimordial with truth. However, for a true poetic metaphysics, and one built on the concept of univocity, the requirement is that being be always and only *being as.* The expression "being as" must be understood in its neutrality. The being of beings is not tied in a special way to this or that particular being. Rather, it is being *as* neither this nor that of all particular beings, yet *as,* potentially, any and all of them.

5. The limits of analogy are shown by Hegel with reference to experimental science, but they are as important in ontology. For Hegel, "analogy not only does not give a perfect right, but on account of its nature contradicts itself so often that the inference to be drawn from analogy itself is rather that analogy does not permit any inference to be made" (1977: 152).

6. In this respect, see Vincent (1987).

7. Heidegger does not use the adjective "radical" to define the turn in *What Are Poets For?* However, as I have noted above, in *The Nature of Language* he says: "Thinking is more thoughtful in proportion as it takes a more radical stance, as it goes to the *radix,* the root of all that is" (1971a: 71). I have already called attention to the importance of the root(s) in *Being and Time* too.

8. In his *Letter on Humanism,* Heidegger says that "there is a thinking more rigorous than the conceptual" (1977: 235).

9. The first meaning of *ziehen* is "pull, draw" as of a line, lot, or conclusion. Another meaning is "dig, cut" as of a ditch. There are other several meanings, all of which, it

seems to me, relate to some concrete labor activity; for example, "cultivate," "build, erect (a wall)," "describe (a circle)," and so on.

10. I put "the grant" in brackets because it is not in the German text, which reads: "... das Fragen nicht die eigentliche Gebärd des Denkens ist, sondern–das Hören der Zusage dessen, was in die Frage kommen soll" (1959: 175).

11. See *La ginestra, o il fiore del deserto* (Leopardi 1997: 78).

12. I owe the play of prepositions (in/on) to a Philadelphia graffiti artist who remains anonymous.

13. Here, in a very interesting way, Hardt and Negri also see fundamentalism as a postmodern, rather than premodern, mode of thought.

14. This is a conception that, especially after the recent events related to the "war against terrorism," needs to be challenged. Guantánamo Bay and the Abu Ghraib prison in Iraq come to mind. Giorgio Agamben is right when he says, "The fundamental categorical pair of Western politics is not that of friend/enemy but that of bare life/political life, *zoē/bios,* exclusion/inclusion" (Agamben 1998: 8).

15. Unless, of course, one uses the word "transcendent" in the Sartrian sense.

16. In this respect, see Kuspit (1993).

Bibliography

Adorno, Theodor W. 1973. *Negative Dialectics*, trans. E. B. Ashton. New York: Continuum.
_____. 1997. *Aesthetic Theory*, trans. Robert Hullot-Kentor. Minneapolis: University of Minnesota Press.
Agamben, Giorgio. 1998. *Homo Sacer: Sovereign Power and Bare Life*, trans. Daniel Heller-Roazen. Stanford, CA: Stanford University Press.
_____. 1999a. *The Man without Content*, trans. Georgia Albert. Stanford, CA: Stanford University Press.
_____. 1999b. *Potentialities: Collected Essays in Philosophy*, trans. Daniel Heller-Roazen. Stanford, CA: Stanford University Press.
_____. 2000. *Il tempo che resta. Un commento alla Lettera ai Romani*. Torino. Bollati Boringhieri.
_____. 2003. *Stato di eccezione*. Torino: Bollati Boringhieri.
Alliez, Éric. 1996. *Capital Times. Tales from the Conquest of Time*, trans. Georges Van Den Abbeele. Minneapolis and London: University of Minnesota Press.
Almeida, Bira. 1986. *Capoeira: A Brazilian Art Form. History, Philosophy, and Practice.* Berkeley, CA: North Atlantic Books.
Amin, Samir.1997. *Capitalism in the Age of Globalization: The Management of Contemporary Society.* London and New York: Zed Books.
Arendt, Hannah. 1958. *The Human Condition.* Chicago: University of Chicago Press.
Aristotle. 1941. *Politics* and *Nicomachean Ethics*, in *The Basic Works of Aristotle*, ed. Richard McKeon. New York: Random House.
_____. 1979. *Metaphysics*, trans. Hippocrates G. Apostle. Grinnell, IA: The Peripatetic Press.
Aronowitz, Stanley. 1981. *The Crisis in Historical Materialism.* Minneapolis: University of Minnesota Press.
_____. 2003. *How Class Works: Power and Social Movement.* New Haven, CT, and London: Yale University Press.
_____ and William Di Fazio. 1994. *The Jobless Future: Sci-Tech and the Dogma of Work.* Minneapolis: University of Minnesota Press.
Augustine. 1942. *Confessions*, trans. F. J. Sheed. Indianapolis: Hackett.
Balibar, Étienne. 1995. *The Philosophy of Marx*, trans. Chris Turner. London: Verso.
Bastiat, Frederic. 1964. "Protectionism and Communism," in *Selected Essays on Political Economy*, trans. Seymour Cain, ed. George B. de Huszar. New York: William Volker Fund.
Baudrillard, Jean. 1975. *The Mirror of Production*, trans. Mark Poster. St. Louis: Telos Press.
Benjamin, Walter. 1969. *Illuminations*, trans. Harry Zohn. New York: Schocken Books.
Bernstein, Richard J. 1992. *The New Constellation. The Ethical-Political Horizons of Modernity/Postmodernity.* Cambridge, MA: MIT Press.
Bloch, Ernst. 1991. "Non-Contemporaneity and Obligation to Its Dialectic" in *Heritage of Our Times*, trans. Neville and Stephen Plaice. Berkeley and Los Angeles: University of California Press.
_____. 1995. *The Principle of Hope*, 3 volumes, trans. Neville Plaice, Stephen Plaice and Paul Knight. Cambridge, MA: MIT Press.

_____. 2000. *The Spirit of Utopia*, trans. Anthony A. Nassar. Stanford, CA: Stanford University Press.

Bobbio, Norberto. 1987. *Which Socialism?*, trans. Roger Griffin. Minneapolis: University of Minnesota Press.

Bookchin, Murray. 1971. *Post-Scarcity Anarchism.* Berkeley: Ramparts Press.

Braudel, Fernand. 1995. *The Mediterranean and the Mediterranean World in the Age of Philip II,* Vol. II, trans. Siân Reynolds. Berkeley: University of California Press.

Bukharin, Nikolai. 1969. *Historical Materialism: A System of Sociology.* Ann Arbor: University of Michigan Press.

Burnet, John. 1957. *Early Greek Philosophy.* New York: Meridian Books.

Celan, Paul. 1996. *Light-Force,* trans. Jack Hirschman and Angela Beske. San Francisco: Deliriodendron Press.

Condillac, Abbé Étienne Bonnot de. 1984. *Traité des sensations.* Paris: Fayard.

Debord, Guy. 1995. *The Society of the Spectacle,* trans. Donald Nicholson-Smith. New York: Zone Books.

Deleuze, Gilles. 1994. *Difference and Repetition,* trans. Paul Patton. New York: Columbia University Press.

Duns Scotus, John. 1986. *On the Will and Morality,* trans. Allan Wolter. Washington, DC: Catholic University of America Press.

_____. 1987. *Philosophical Writings,* trans. Allan Wolter. Indianapolis and Cambridge: Hackett Publishing Company.

Emmons, Willis. 2000. *The Evolving Bargain: Strategic Implications of Deregulation and Privatization.* Boston: Harvard Business School Press.

Foucault, Michel. 1965. *Madness and Civilization: A History of Insanity in the Age of Reason,* trans. Richard Howard. New York: Vintage.

_____. 1970. *The Order of Things: An Archaeology of the Human Sciences.* New York: Vintage.

_____. 1977. *Discipline and Punish: The Birth of the Prison,* trans. Alan Sheridan. New York: Vintage.

_____. 1997. *Essential Works of Foucault 1954–1984, Vol. I, Ethics: Subjectivity and Truth,* ed. Paul Rabinow. New York: New Press.

_____. 2000. *Essential Works of Foucault 1954–1984, Vol. III, Power,* ed. James D. Faubion. New York: New Press.

Gilson, Étienne. 1952. *Jean Duns Scot: Introduction a ses positions fondamentales.* Paris: Librairie Philosophique J. Vrin.

Godin, Christian. 1997. *La totalité. Prologue: Pour une philosophie de la totalité.* Seyssel: Éditions Champ Vallon.

Gorz, André. *Farewell to the Working Class,* trans. Michael Sonenscher. London: Pluto Press.

Gramsci, Antonio. 1971. *Selections from the Prison Notebooks,* ed. and trans. Quintin Hoare and Geoffrey Nowell Smith. New York: International Publishers.

_____. 1990. *Selections from Political Writings, 1910–1920,* ed. Quintin Hoare, trans. John Mathews. Minneapolis: University of Minnesota Press. (First published in 1977 by Lawrence and Wishart).

Guevara, Ernesto Che. 1997. *Che Guevara Reader. Writings on Guerrilla Strategy, Politics and Revolution,* ed. David Deutschmann. Melbourne: Ocean Press.

Gullì, Bruno. 1999. "The Labor of Fire: On Time and Labor in the *Grundrisse.*" *Cultural Logic.* Volume 2. <http://eserver.org/clogic/2–2/gulli.html>.

_____. 2003. *An Art Hidden in the Forest of the Earth: Labor between Economy and Culture.* Ph.D. dissertation, City University of New York.

Hardt, Michael, and Antonio Negri. 1994. *The Labor of Dionysus: A Critique of the State-Form.* London and Minneapolis: University of Minnesota Press.

_____. 2000. *Empire.* Cambridge, MA, and London: Harvard University Press.

_____. 2004. *Multitude: War and Democracy in the Age of Empire.* New York: Penguin.

Harvey, David. 1989. *The Limits to Capital.* Chicago: University of Chicago Press—Midway Reprint.

Hegel, G.W.F. 1977. *Phenomenology of Spirit,* trans. A. V. Miller. Oxford: Oxford University Press.

_____. 1989. *The Science of Logic,* trans. A. V. Miller. Atlantic Highlands, NJ: Humanities Press International, Inc.

_____. 1991. *The Encyclopedia Logic. Part I of the Encyclopedia of Philosophical Sciences,* trans. T. F. Gereats, W. A. Suchting, and H. S. Harris. Indianapolis: Hackett Publishing Company.

Heidegger, Martin. 1959. *Unterwegs zur Sprache.* Tübingen: Neske.

_____. 1968. *Existence and Being,* ed. W. Brock. Chicago: Regnery.

_____. 1971a. *On the Way to Language,* trans. Peter D. Hertz. New York: Harper and Row.

_____. 1971b. *Poetry, Language, Thought,* trans. Albert Hofstadter. New York: Harper and Row.

_____. 1972. *On Time and Being,* trans. Joan Stambaugh. New York: Harper and Row.

_____. 1977. *Basic Writings,* ed. D. F. Krell. New York: Harper and Row.

_____. 1979. *Nietzsche. Volume I: The Will to Power as Art,* trans. David Farrell Krell. New York: Harper and Row.

_____. 1982. *Nietzsche. Volume Four: Nihilism,* ed. D. F. Krell. San Francisco: HarperCollins.

_____. 1984. *Nietzsche. Volume Two: The Eternal Recurrence of the Same,* trans. D. F. Krell. San Francisco: HarperCollins.

_____. 1996. *Being and Time,* trans. Joan Stambaugh. New York: State University of New York Press.

Hobsbawm, Eric. 1962. *The Age of Revolution: 1789–1848.* New York: Mentor.

_____. 1994. *The Age of Extremes. A History of the World, 1914–1991.* New York: Vintage.

_____. 1999. *Industry and Empire: The Birth of the Industrial Revolution.* New York: The New Press. (First published in 1968 by Weidenfeld & Nicholson.)

_____. 2000. *Bandits.* New York: New Press.

Hölderlin, Friedrich. 1984. *Hymns and Fragments,* trans. Richard Sieburth. Princeton, NJ: Princeton University Press.

Jay, Martin. 1984. *Marxism and Totality. The Adventures of a Concept from Lukács to Habermas.* Berkeley and Los Angeles: University of California Press.

Kant, Immanuel. 1929. *Critique of Pure Reason,* trans. Norman Kemp Smith. New York: St. Martin's Press.

Kuspit, Donald. 1993. *The Cult of the Avant-Garde Artist.* Cambridge: Cambridge University Press.

Labriola, Antonio. 1965. *La concezione materialistica della storia.* Introduction by Eugenio Garin. Bari: Laterza.

Lazzarato, Maurizio. 1996. "Immaterial Labor," in Paolo Virno and Michael Hardt, eds., *Radical Thought in Italy: A Potential Politics.* Minneapolis and London: University of Minnesota Press.

Leopardi, Giacomo. 1997. *Selected Poems,* trans. Eamon Grennan. Princeton, NJ: Princeton University Press.

Locke, John.1980. *Second Treatise of Government.* Indianapolis: Hackett Publishing Company.

Lucretius. 2001. *On the Nature of Things,* trans. Martin Ferguson Smith. Indianapolis/Cambridge: Hackett Publishing Company.

Lukács, Georg. 1971. *History and Class Consciousness. Studies in Marxist Dialectics,* trans. Rodney Livingstone. Cambridge, MA: MIT Press.

_____. 1980. *The Ontology of Social Being: 3. Labour,* trans. David Fernbach. London: Merlin Press.

Mallet, Serge. 1975. *The New Working Class,* trans. Andre and Bob Shepherd. Bristol: Spokesman Books.

Marcuse, Herbert. 1964. *One-Dimensional Man: Studies in the Ideology of Advanced Industrial Societies.* Boston: Beacon Press.

_____. 1969. *An Essay on Liberation.* Boston: Beacon Press.

_____. 1972. "The Foundation of Historical Materialism" (1932), in *From Luther to Popper.* London and New York: Verso.

_____. 1972b. *Counter-Revolution and Revolt.* Boston: Beacon Press.

Marx, Karl. 1973. *Grundrisse: Foundations of the Critique of Political Economy,* trans. Martin Nicolaus. New York: Vintage Books.

_____. 1975. "Economic and Philosophical Manuscripts (1844)," in *Early Writings,* trans. Rodney Livingston and Gregor Brenton. New York: Vintage Books.

_____. 1977. *Capital. Vol. I,* trans. Ben Fowkes. New York: Vintage Books.

_____. 1978. *Capital. Vol. II,* trans. David Fernbach. New York: Vintage Books.

_____. 1981. *Capital. Vol. III,* trans. David Fernbach. New York: Vintage Books.

_____. 1994. *Selected Writings,* ed. Lawrence H. Simon. Indianapolis and Cambridge: Hackett.

_____. 2000. *Theories of Surplus Value, Vol. I,* in *Theories ... Books I, II, and III.* Amherst, NY: Prometheus Books.

_____ and Frederick Engels. 1947. *The German Ideology.* New York: International Publishers.

_____. 1986. *Selected Works in One Volume.* New York: International Publishers, Ninth Printing.

Mauss, Marcel. 1990. *The Gift: The Form and Reason for Exchange in Archaic Societies,* trans. W. D. Halls. New York, London: W.W. Norton.

McLaren, Peter. 2000. *Che Guevara, Paulo Freire, and the Pedagogy of Revolution.* Boulder, CO: Rowman & Littlefield.

Méda, Dominique. 1995. *Le Travail. Une valeur en voie de disparition.* Paris: Aubier.

Milbank, John. 1991. *The Religious Dimension in the Thought of Giambattista Vico, 1668–1744. Part I: The Early Metaphysics.* Lewiston, NY: Edwin Mellen Press.

Mumford, Lewis. 1934. *Technics and Civilization.* New York: Harcourt Brace & Company.

_____. 1938. *The Culture of Cities.* New York: Harcourt Brace & Company.

_____. 1961. *The City in History: Its Origins, Its Transformations, and Its Prospects.* New York: Harcourt.

_____. 2000 (1952). *Art and Technics.* New York: Columbia University Press.

Munck, Ronaldo. 2002. *Globalization and Labour: The New "Great Transformation."* London and New York: Zed Books.

Nancy, Jean-Luc. 1991. *The Inoperative Community,* ed. Peter Connor. Minneapolis and London: The University of Minnesota Press.

_____. 1993. *The Experience of Freedom,* trans. Bridget McDonald. Stanford, CA: Stanford University Press.

Negri, Antonio. 1987. *Lenta ginestra. Saggio sull'ontologia di Giacomo Leopardi.* Milano: Sugarco Edizioni.

_____. 1991a. *Marx beyond Marx. Lessons on the* Grundrisse, trans. Harry Cleaver, Michael Ryan, and Maurizio Viano. New York: Autonomedia, Inc.

_____. 1991b. *The Savage Anomaly: The Power of Spinoza's Metaphysics and Politics,* trans. Michael Hardt. Minneapolis and Oxford: University of Minnesota Press.

_____. 1992. *Il potere costituente: saggio sulle alternative del moderno.* Varese: Sugarco Edizioni.

_____. 1999. *Insurgencies: Constituent Power and the Modern State,* trans. Maurizia Boscagli. Minneapolis: University of Minnesota Press.

Nietzsche, Friedrich. 1967. *The Birth of Tragedy,* trans. Walter Kaufmann. New York: Random House.

_____. 1968. *The Will to Power,* trans. Walter Kaufmann and R. J. Hollingdale. New York: Vintage.

_____. 1969. *On the Genealogy of Morals and Ecce Homo,* trans. Walter Kaufmann and R. J. Hollingdale. New York: Random House.

_____. 1974. *The Gay Science,* trans. Walter Kaufmann. New York: Random House.

_____. 1978. *Thus Spoke Zarathustra,* trans. Walter Kaufmann. New York: Penguin Books.

_____. 1990. *Twilight of the Idols / The Anti-Christ,* trans. R. J. Hollingdale. New York: Penguin Books.

Overy, Paul. 1991. *De Stijl.* New York: Thames and Hudson.

Pashukanis, Evgeny, B. 1978. *Law and Marxism: A General Theory. Towards a Critique of the Fundamental Juridical Concepts,* trans. Barbara Einhorn. London: Ink Links.

Polanyi, Karl. 1944. *The Great Transformation: The Political and Economic Origins of Our Time.* Boston: Beacon Press.

Ponting, Clive. 1991. *A Green History of the World: The Environment and the Collapse of Great Civilizations.* New York: Penguin Books.

Postone, Moishe. 1996. *Time, Labor, and Social Domination: A Reinterpretation of Marx's Critical Theory.* Cambridge: Cambridge University Press.

Read, Jason. 2003. *The Micro-Politics of Capital: Marx and the Prehistory of the Present.* Albany: State University of New York Press.

Rediker, Marcus. 1987. *Between the Devil and the Deep Blue Sea: Merchant Seamen, Pirates, and the Anglo-American Maritime World, 1700–1750.* Cambridge: Cambridge University Press.

Rifkin, Jeremy. 1995. *The End of Work: The Decline of the Global Labor Force and the Dawn of the Post-Market Era.* New York: G.P. Putnam's Sons.

Rosdolsky, Roman. 1977. *The Making of Marx's 'Capital'*, trans. Pete Burgess. London: Pluto Press.

Rubin, Isaak Illich. 1972. *Essays on Marx's Theory of Value*, trans. Miloš Samardïija and Fredy Perlman. Detroit: Black and Red.

Saussure, Ferdinand de. 1986. *Course in General Linguistics*, trans. Roy Harris. La Salle, IL: Open Court.

Schmitt, Carl. 1996. *The Concept of the Political*, trans. George Schwab. Chicago: University of Chicago Press.

Schumpeter, Joseph A. 1950. *Capitalism, Socialism and Democracy*. Third Edition. New York: Harper & Row.

Simmel, Georg. 1990. *The Philosophy of Money*, trans. Tom Bottomore and David Frisby. Second Enlarged Edition. London and New York: Routledge.

Spengler, Oswald. 1991. *The Decline of the West* (1918), An Abridged Edition, trans. C. F. Atkinson. New York, Oxford: Oxford University Press.

Steger, Manfred B. 2003. *Globalization: A Very Short Introduction*. Oxford: Oxford University Press.

Tronti, Mario. 1977 (1966). *Operai e capitale*. Torino: Reprints Einaudi.

Trotsky, Leon. 1959. *The Russian Revolution: The Overthrow of Tzarism and the Triumph of the Soviets*. Selected and edited by F. W. Dupee from *The History of the Russian Revolution*. New York: Doubleday.

Vico, Giambattista. 1968. *The New Science*, trans. Thomas Goddard Bergin and Max Harold Fisch. Ithaca, NY: Cornell University Press.

——————. 1983. *Autobiografia. Poesie: Scienza Nuova*. Milano: Garzanti.

——————. 1988. *On the Most Ancient Wisdom of the Italians Unearthed from the Origins of the Latin Language. Book One: Metaphysics*, trans. L. M. Palmer. Ithaca, NY: Cornell University Press.

Vincent, Jean-Marie. 1987. *Critique du travail: Le faire et l'agir*. Paris: Presses Universitaires de France.

Virno, Paolo. 1996. "Notes on the 'General Intellect,'" in Saree Makdisi, Cesare Casarino, and Rebecca E. Karl, eds., *Marxism beyond Marxism*. New York and London: Routledge.

——————. 2002. *Grammatica della moltitudine: Per un'analisi delle forme di vita contemporanee*. Roma: DeriveApprodi.

——————. 2004. *A Grammar of the Multitude: For An Analysis of Contemporary Forms of Life*, trans. Isabella Bertoletti, James Cascaito, and Andrea Casson. New York: Semiotext(e).

Williams, Eric. 1944. *Capitalism and Slavery*. Chapel Hill: University of North Carolina Press.

Willis, Paul. 1977. *Learning to Labor: How Working Class Kids Get Working Class Jobs*. New York: Columbia University Press.

Index

Readable passages
p.112 ; Capoeira ...
p.125 ; "Potency" vs. "labor power"

p.134 ; "...we have to reach back..."
p.183 : "...once labor and art speak with one voice..."

BRUNO GULLÌ teaches philosophy at Long Island University, Brooklyn Campus, and at Kingsborough Community College.

Philosophical statement of Marx's "supreme contradiction" of CMP (p197): 79.

An incidental def. of "pure labor"?
                                    p. 178
"The renewed concept of labor we have
    presented here." p. 185